P
3/11/05

Online Therapy

More Advance Acclaim for
Online Therapy:
A Therapist's Guide to Expanding Your Practice

"Online therapy has provided my traditional practice with new options I had never dreamed possible. I realized the potential for my practice when I first attended an online therapy seminar presented by Dr. Kathleene Derrig-Palumbo. The information I received helped me to expand my horizons and better serve my clients. This is the first book I've read about online therapy that is easy to understand and provides clear steps that are simple to implement. *Online Therapy: A Therapist's Guide to Expanding Your Practice* empowers therapists with the detailed information and know-how necessary to expand their practices and reach people that would otherwise go unserved."
—Marina Skegin-Sipes, M.A., MFT

A Norton Professional Book

Online Therapy

A Therapist's Guide to Expanding Your Practice

Kathleene Derrig-Palumbo

Foojan Zeine

W. W. Norton & Company
New York • London

For information about permission to reproduce selections from this book,
write to Permissions, W. W. Norton & Company, Inc., 500 Fifth Avenue,
New York, NY 10110

Manufacturing by Quebecor World—Fairfield Division
Production Manager: Benjamin Reynolds
Design by Anna Oler
Composition by PennSet, Inc.

LIBRARY OF CONGRESS CATALOGING-IN-PUBLICATION DATA

Derrig-Palumbo, Kathleene.
Online therapy : a therapist's guide to expanding your practice /
Kathleene Derrig-Palumbo, Foojan Zeine.
p. cm.
"A Norton professional book."
Includes bibliographical references and index.

ISBN 0-393-70452-1

1. Internet in psychotherapy. 2. Psychotherapy—Practice. I. Zeine,
Foojan. II. Title.

RC489.I54D47 2005
616.89'14—dc22
2004063592

W. W. Norton & Company, Inc., 500 Fifth Avenue, New York, N.Y. 10110
www.wwnorton.com

W. W. Norton & Company Ltd., Castle House, 75/76 Wells St.,
London W1T 3QT

1   3   5   7   9   0   8   6   4   2

Contents

Part I: Clinical, Theoretical, and Research Bases for Online Therapy

Part II: Setting Up an Online Practice: Business, Legal, and Ethical Issues

Appendices

Foreword

This is a remarkably comprehensive book on how a professional therapist or counselor can use the computer to do online therapy with her or his clients. Because this form of therapy is relatively new and unique, the reader will have many questions about how to do it, how to build a practice, techniques of therapy that can best be employed, legal and ethical issues, online therapy research, and so on. Fortunately, the authors courageously and honestly tackle these questions, and answer them out of their own online therapy experience and out of the careful study they have done of the literature on the subject. If they have omitted anything of great importance, I have yet to find it.

As I note in the interview in the book that the authors had with me, I don't pretend to have done many online therapy sessions with my clients, but for more than 45 years I have done countless phone sessions with them with excellent results. A big myth in psychotherapy is that, in order to relate well to your clients, you have to show them fine empathy, support, and acceptance, and you have to see them face to face.

Nonsense! I have found that most clients are quite appreciative when they don't have to come to my office and are delighted to tell me their troubles over the phone. They listen intently, question me just as they would do if they were in my office, and tell me very private things about themselves exactly as if we were face to face. Sometimes, in fact, they see that they have more privacy during phone sessions than if they visit me in my office. If clients are concerned about privacy, distance therapy is great!

How about my own loss when I can't see my clients face to face and therefore cannot watch their facial expressions or body gestures? I miss something—but not very much. As long as clients speak expressively—which most of them do—I can easily hear the nuances of their verbal expressions, and I rarely lose touch with their real feelings. Moreover, I can concentrate on their oral presentation and get almost as much of my clients' thoughts, emotions, and behaviors as I would be able to do if I had sight of them.

For many years, then, I have done hundreds of phone sessions, and both I and my clients have benefited from them. If we were a little bit limited by not being face to face, we were able to overcome the much more significant limitations of sickness, disability, distance, or other factors that would have kept us from seeing each other. Occasionally I have had sessions with my clients when they made a tape recording and I answered with a return recording. Occasionally, too, clients have written me and I have replied by mail (or e-mail) and that has worked out therapeutically. It is now also possible to hook up video cameras to the computer and in that manner both see and hear clients at a distance. I have only had a couple of sessions using that kind of equipment, but they have worked quite well. I think that doing things that way will become very popular and advantageous in the future.

To sum up: Psychotherapy sessions by phone, by computer, and by computer and video are all practical when face-to-face sessions are not feasible. *Online Therapy* by Kathleene Derrig-Palumbo and Foojan Zeine is an excellent pioneering book that tells you all you want to learn about it—and more! By all means read it.

Albert Ellis, Ph.D., President
Albert Ellis Institute
New York City

Introduction

According to *Mental Health: A Report of the Surgeon General* (Surgeon General, 1999), traditional therapy is inaccessible to many people because of the stigma associated with it. The report states that nearly two-thirds of people who need mental health care never receive it because they are too embarrassed to make in-person contact with a therapist. The report suggests that online therapy is a possible solution because the nonvisual environment offers these clients a sense of security and freedom to express their innermost thoughts. People feel an enhanced sense of privacy when engaging in online therapy. Also, the structure and procedures employed by HMOs and the mental health industry continue to make it difficult for many people to get the care they need. Presently, HMOs severely limit the number of face-to-face therapy sessions, pressuring therapists to transition clients to medications at the earliest opportunity.

Online therapy is being used to treat many underserved client populations. Many of the clients seen by online therapists include teenagers, people living in rural areas where access to therapy is nearly nonexistent, people housebound by reason of physical disabilities, victims of domestic violence, and issue-oriented people who want personal growth and fulfillment but don't see themselves in face-to-face therapy.

We define online therapy as the practice of psychotherapy using the Internet as the medium of communication between therapist and client. It is important to remember that only the medium, the Internet, is different from traditional therapy. The Web-based tools used for the practice of online therapy include message boards; public chat rooms and real-time chat rooms, which allow individuals or groups to type messages back and forth; e-mail; Internet telephone; and web-based audio- and videoconferencing. Using these online tools, mental health practitioners are able to interact with clients either exclusively online or in a combination of online and face-to-face therapy.

Online therapy has actually been in existence since the early days of the Internet. Therapists using telephone therapy found the transition to online therapy a smooth one, and in fact one of the first demonstrations of the Internet was a simulated psychotherapy session between computers at Stanford University and the University of California, Los Angeles, during the 1972 international conference on computer communication. So, in the early 21st century, online therapy has quite a substantial history behind it.

Therapists interested in treating clients online have two options: either to set up an individual Web site or to join one of the e-clinics (Web sites that provide the technology for therapists to meet with their clients). Many people find e-clinics a good choice because the technical aspects of setting up the Web site, creating a home page, billing and accounting, advertising and marketing, security and confidentiality are taken care of by the site's administration. Clearly, therapists contemplating doing online therapy need to do a great deal of research to discover the best option. For example, if a group therapist joins an e-clinic with a big listing of group therapists, the Web site will probably be well set up to handle this kind of work in an expeditious manner, but on the downside, there will be a lot of competition. It might be a better personal, business, and clinical decision to find an e-clinic which lacks the therapist's particular specialty. In addition, a therapist may wish to join an e-clinic that screens therapists, which means that prospective clients are better protected.

Professional acceptance of online therapy is best demonstrated by the development of online therapy principles and standards. Some of the major professional organizations have developed or are developing guidelines for online therapy, including the International Society for Mental Health Online, American Medical Informatics Association, American Psychological Association, National Board of Certified Counselors, and the American Counseling Association (see Appendix C).

It should be emphasized that online therapy is not an either-or situation: Clients can indeed be treated exclusively online, but they can also be treated with a combination of online and face-to-face. Some therapists have found that face-to-face clients who reach a point where they are "stuck" can find a way through by discussing their issues online. There is a strong sense for many clients of both the privacy of online therapy and a feeling of connection with the therapist. Therapists contemplating online therapy often worry first and foremost about the therapeutic alliance, but it can be as strong or stronger than in face-to-face therapy. The discipline imposed by typing, that is of necessity more succinct in presentation than the spoken word, can bring issues to the table more rapidly than in the case of traditional therapy. Some clients have reported that text messaging gives them time to collect their thoughts prior to typing a response. The alleviation of a perceived need to immediately respond allows additional time for reflection. In addition, issues may be discussed candidly, without fear of judgment.

There are certain diagnoses that are difficult to treat online. A suicidal client may be more safely treated in face-to-face therapy. Certainly, therapists may want to consider a face-to-face referral, especially if they are contacted by a suicidal client who lives in another state. Schizophrenia, thought disorders, and psychosis are not amenable to online therapy.

Another concern surrounding online therapy is the legitimacy of individuals claiming to be therapists. Clearly, online therapy can only be as reliable as its practitioners. Online therapists are considered to be qualified and legitimate when they are in good standing with their licensing board and have current malpractice insurance. A therapist offering services from an individual Web site would be well advised to have his or her licensing information, academic credentials, training, and specialties prominently displayed on their home page, so that prospective clients can see at once whether this is a therapist who has the background to help them.

THE INTERNET AND MENTAL HEALTH

What is the essence of therapy? If we go beneath its many forms, schools, and theories, therapy can be seen as a guided conversation. As a conversation, therapy includes the richness of personal interactions, the use of visual, audio, and kinesthetic resources, as well as the application of both spoken and written word. Therapy is one of the richest forms of interpersonal communication yet developed by human beings. And it is this richness and depth that brings healing.

Communication has changed as technology has changed throughout history. We stand today amidst an unquestioned communications revolution brought about by the staggering power of computer-to-computer communication. This revolution in technology, like so many others, has its critics as well as proponents. But we can all agree that, while computers can in fact exchange information, it is the human mind that both facilitates and adds depth and spirit to electronic communication. It stands to reason, then, that therapists—who open the doors of perception through guided communication with their clients—can be dramatically empowered by embracing the use of the computer and Internet in their practices. Computer-assisted therapy will not "replace" office visits any more than automobiles have replaced walking. Technology will not destroy intimacy in the therapeutic setting any more than telephones replaced family get-togethers. The very debate about whether computers and the Internet are "good" or "bad" for therapy becomes ever more stale as time passes. The significant questions today are about *how* to incorporate these tools into the therapeutic setting, not *if* they should be incorporated.

The Internet has become an accepted and ubiquitous part of everyday life (Employment Policy Foundation, 2001; Harris Poll, 2001; Pastore, 2000b; Pew Internet and American Life Project, 2002). The Internet is now a common source of information about and delivery of healthcare services, including mental health (Harris Poll, 2001; Internet and American Life Project, 2002; Maheu & Gordon, 2000; Pastore, 2000c). This has profound implications for the practices of many mental health practitioners who have a professional stake in the theory and practice of psychology. Mental health professionals are affected by both the dissemination of information related to mental health and the actual provision of mental health services through electronic media. Empirical research with regard to this growing method of providing mental health information and services has been slow to meet this need. The scarcity of existing empirical studies calls for researchers and clinicians to fill this research gap. However, thus far, the research points to the consumer benefiting from many computer-mediated methods of mental health services (Glueckauf, Pickett, Ketterson, Loomis, & Rozensky, 2003; Keefe & Blumenthal, 2004; Ritterband, Gonder-Federick, Cox, Clifton, West, & Borowitz , 2003).

A Harris Poll (2000) found that more than 60 million people searched for health information online in 2000 and 40% of them were looking for information about mental health. As the

Internet continues to affect and change the lives of people around the world, online therapy is reaching more people every year. The following are some data that reflect the growth of the Internet, and along with it, the growing of online therapy.

Fifty-six percent of all adults in the United States (approximately 114 million people) are online at home, work, or school. Of these, 86% report seeking information on healthcare or specific diseases, up from 71% in 1998 (Harris Poll, 2000).

Cyber Dialogue reports 36.7 million adults in the United States using the Internet to search for health-related content (Pastore, 2000c).

A survey of behavioral telehealth practitioners who provide behavioral health services on the Internet shows that the media used is "evenly distributed between e-mail, Web sites, and real-time interactive communication, including chat rooms and videoconferencing" (Maheu & Gordon, 2000, p. 485).

In 1995 there were approximately 12 e-therapist sites on the Internet. By 2001 there were approximately 300 private practice Web sites and e-clinics where e-therapists offered services. Based on feedback from attendees and our international workshops who use email therapy and chat therapy, as well as reports from our own and other e-clinic membership, there are more than 5,000 e-therapists active in 2005.

Seventy percent of consumers of Internet services are 20 to 50 years old.

The Pew Internet and American Life Project (2000) found that on a typical day at the end of 2004, some 70 million American adults logged onto the Internet for general use. That represents a 37% increase from the 51 million Americans who were online on an average day in 2000 when the Pew Internet and American Life Project began its study of online life. Sixty-five percent of consumers seek information about nutrition, exercise, or weight control; 39% seek mental health information (Raine & Horrigan, 2005).

The National Advisory Mental Health Council indicates that

the National Institute of Mental Health public information Web site receives an average of 5 to 6 million hits in a typical month (NIMH, 2002).

According to Alexa.com, a Web ranking service, the National Institute of Mental Health receives an average of 2–4 million hits per day. (http://www/alexa.com/data/details/traffic_details? q=&url=http://www.nimh.nih.gov/publicat/index.cfm)

As the data come in, and the expenses of both mental health care providers and clients grow, the scope of application and the premise of effectiveness for online therapy appears significant.

Are there challenges? Absolutely. Are we engaged in a sort of worldwide laboratory about how best to use these tools? Definitely. Do we have all the answers? No. We do know a few vitally important things, however. We know that some people can have dramatic breakthroughs using computer and Internet-based communication with mental health professionals. We know that successes have occurred in both mediated and nonmediated technology-augmented therapy. We know the Internet is a means to reach people who would not otherwise receive treatment. We also know that the technology is already here, already in use, and that if we, as a profession, do not learn to use it wisely, responsibly, and ethically, we will fail to meet the very real needs of our society.

THE JOURNEY

The thought of creating an online therapy clinic came to me, Kathleene Derrig-Palumbo, in 1994, when I first became exposed to the Internet. I immediately saw how the Internet was affecting communication, and it amazed me how quickly it was being adopted. Seeing people eagerly using chat rooms and sending emails was a clear sign that the Internet would revolutionize communications. I recognized that the anonymity afforded by the Internet would be a significant component in bringing therapy services to people who would not otherwise go to therapy.

At the time, the idea of conducting therapy via the Internet was so new that the most prevalent reaction from members of the profession bordered on horror. My colleagues would say things like, "Kathleene, you can't treat someone you can't see!" Other people instantly took the leap to infer that online therapy was an attempt to replace traditional, face-to-face therapy. I knew of a few visually impaired therapists, however, and their inability to "see" the client certainly did not affect their ability to provide effective therapy. I also realized that people had been making strong connections using only the written word for thousands of years.

The skeptics and cynics certainly offered me important issues to understand and work through, but my vision remained clear and I focused on moving forward. My primary mission was to gather as much information and become as knowledgeable as possible about this new modality. The following six years were dedicated to learning as much as possible about computers and telemedicine (i.e., health care services provided from a distance using audio, video, and computer technology). I analyzed the marketplace with the help of specialized consultants and once my team had garnered the information we needed, we created the MyTherapyNet.com business plan.

We resisted advice to start the company in 1998. At that time, everyone was talking about starting Internet companies, taking them public, and then cashing out. We recognized two problems with this business approach. First soliciting venture capital often meant losing control of your company and, in our case, this meant losing control of the process of providing mental health care. There was no way that we could have someone from outside the profession come in and tell us how to provide therapy services. It would be unethical. Second, we recognized that this particular "exit strategy" would mean that I would be allowed to give birth to my baby, only to have it torn from my arms. The prospect of building the company, just to have it sold off to the highest bidder, was not an option I was willing to consider.

In February of 2000, I quit my job as COO of a corporation that provided psychiatric programs to hospitals and began to assemble my management team for our project. I created a solid management team with expertise in all of the pertinent areas. I had seen two other competitors start up around that time, and I quietly recognized that they were headed for trouble for lack of planning. Others followed, and the vast majority of failed or unsuccessful online therapy endeavors fell into two categories—1) those who were business people with no knowledge of therapy, and 2) those who were therapists who had no knowledge of entrepreneurial business. By early April, I had assembled my dream team of experts in mental health, business, technology, law, and education.

We built the training division of MyTherapyNet.com, including an Online Therapy Certification program as well as a host of other courses. We traveled the country conducting workshops and seminars, as well as attending State Mental Health Regulatory Board meetings to help regulators understand online therapy from a proactive perspective. Soon we were also providing seminars for other organizations, companies, educational institutions, and associations, including Pepperdine University, Glendale Unified School District, and the American Association of Marriage and Family Therapists.

Besides addressing the issue of educating mental health professionals about online therapy, the first year was spent building and testing the Web site. We organized a focus group of 200 people to provide feedback for everything from the design and look of the site to the functionality of receiving online therapy services. We consulted with one of the foremost mental health legal experts in the nation, Richard Leslie, to be certain that our approach was absolutely correct, both legally and ethically.

In that first year, we quickly established ourselves as a responsible trendsetter, and MyTherapyNet.com was the first company to offer online therapy training to therapists. We wanted to be certain that once our service would be opened for business, the practitioners available at MyTherapyNet.com would be skilled in providing services using this new modality. We sent out brochures to therapists across the United States to recruit qualified therapists who were interested in having a virtual office in addition to their traditional face-to-face practice. We also placed advertising in the major therapist-oriented mental health journals. Articles were written about us, and the word was spreading quickly.

In May of 2001, after a year of intensive development, we launched the MyTherapyNet.com Web site. From that moment in time we have never stopped improving and innovating the service. Having long ago met our goal of providing an easy-to-use virtual office for both clients and therapists, we continue to focus on improving the interface, the online location where therapy takes place, and adding new technologies and functionalities as they become available. A virtual office contains the functionality of a real office such as meeting rooms, billing services, message centers, notebooks and accounting systems. The only difference between a traditional office and a virtual office is that a virtual office is located online. By automating processes, the virtual office aggregates as many practice management and maintenance tools as possible.

The journey has been a remarkable one. We set out to make a difference and found that we were having a much more pronounced effect than we ever had imagined. Our basic commitment is that anyone, anywhere, who needs help must have access to that help. People are indeed seeking help that otherwise would have never considered doing so. Others are getting benefits from online therapy that revolve around the nature of chat therapy—i.e., they get to their issues quicker and they are making greater progress than they were able to do in traditional face-to-face therapy. Online therapy also means being able to share thoughts with a therapist between sessions, keeping tabs on old clients, and providing access to therapy when on vacation or away on business. Online therapy means different things to different people, and it is appropriate in some circumstances as well as not appropriate in others. One thing is certain—there is a growing number of people worldwide who attest to the effectiveness of this new modality.

THIS BOOK

This is not the first book to be published about computer and Internet technology and therapy. However, unlike past publications this book focuses on the *practical* steps to take to implement the technology as a business development tool and use it as a healing tool. This is not a theoretical treatment of the "benefits" of computer-assisted therapy, but a theoretical underpinning is at the core. This is not merely a compendium of case studies, but compelling examples of the healing benefits of computer-based therapy are found throughout. Other books on the subject spend an inordinate amount of space—we think—on either the cost–benefit analysis or the details of how intricate technologies are used to foster communication. Certainly, both of these subjects merit study. However, the practical need for mental health care professionals is how to use it. Moreover, while other books provide an exhaustive debate about the merits and pitfalls associated with using computers and the Internet in practice, this book simply debunks the myths and moves directly into implementation and usage. After all, it is *already here!*

The book is divided into two parts: Part I, Clinical, Theoretical, and Research Bases for Online Therapy, opens with a chapter on "The Most Effective Therapeutic Approaches for Online Therapy," discussing some of the brief therapies that work best with online therapy: Albert Ellis's rational–emotive–behavioral theory, Aaron Beck's cognitive–behavioral theory, solution-focused theory, and family brief therapies. Chapter 2 discusses "Some Common Questions about Online Therapy," including such topics as privacy and confidentiality, the therapeutic alliance, and whether or not online therapy can be used with serious disorders. Chapter 3, "Clinical Guidelines and Approaches," discusses online therapy as an extension of face-to-face therapy, pointing out that it is the *medium* that is different, but that therapists draw upon the same tools of their trade in both forms of therapy. The stages of therapy are discussed from initial contact to termination. Chapter 4, "The Effectiveness of Different Modes of Online Therapy," presents some of the tentative research findings regarding online therapy.

Part II, Setting Up an Online Practice: Business, Legal, and Ethical Issues, covers the nuts-and-bolts issues of the therapist's decision to move into online practice, either exclusively or in addition to an existing face-to-face practice. The section opens with Chapter 5, "Is It Time to Go Online?," which covers the myriad questions a therapist must ask him- or herself regarding the effect an online therapy practice would have on personal lifestyle issues, business decisions, and clinical matters. Chapter 6, "Going Digital," walks the reader through the various technological issues involved in setting up an individual Web site or joining an e-clinic. Sample pages from existing Web sites are shown throughout the chapter to illustrate the points under discussion. Chapter 7, "Maintaining an Online Practice," discusses marketing, advertising, and pricing of therapy services. Chapter 8, "Legal and Ethical Issues," presents the main issues governing the practice of online therapy, including confidentiality, payment for referral, treating clients in other states, reporting abuse, relevant legislation to manage HIPAA, telemedicine law, ethics, and unprofessional conduct.

The book also features four appendices: Appendix A discusses in greater detail the issues involved in purchasing hardware and software for an online therapy practice; Appendix B lists some online therapy sites, educational sites, self-help sites, and emergency resources; Appendix C presents the online therapy guidelines published by the major professional groups listed above; and Appendix D offers information on education in online therapy. There is also a glossary of key terms for handy reference and definition. In this book each glossary term appears in boldface type on first usage.

Challenges abound in the new field of online therapy, and using computer and Internet-based communication with mental health professionals is still required. This book sets out to both educate mental health professionals about the tools and technologies available, as well as to explain how to use them. We hope it will encourage more mental health professionals to investigate the benefits of online therapy, and perhaps reach clients they would not otherwise have been able to help.

Acknowledgments

I dedicate my work to my very loving and caring family . . . you are my heroes.

To my husband, Gregori, whose unwavering support and love acts as a guiding light through my life journey. You have inspired me to fulfill my goals and dreams. With you by my side, I will accomplish anything to which I set my mind. I would like to also thank you for living life the way it was meant to be lived. You are not only my husband, but my best friend. Thank you so very much for being everything that I have ever dreamed.

To my daughter, Sophia, thank you for being my inspiration during this time. You are my little angel.

To my parents, Dr. John and Sheila Derrig, who have always believed in me and supported my goals. Thank you for always reminding me what I can achieve through perseverance. Dad, you have taught me about the healing quality of laughter and how important it is to be happy in life. Thank you to you and Mom for all my great childhood memories. Mom, you have provided me with the strength and knowledge necessary to spread my wings and soar through life. Most of all, Mom, thank you for showing me the power and beauty of being a woman.

Kathleene Derrig-Palumbo, Ph.D.

This is a great opportunity for me to express my gratitude to the people in my life who have been the source of love, encouragement, power, vision, clarity, and abundance for me.

To my mother, Forouzandeh Arbaby, and my godmother, Anvar Lajevardi, you two have been the source of unconditional love and unresting drive. I thank you for all that you have taught me and for being great role models as women. Reza Broomand, thank you for your love, understanding, support, allowing me to be who I am, and always being there for me. Thank you to all my friends who have always been cheering for me, supporting and sharing my vision—Golpar Nourkhah, Maryam Molavi, Khotan BaniAmam, Alex Farhadi, Amanollah Ghahraman, Farokh Tofighi, Dr. Shavash Safvati, Farhad Abolfathi, and Elaheh and Sharon Yousefian. To all my mentors who have guided me and have always believed in me—Dr. Rhoda Codner, Dr. Fereshteh Mirhasehmi, Dr. M.A. Shamie, and Steve Baghoomian—you are a great reason that I am where I am in my life.

My deepest gratitude and love are with all of you who have been in my life and have affected me in the most beautiful way. You are always in my heart.

Foojan Zeine, Psy.D.

In addition, we would like to honor and thank the following people for their support and guidance throughout the wonderful journey of writing this book and for their historical contributions to this new frontier—online therapy.

Dr. Albert Ellis, we would like to thank you for the opportunity to meet and interview you at your institute. We are tremendously honored that you allowed us to incorporate your work into our book and that you have honored our work by contributing so much of yourself to this project. Professionally, we will be forever grateful that you have brought your eminent expertise to bear upon this book. Personally, your enthusiasm for this project will forever be in our hearts and minds.

Drs. Donald Meichenbaum, Scott Miller, David Epston, Harville Hendrix, and Shelley Green—we would like to thank you for all of your time and energy. Your contributions are invaluable.

Dr. G. Frank Lawlis, we thank you for your faith and unwavering support in the development of our company, this book, and our profession. Your vast experience has allowed us to expand our horizons. We are grateful to you for introducing us to the work of Dr. Phillip McGraw and for building a relationship in which My TherapyNet.com therapists provide support to Dr. Phil's guests and viewers. We would also like to extend a personal thank you to Dr. Phillip McGraw for acknowledging the importance of our work and having us as professional guests on his "Dr. Phil" show.

We are overwhelmingly grateful to the unbelievable support, guidance, and hard work of Gregori Palumbo, Liza Eversol, and Paul Andrews. Without you this book would not have been possible. You three take the concept of team to a whole new level. A special heartfelt thank you to Sheila Derrig for her amazing attention to detail, input, and support. We would like to honor a few of the outstanding individuals from Mytherapynet.com whose combined skills and knowledge have created the company's exceptional standards—Roger Gomez, Danilo "Jay Jay" Napalan, Edward Rholl, J.D., Fred Ferrier, and Derek Keegan.

We would like to thank all the following angels who have supported us through this process in many different ways—Chris Carnell, Dr. Debora Cooper, Dr. and Mrs. Derrig,

Amanollah Gharahman, Travis Gemoets, Dr. Pedram Majidshad, Dr. Fereshteh Mirhashemi, Fabrizio Munoz, Golpar Nourkhah, Katherine Petriack, David Sipes, Marina Skegin-Sipes, Dr. Daniel Stern, and Monica Vallado. We would also like to extend a special thank you to Galilay Entertainment for providing us with the initial financial support to begin this venture.

Thank you to all the therapists who have recognized the importance of online therapy, and who have had the patience and the endurance to play such an important role in this emerging modality.

To the American Association of Marriage and Family Therapy, whose openness, willingness and unbiased outlook have provided us with the opportunity to educate therapists about this new medium of therapy, we would like to commend you in your dedication to the field of psychotherapy and in your resolve to provide your membership with a complete perspective of the field. Karen Gautney, Dr. Bill Northey, Dawn Berry, the AAMFT board, the president, and all the support staff—we thank you. We also would like to thank Richard Lesley, J.D., for his vast knowledge and expertise in the area of psychotherapy law. His intimate familiarity with the law allows him to see clearly in uncharted territory. You are truly a gift to our profession.

Michael McGandy, thank you for believing in us and giving us the opportunity to share our vision in this book. Your patience, guidance, and input have made this process a memorable and remarkable experience.

Kathleene Derrig-Palumbo, Ph.D.
Foojan Zeine, Psy. D.

Online Therapy

PART I

Clinical, Theoretical, and Research Bases for Online Therapy

CHAPTER 1

The Most Effective Therapeutic Approaches for Online Therapy

Online therapy is neither a theory nor a style of therapy; rather it is a medium which therapists can use to treat clients. Therapists can remain true to their style and orientation while using this new medium. Online therapy has its clinical benefits, and it has its limitations. This chapter reviews the benefits and limitations of the main theories best suited for online therapy.

Many of the cognitive-based theories work best with online therapy, and several theorists and practicing clinicians offer insights and guidelines for using their theories and associated interventions. They are divided into three theoretical approaches: cognitive–behavioral, narrative, and client-centered. Cognitive–behavioral includes Albert Ellis's rational–emotive behavioral therapy, Aaron Beck's cognitive–behavioral theory, solution-focused theory, and family brief therapy. These theories are also known as *brief therapies*.

The second theoretical approach discussed is *narrative therapy*. This approach is very well suited for online therapy owing to the emphasis on writing as the main intervention. The third theoretical approach discussed is client centered and includes information about clinicians who are successfully using client-directed outcome-informed clinical work and transpersonal theory. Harville Hendrix also presents imago therapy, which can be used with couples online.

RATIONAL EMOTIVE BEHAVIOR THERAPY

Created in 1955 by Albert Ellis, rational emotive behavior therapy (REBT) is an action-oriented, psychoeducational therapeutic approach that creates emotional growth by guiding clients to replace their self-defeating thoughts, feelings, and actions with new and more effective ones. REBT educates individuals to take responsibility for their own thoughts and emotions and to exercise the power to change unhealthy behaviors that interfere with the ability to function in day-to-day life.

Ellis's first book on REBT was *How to Live with a Neurotic* (1957/1986); then came *The Art and Science of Love* (1960/1970). He has now published 75 books and over 700 articles on REBT, sex, and marriage. He is currently president of the Institute for Rational Emotive Therapy in New York, which offers a full-time training program and operates a large psychological clinic (http://www.rebt.org).

REBT is a practical, action-oriented approach to coping with problems and enhancing personal growth, and it is easily adapted to online therapy, especially using **real-time chat**, videoconferencing, and **Internet phone**. Using these methods, online therapists are able to use REBT techniques that place a good deal of focus on the present. Currently held attitudes, painful emotions, and maladaptive behaviors that can sabotage a fuller experience of life are easily challenged online. REBT therapists also provide their online clients with an individualized set of proven techniques for helping them to solve problems.

As with traditional therapists, online REBT therapists work closely with people, seeking to help uncover their individual set of beliefs (attitudes, expectations, and personal rules) that frequently leads to emotional distress. Among the variety of REBT methods that is successfully applied to online therapy, Ellis outlines techniques such as "disputing" to help people reformulate their dysfunctional beliefs into more sensible, realistic, and helpful ones. Both traditional and online REBT approaches help people to develop a philosophy and approach to living that can increase their effectiveness and happiness at work, in living successfully with others, in parenting and educational settings, in making our community and environment healthier, and in enhancing their own health and personal welfare.

REBT Model

The following model is Ellis's step-by-step approach to REBT. The model is derived from watching Ellis in an eloquent interaction with a patient at his institute.

1.   Identify troublesome situations that your client is most disturbed about, the ones that are emotionally charged. Choose one. Explore the criticism about the situation.
2.   Identify the attitudes, beliefs, and thoughts about the criticism.
3.   Explore the reaction that comes in response to the belief, the feelings that arise from holding onto that belief.
4.   Dispute, question, and challenge the irrational beliefs.
5.   Help the client to rationally, logically, and sensibly respond to the dispute.
6.   Help the client to distinguish and choose to detach from the irrational belief, which will also change the feeling from intense emotion to minor frustration or annoyance.
7.   Give instructions to the client to practice daily for

30 days. For example, ask the client to look in the mirror for the next 30 days and say "I am a great person and I am deserving."

8. Assign rewards and consequences for the daily practice session. For example, ask the client to do the following: "Every day you do the assignment, give yourself a point. If you did not do the assignment, take away a point. Add up all your points at the end of week to see if you've earned enough points for a reward, such as treating yourself to something wonderful.

The following transcript is from an interview conducted with Ellis about online therapy in January 2004.

Q: How would you approach a client online for the first session?

Ellis: I approach it the same way I approach clients in person. I would find out what the external problem is and show them that, largely, they are creating the problem. They don't merely get disturbed, they also disturb themselves with what they tell themselves about bad events. If they listen to me, I'll tell them how they are making themselves disturbed and how to stop doing so.

Q: How would the therapeutic alliance be created via chat without seeing the client?

Ellis: It is a myth that you have to see the clients. By voice or by words you need to show the clients that you are interested in them. Be vitally interested in showing the client how not to disturb him- or herself, and how the client ends up disturbing him- or herself without realizing it. It can be done without face-to-face contact if you think it can be done, and if you think it cannot be done, then you will be ineffective and you won't arrange a good therapeutic alliance.

Q: How would you approach the client's emotions over the Internet?

Ellis: Get clients to talk about their feelings. Show them how when something happens to them, they feel something about it. There are two kinds of feelings: appropriate and healthy feelings (sorrow, regret, frustration), and unhealthy feelings. Everyone is born and reared so that when they think about something that happens, they often create disturbing feelings about it. It has little to do with their childhood experiences. That is something that therapists frequently invent and believe. Teach clients that they can feel healthy feelings such as frustration and annoyance but that they don't need to feel depressed and anxious. Clients need to realize that they created all those reactions to unfortunate events, and they can undo their reactions.

Q: What interventions are best suited for online therapy?

Ellis: It all depends on the person. Normally we need to show clients that their thinking is crooked, and that makes them feel upset and bad. Then their behavior also becomes dysfunctional. Many thinking, feeling, and behavioral interventions are used which can be applied to different people. Some interventions can be similar and yet lead to different results.

Q: Would any specific intervention be better in chat therapy vs. **audiotherapy** vs. **videotherapy**?

Ellis: Nobody knows. You try different ones and see what suits the particular person. No one knows until you try it and see what works. Maybe later on we will have data on which one works better for certain kinds of people, but it still depends on the client and on the therapist's style.

Q: How would you approach couples online?

Ellis: Same as face-to-face. You ask what they see the

problem to be, show them that they are getting up-set about their mate, but show that the mate is not upsetting them. They are usually upsetting them-selves by *demanding* that their mate be different in-stead of *wishing* that he or she be more loving and receptive.

Q: How would you approach adolescents online?

Ellis: Same as face-to-face. You find the adolescents' prob-lems and show them that they are upsetting them-selves by their irrational beliefs about how others and the world absolutely must be.

Q: How would you approach family therapy online?

Ellis: That might be more difficult for everyone to have access to the computer. Overall, as with the other categories, find out how each one of them bothers him- or herself regarding another family member. It is best not to do typing if it slows people down. Au-dio is the best.

Q: How would you assess for diagnosis and formulate treatment goals online?

Ellis: The same way you assess in **face-to-face therapy**. You get patient information about their goals, values, and their distorted reactions when these are thwarted.

Q: Would you have any legal and ethical considera-tions?

Ellis: Making sure that no one is listening. Besides that, the same ethical issues as when in face-to-face therapy.

Q: How would you terminate with a client online?

Ellis: Same as in face-to-face therapy. You check what is bothering the client, make the symptoms less debil-itating, make the sessions less frequent, see that they have much less disturbances for a couple of months, and then terminate.

Q: Would any of your answers to the above questions

be different for traditional therapy vs. online therapy?

Ellis: Very little difference.

Q: Do you have any concerns about online therapy?

Ellis: When I have tried it, it took time to use typing. I am
very comfortable using the audio. Just like telephone therapy, I have done thousands of telephone
sessions and I find them quite useful.

Q: When you do phone sessions, do you only have
clients in New York state or nationwide?

Ellis: Nationwide and some foreign countries.

Q: In your opinion, where do you think therapy takes
place, where the therapist is or where the client is?

Ellis: Both, where the therapist is and where the client is.

Q: For state criteria purposes, if you had to pick one,
where do you think therapy takes place?

Ellis: Who cares? The important factor is that therapy
takes place where the client and therapist are.

Q: What do you think about the innovation that technology brings to therapy?

Ellis: It widens the scope. You can see all sorts of people
that you never had access to seeing before.

In the interview with Ellis, it was apparent that REBT can be
utilized effectively via the online medium.

COGNITIVE–BEHAVIORAL THERAPY

Cognitive–behavioral therapy (CBT) focuses on changing certain thought patterns. As with traditional therapy, the premise
of online cognitive therapy is that the way we perceive situations influences how we feel emotionally (Beck, 1979). By helping online clients change their thoughts and their stories, their
behaviors will also change. The online cognitive–behavioral
therapist establishes and maintains a therapeutic alliance, and

educates the patient about the problem and possible solutions. With Socratic interventions, artful questioning, the use of patients' self-monitoring, modeling films, the use of "teaching stories," and the like, the therapist helps the patient reconceptualize his or her problem in a more hopeful fashion. Other core tasks of therapy include nurturing patients' hope, teaching skills, and ensuring the likelihood of generalization. The therapist needs to ensure that not only do patients have intra- and interpersonal skills, but also that they apply them in their everyday experience. Patients also need to come to see the connections between their efforts and resultant consequences. Moreover, given the high likelihood of patients reexperiencing their problematic behaviors and given the episodic nature of chronic mental disorders, there is a need to help patients develop relapse prevention skills (Meichenbaum, 2000). The client usually must do considerable work, such as homework, writing assignments, and practice techniques learned in the session. All of these may be effectively accomplished online and submitted to the therapist between sessions. As with traditional therapy, a client's failure to complete tasks as assigned is taken as a lack of motivation and unwillingness to change behaviors. Online therapy allows for greater accountability because sessions can be more frequent and records of text communications can be stored.

In a research article (Proudfoot, Goldberg, Mann, Everett, Marks, & Gray, 2003), the authors found that a computerized **interactive** program may provide effective cognitive–behavioral therapy (CBT) to patients with anxiety and depression, thereby increasing the availability of this technique. One CBT computer **program**, Beat the Blues (BtB), uses interactive, **multimedia** techniques, teaching clients suffering from anxiety or depression about the nature of their symptoms and ways to treat them using cognitive–behavioral techniques. This research demonstrates applicability, when using this program, as an adjunct to pharmacotherapy or with patients who do not wish to take medication. Results indicated a greater reduction in symptoms using BtB therapy as compared to standard therapy. This research points to the use of CBT interventions as a means to improve clients' work and social adjustment.

Donald Meichenbaum, a prominent cognitive–behavioral theorist, stated in an interview about online therapy that it is crucial for patients to have a choice in learning about their treatment options. Meichenbaum is a distinguished professor emeritus, clinical psychologist, research director, and a founding member of the Melissa Institute.

Q: How do you see online therapy as being effective for clients?

Meichenbaum: I would like to explore online therapy from the psychoeducational perspective. I think that psychoeducational **Web sites** can be utilized as a prescriptive treatment where the physician prescribes the Web site address to the patient, which enables the patient to engage in the behavioral activation as a conjoint with already existing treatment. These Web sites offer programs that are tailored to the individual patient's needs. The mechanics of the Web sites need to be user friendly and stated in a language that is comfortable and familiar to the public.

Q: How could online psychoeducational treatment be effective for clients?

Meichenbaum: Patients who are depressed or have a high level of anxiety often go to their primary physician. The only treatment option that is relayed to them is medication management for their symptoms. Patients have the right to receive information and be a part of the decision-making process regarding their treatment options. Patients seeking treatment or information should be asked a series of questions and be guided to different assessment tools, such as a small test, to assess for depression, anxiety, or other diagnosis. Patients can then access a diagnostic tree and choose their responses and path, step-by-step, to see what their treatment options would be. One model treatment option can be a video about cognitive interventions. This intervention could be demonstrated through the use of role-play by both the clinician and the client.

Q: Are there any psychoeducational Web sites that are available for clients?

Meichenbaum: There are existing educational sites such as http://www.feelbetter.org, which offers six sessions of cognitive–behavioral interventions; The Melissa Institute (see its Web site http://www.melissainsti tute.com) offers interventions and education regarding violence protection.

As Meichenbaum explained, self-help psychoeducational sites can be very therapeutic as an adjunct to medication management, face-to-face therapy, and online chat **real-time** therapy. We also believe that cognitive–behavioral interventions can easily be utilized in online therapy. The two clinical handbooks written by Meichenbaum are very useful psychoeducational resources: *A Clinical Handbook/Practical Therapist Manual for Assessing and Treating Adults with Posttraumatic Stress Disorder (PTSD)* (2000) and the other focuses on *The Treatment of Individuals with Anger-Control and Aggressive Behavior* (2003).

SOLUTION-FOCUSED BRIEF THERAPY

There are a number of solution-oriented models that have many parallels, but do vary slightly in their emphasis on language. All of these models can be used effectively online via **chat**, audio, or video. The work of O'Hanlon, Weiner-Davis, and Wilk (O'Hanlon & Weiner-Davis, 1989, O'Hanlon & Wilk, 1987) addresses the framework of language that people are caught in without questioning the underlying assumptions. It is convenient for the client and the therapist to address the language in a text that a client has typed.

Using habitual language patterns prevents the discovery of new solutions if people cannot see outside their routine frame of reference. Solution-focused therapists believe that meaning and perception are embedded in language, and that language becomes the vehicle of change. As with face-to-face therapy, in online solution-focused brief therapy, there are no preformed judgments about the right or wrong way to live, but rather attempts to call forth the client's resources and bring them to bear on a problematic situation, so that ultimately a person can view that situation from a different perspective and act accordingly.

Solution-focused brief therapy (SFBT) was developed in America in the 1980s by Steve de Shazer and Insoo Kim Berg. After spending many years studying problem behavior and trying to change it, they switched to studying solution behavior and how to promote it. Two simple ideas underlie solution-focused brief therapy:

1. Everyone experiences times in their lives in which they have not achieved a goal or have been consumed with a problem or issue. Likewise, everyone also experiences times in which they solve their problems and achieve their goals. These times are what de Shazer and Berg called *exceptions*. The skills that the person makes use of during these exceptional times are the basis for potential solutions.

2. Having a clear goal facilitates the path toward the solution. Often, people focus upon what they do not want and subsequently are only attentive to getting out of their immediate situation rather than prioritizing what they desire. (de Shazer, 1985)

A solution-focused brief therapist's task is to discover the person's skills that can contribute to resolution of the presenting problem. They will ask many questions about how life will be when the problem is resolved. As the answers to these questions gradually unfold, the clearer the possibility of the resolution appears.

Berg described SFBT as an approach that sees the future as created and negotiated rather than as an unchangeable consequence of past events. In this approach in spite of the person's past traumatic events, she or he can negotiate and implement strategies that would lead to a more satisfying life. SFBT also assumes that clients possess all the necessary resources, skills, and knowledge to make their life better if they so choose. Small changes can and do lead to big differences in the future (Berg, 2004).

Many of the solution-focused therapy interventions can be used online. The miracle question, "Suppose that one night there is a miracle and while you were sleeping the problem that brought you to therapy is solved: How would you know? What would be different? What will you notice different the next morning that will tell you that there has been a miracle? What will your spouse notice?" (deShazer, 1985) The miracle question helps a client to discover what would be different without the problem situation, and therefore contributes to the setting of salient goals. This is generally done at the beginning of therapy, but can be used throughout to reevaluate goals. In this way the client is helped to move away from being stuck in the problem with all of its feeling states and causes and ramifications, toward envisioning a picture of what could be.

Utilization is another intervention that involves meeting the clients where they are and moving forward with them from that point. Rather than stating a different viewpoint or goal, the therapist accepts the client's position and starts there. This helps with the joining process and essentially builds a bridge from where the client is now, to the eventual goal (O'Hanlon & Wilk, 1987).

For the purpose of convenience and speed in the therapy

process, solution-focused therapies are effective and convenient for many clients who use computers.

FAMILY BRIEF THERAPY

Shelley Green is an Associate Professor, Department of Family Therapy, School of Humanities and Social Sciences, Nova Southeastern University. In an interview, she discusses how she could utilize online therapy with the families that she sees in therapy.

Q: Could you let us know about your experience with online therapy?

Green: My experience of online conversations began with teaching online. To my surprise, my students created and developed intense relationships over the **Internet** and through the use of chat. I witnessed many in-depth conversations that created intimacy among my students. However, I have not directly conducted online therapy with my clients yet.

Q: With your online teaching experience how would you propose conducting brief family therapy online with a client?

Green: In working with families online, I would ask the family to **log onto** a group chat session from different computers. Through this approach, all of the family members may read and be involved with each other's conversation. The interaction between the family members can be observed by the therapist and reflected upon. Family members would be encouraged to e-mail and chat with each other several times a week to create an ongoing conversation. Videoconferencing can also be used within the family session by having one camera for the family and a second camera for the therapist.

Q: What interventions do you think would be effective in family online therapy?

Green: I could see the possibility of using Milan circular questioning (Boscolo, Cecchin, Hoffman, & Penn, 1987) as well as other interactional questions that could take advantage of the online environment. An example of that type of questioning might be, "How do you think your father would describe this situation if he were here?" At that point the family would be brought back together to see what the other family member has written in response to the question. The response may create a different interactional perspective that opens up possibilities for change.

Q: With adolescents using chat to communicate constantly, how would you see online therapy being effective for them in family therapy?

Green: In my experience working with adolescents, I have found that they have a great sense of familiarity with chatting online and **instant messaging**. At times, adolescents may feel intimidated by a certain setting, when they feel an adult may be there to judge them, or put them under a microscope. Because adolescents do not have the same biases as some adults about communicating online, it may be easier to create intense relationships when conducting online therapy with them.

Q: How do you see a therapeutic alliance being built in online therapy?

Green: I was surprised watching my students bonding and relating so quickly and so intensely. I witnessed many thought-provoking questions and intimate responses presented. I would assume that whether in **real-time chat** or **e-mail**, the client or the therapist may address a question or a statement and compose a thoughtful and meaningful response and create profound therapeutic moments.

Q: Do you have any concerns about online therapy?

Green: Online therapy creates the opportunity to treat clients across state boundaries or internationally, so it is important to pay careful attention to ethical and legal considerations that might vary by state or country. It will also be important to learn about the client's cultural context. Online therapy legislation should be drafted to protect confidentiality and to address ethical concerns in this modality.

As a brief therapist, Green stated that it made sense to use brief therapy online. Her approach is for the family to initiate and terminate therapy in a convenient and workable way. Family brief therapy would be a good choice for online therapy.

NARRATIVE THERAPY

Narrative therapy is an approach to counseling and community work. It centers people as the experts in their own lives and views problems as separate from people. Narrative therapy assumes that people have many skills, competencies, beliefs, values, commitments, and abilities that will assist them to reduce the influence of problems in their lives. The word *narrative* refers to the emphasis that is placed upon the stories of people's lives and the differences that can be made through particular telling and retelling of these stories. Narrative therapy involves ways of understanding the stories of people's lives, and ways of reauthoring these stories in a collaboration between the therapist/community worker and the people whose lives are being discussed. It is a way of working that draws on the client's history and the broader context that affects people's lives and the ethics or politics of therapy.

In an electronic correspondance, Epston stated that "with ingenuity, online therapy allows for virtuality in terms of very invigorating conversations along with the apprenticing of therapists who can join in such ventures. Such conversations seem to conflate training, supervision, consultation with the very practice" (personal correspondence, April 23, 2004). For more information on narrative therapy in an online context, including transcripts of e-mail correspondence, see www.narrative approaches.com and specifically "The Archive of Resistance" that features correspondence regarding anorexia/bulimia.

Because narrative therapy relies on writing and places its value on written words, online chat therapy is an ideal medium for this approach.

CLIENT-DIRECTED, OUTCOME-INFORMED CLINICAL WORK

In a telephone interview with Scott Miller, a therapist who also lectures and trains in client-directed, outcome-informed clinical work and other time-sensitive therapeutic approaches, we explored how online therapy can benefit this approach. Miller cofounded the Institute for the Study of Therapeutic Change and offers pro bono services at a clinic dedicated to serving the underserved (see http://www.talkingcure.com).

Q: How do you see online therapy being effective for your approach?

Miller: Outcome-Informed clinical work can easily be conducted online. In fact, the largest studies on the approach have been conducted in a telephonic EAP setting (you can find these by the way at: www.talk ingcure.com). Working in this fashion merely requires the therapist to seek valid and reliable feedback regarding the alliance and outcome of treatment at each session. We call this "practice-based evidence"—using data generated during the session to structure and guide therapy.

Q: Could you please tell us about your approach and how online therapy can facilitate the implementation of this model?

Miller: We describe the outcome-informed process in numerous articles and in detail in our most recent book *The Heroic Client* (Duncan, Miller, & Sparks, 2000). Our most recent study involving over 6500 completed cases of treatment found that providing therapists with real-time feedback regarding the client's experience of the alliance and progress of treatment decreased drop out rates and improved the overall effect size by 65%. Such results were obtained, by the way, without training the therapists in any new treatment or diagnostic skills. Indeed, therapists were free to work in whatever way they preferred. The only constant in an otherwise diverse clinical setting was the availability of formal client feedback. When outcome-informed, therapists have an ongoing quality control system, monitoring the engagement and effectiveness of treatment on a session-by-session basis. Therapists working online can simply incorporate the feedback tools into their work. Depending on their circumstances and resources, they can use a web-based or end-user **software** program that administers, scores, and interprets the measures.

Q: Could you please explain about the tools and the role of online therapy in implementation of these tools?

Miller: My colleague, Barry Duncan, Psy.D., and I developed two feasible and reliable clinical tools. The Session Rating Scale 3.0 (SRS) (Johnson, Miller, & Duncan 2000), is a brief, four-item measure of the therapeutic alliance completed by the client and discussed with the therapist at the end of each session. The second measure is the Outcome Rating Scale (ORS), (Miller & Duncan, 2000), a brief, four-item measure of change completed by the client and discussed with the therapist at the beginning of each visit. (You may download both Rating Scales from www.talkingcure.com/measures.htm.) The SRS is administered at the end of each visit, either face-to-face or online. The ORS is administered at the beginning of each session. The scales can be used, regardless of the therapist's orientation, to create more effective therapeutic relationships and enhance treatment results.

Q: In comparison with face-to-face therapy, obviously non-verbal cues will be missing in an online therapy sessions. Could you please explain how your approach will enhance the process of receiving more information?

Miller: The measures, while not non-verbal in nature, are valid and reliable. Moreover, since both are relatively brief (requiring less than a minute to give and score) they can be completed at the time the service is offered. The availability of real-time feedback provides a crucial window of opportunity. The therapist can know whether to continue with more of the same or modify the treatment being offered. Whether online or face to face, available evidence indicates that taking the time to seek and discuss the client's experience of care enhances retention and outcome.

Miller states that the Client-Focused Outcome-Informed Clinical approach can be utilized with adults and adolescents, face-to-face, online, and over the telephone, anywhere in the world.

IMAGO RELATIONSHIP THERAPY

Imago relationship therapy is the theory and practice of the dynamics of committed partnerships with a focus on marriage.

It had its origins in the personal and intellectual partnership of Harville Hendrix and Helen LaKelly Hunt. After their marriage in 1982, they co-founded the Institute for Imago Relationship Therapy in 1984 to offer workshops for couples and training for interested professionals.

While imago relationship therapy originated as a clinical theory of marriage and marital therapy, reflection upon the larger implications of the unconscious dynamics of marital interaction led to the development of a set of metatheoretical assumptions. These assumptions are about the nature of the universe (cosmology), and thus of human nature (anthropology), which accounts for how such unique interactions could occur. Using inferential analysis from the clinical observation of couples moving from unconscious reactivity to conscious intentionality in their relationship, the authors posit that we live in an evolving, conscious universe that is in the process of self-completion, self-expansion, self-repair, and self-awareness. They continue this theory by explaining that these processes are evident in and facilitated by human species and personal evolution, self-reflection and healing, and are involved in marital dynamics and the healing process.

We interviewed Hendrix about online therapy by telephone and e-mail.

Q: How do you approach clients online for the first session?

Hendrix: I would ask them why they chose online therapy versus face-to-face therapy and why they chose me. Is there anything they want to know about me before we start? I would also talk with them about the limits and value of online therapy. I would indicate that not being able to see them limits my awareness of nonverbal conversation, but that writing has the advantage for them of being able to reflect on their feelings and thinking without the intrusion of nonverbal signals from me, and vice versa.

Given that I only do couples therapy, I would want them both to be online at the same time and all the time. I would ask if they could do that and if they are willing to do it. I would have to solve the problem of how I could see both of them online at the same time.

Then I would want to know what their goals were, and what they would like to achieve in this process. This would no doubt invite them to tell me their problem, but I would insist that they begin by talking about how they would want it to turn out. What would be different in their lives that would make this process successful for them? What is their view of a dream marriage?

I always want to know their vision of a successful outcome. That gives me a chance to assess how realistic their goals are, and if realistic, it guides me in knowing how to work with them around their goals. The discussion would include my views about the value of a marital vision, and then when we settled on realistic goals, we would work out a contract about outcome. I would tell them what I believe I can and cannot do, and we would discuss the limitations and values of online therapy (i.e., I cannot see them).

Then I would tell them how I work: that I use dialogue as the primary therapy process, that I would like to introduce them to my methodology by sending them a diagram of the process, then demonstrating it, and, finally, ask them to practice it by mirroring me, and then I would facilitate them in practicing it with each other. I would ask them to begin by stating something positive about each other, rather than starting with a negative. This would help them associate dialogue with all transactions rather than only with problems.

Q: How would the therapeutic alliance be created via chat without seeing the clients?

Hendrix: I think the beginning of the therapeutic alliance would be created by the above discussion of goals. In addition, in the first session, I would like to know something about them, where they live, what they look like, family, what kind of room they are in, how their computers are set up, are they together or separate? And I would ask if they wish a description of my context. I would ask if they have been in therapy before and what the outcome was? Then I would like to work with them to set up a goal for this first session. Find out what they would like to accomplish and we would work to make that realistic.

Q: How would you assess for diagnosis and formulate treatment goals online?

Hendrix: I tend not to do much diagnosis. I find the diagnosis evolves over time. But I always ask if there are any reasons why they may not be able to do therapy: medications, physical health, and so on. I would check for abuse patterns, if any. I would also want to know what they do when they are upset. One tends to isolate and the other to be intrusive, one to withdraw and the other to explode, and I would want to know about the intensity (i.e., how they handle conflict).

The techniques of imago relationship therapy are all designed to help couples finish childhood in their relationship by intentionally meeting the needs that were not met by their caretakers. The traditional role of the therapist as expert/authority in a hierarchical system is replaced in imago therapy by a more egalitarian model of therapist as facilitator of a healing process that is centered on the partners in a relationship rather than on the client–therapist relationship. The locus of healing is in the relationship. In fact, much of the interaction that traditionally constitutes the client–therapist relationship is shifted to the partner–partner relationship, but with some radical changes.

Q: How are couples given psychoeducation?

Hendrix: These are the bedrock issues.

1. We discuss the impact of childhood on the issues in their marriage, and how nonattuned parenting ruptures connection with their parents, within themselves, and with their context, including the cosmos.

2. Their attention is directed toward the unconscious purpose of the selection process (i.e., how their emotional incompatibility, the complementarity of their defenses, and the similarity of their wounds were factors in their romantic attraction to each other).

3. It is important that the couple understands that marriages go through stages. They usually begin with romantic love and go into a power struggle. The stage they are in is usually the power struggle, so they are helped to grasp what they are unconsciously trying to get done. The goal is to help them get that done, using processes that will be successful.

4. By concept and demonstration, the couple is taught the procedures of the dialogue process and how it achieves resolution through connection and maintains connection. To do this, they must learn how to create and sustain safety in their relationship. In the process they learn, and come to experience, that to resolve their issues, they must become surrogate parents to each other and stretch into new behaviors that will not activate childhood issues but instead reciprocally address them and resolve them.

Q: How would you approach clients' emotions over the Internet?

Hendrix: I would simply ask them how they feel about therapy, especially online therapy. I would check out what feelings they are having right now, whether they are relaxed or tense, and how they would like to feel. And I would ask them to take a break, go inside their bodies, and see where their tensions are. Then breathe deeply and imaginatively direct their attention to the body point and imagine that it has a message, and what it is.

Q: What interventions are best suited for online therapy?

Hendrix: I would ask them to write out what they are feeling, using only *I* language. They would be helped to know how to state their frustrations as desires rather than criticisms, and to be clear about what behaviors they want changed and what they are willing to do to change their behavior in order to get what they want. I would intervene in any criticism they might express and ask them to change it into a statement of a request rather than a complaint.

In my practice, we use dialogue as the main therapeutic intervention, and I would ask them to use that online. Essentially, I would ask them to send messages to each other, and the receiver would mirror the message, validate it, and express empathy before he or she responded. This would be a firm guideline and I would intervene in any attempt to not be dialogical. I would also dialogue with them.

The *couple's dialogue* is the primary and singular intervention facilitated by the therapist as coach rather than healer or authority, and it can be easily done online. It is facilitated between partners in the psychoeducational process and in the therapy procedures. It consists of mirroring, validating, and empathizing. The mirroring process helps couples create a safe environment in which they can nondefensively learn about each other's needs. It is the beginning of contact, and its structure looks something like this:

Sender sends a message. Receiver mirrors with this sentence stem.

"If I got it right, you said . . ." Then asks: "Is there more?" and continues to mirror and ask, "Is there more?" until there is no more. Then receiver summarizes all that the sender has sent in a summary paraphrase, leading with, "If I got all of that, your main points are . . . ," then asks, "Did I get it all?"

The next step in dialogue is validation, which enables them to differentiate from one another by seeing the point of view of the other, without necessarily agreeing. It looks something like this:

Sender waits for validation. Receiver leads with sentence: "Well, I can see the point you are making. You make sense, given your experience of my behavior, that you would think——I can see that."

In validation, the receiver distinguishes the partner from him- or herself, discovering that the partner is "not me." This differentiation of the other from the self enhances the sense of self of the receiver, a process distinct from traditional forms of differentiation through self-assertion. In the discovery of the "other," the symbiotic fusion is broken and real relationship becomes possible.

Sender waits for empathic statement. Receiver uses sentence stem: "and given all that, I can imagine you might feel . . ." seeking to mirror the partner's feelings, and over time will be able to participate in them. Such empathic attunement would sound like this: "And I am experiencing how difficult that is for you right now. I am sharing your feeling of. . . ."

Through empathic attunement, they make a deep emotional connection that is itself healing. Many couples, after they have engaged in this process for a while, cannot remember the precipitating incident. Whenever they can recall it, they discover that it is always about an actual or threatened connectional rupture, and the dialogue, which restores connection, obviates the need to explore the initiating incident.

As the online therapeutic process progresses, five variations of dialogue are used for specific purposes. An important process is reimagining your partner as wounded rather than bad or dangerous, the *parent–child dialogue*. In this dialogue, one partner assumes the role of the parent and the other the role of themselves as a child. It looks like this:

Sender acts as a child. Receiver acts as if the parent and asks: "What was it like to be a child in your family?" Or, ". . . to have me as your parent?"

Sender as child: Describes, receiver mirrors, asks if there is more, and closes difficulty as a child, with a summary paraphrase. Then the receiver asks, "What was the worst thing that happened to you as a child?"

Sender describes worst. Receiver mirrors, as above. Then asks, "What do you need that would change and heal all that?"

Sender says what he or she needs. Receiver says: "That makes sense, and you deserve to have that."

The *behavior change request dialogue* is designed to help partners communicate their needs without using criticism, devaluation, or intimidation. Instead, they identify the request hidden in the frustration and ask for a behavior change that would satisfy that request. The partner uses the dialogue process to fully understand the root of the frustration in childhood and the current request. The receiving partner then agrees to a concrete, specific, time-limited behavior and grants it as a gift without imposing an obligation for reciprocity. Since we always marry persons who are least capable of meeting our needs, because of our own childhood wounding and defenses, each person has to stretch into unfamiliar and challenging behaviors. We have learned that what one partner needs the most has to come from their partner's undeveloped self. So, when they ask for their deepest need to be met, if the partner responds by meeting it, they will grow into new parts of themselves. In this way, partners call each other into mutual wholeness.

The *container dialogue* is a process that enables couples to deal with their anger and remain connected and convert the energy into passion. It is the most complicated imago process and consists of seven steps.

Reromanticing is the intentional creation of pleasure in the relationship. Partners using dialogue learn from each other what gave them pleasure in the past, what gives them pleasure in the present, and what they would like that would give them pleasure in the future. After the exchange of the information, they agree on behaviors they will engage in on a daily basis that will be a source of pleasure. This creates safety and bonding.

In *revisioning*, couples are helped to create their

dream relationship. They are asked to describe the qualities and behaviors that would exist in the relationship of their dreams. Thus the relationship that is healing and recovers wholeness is created in their acts of intentional connection. All of the above mentioned interventions can easily be facilitated with the clients via chat, audio-, or videotherapy.

Q: Would you have any legal and ethical considerations?

Hendrix: Can't think of any.

Q: How would you terminate with clients online?

Hendrix: Assuming the process was successful, I would ask them for an assessment and would check how consistent their changes were, how related to their goals. I never really terminate, so we might suspend sessions and check in, as they needed, or we would have a schedule of check-ins. I remain available if they wish it.

Q: Please state if any of your answers to the above questions would be different for traditional therapy vs. online therapy.

Hendrix: Not much.

Although couples therapy could be more challenging than individual therapy for the therapist, Hendrix painted a smooth picture of how therapists can implement their personal orientation online and be effective with couples. Hendrix showed that with some accommodations for this new modality, his approach was easily modified to be conducted online. This concept can ease many therapists' concerns about preserving their modality and professional identity while working online.

TRANSPERSONAL THERAPY

G. Frank Lawlis serves as the principal content adviser to the *Dr. Phil* television show. In an interview about online therapy, we explored how his orientation and approach, which are usually known to require a face-to-face setting, can be conducted online. Lawlis has a doctorate in counseling psychology with an emphasis on medical psychology and rehabilitation. He was awarded the diplomate (A.B.P.P.) in both counseling and clinical psychology and he is a Fellow of the American Psychological Association, an honor awarded for his scientific contributions to the field of clinical psychology and behavioral medicine.

Q: How do you think your approach can be implemented online?

Lawlis: Transpersonal applications for the Internet have natural approaches because words themselves are symbols, making the inherent messages from expressions very potent for insight and guidance. My approaches can include homework and personal quests that usually take place between sessions, although there can be breaks in the sessions for real-life experiences. For example, for online approaches, I work with the symbols that come up for the client. We draw them, we taste them, we act them out, and write about them. One of the typical symbols is a white knight that symbolizes the powerful good within us. The client writes a story about the power of this great warrior and what strengths lie beneath the power and when to use them. We write stories (fantasy as well as actual) about how the white knight works to preserve peace. These exercises are very powerful, and clients often keep them for decades.

Q: What interventions from your approach can be utilized in online therapy?

Lawlis: In order to receive the guidance residing in transpersonal space (unconscious or from other realms, such as the collective unconscious), I have used a variety of rituals, depending on the preference of the client. My choices with the greatest impact have been:

- Using lucid dreaming
- Humming for 15 minutes
- Breathing meditation with focus
- Finding a space in nature and staying for 24 hours
- Sitting in total darkness (such as a closet)
- Staring at a candle
- Free drawing, painting, or sculpturing
- Moving (dancing) to music
- Listening to selections of music

There are many more that can be created, but all of them require that the person have no distractions and can listen to his or her images as they come. The same instructions are given online, and that the question they want addressed be clearly defined (written in chat). They are conscious of what symbols are presented throughout the quest period. They are not to try to interpret them or to become discouraged if the answers do not pop up immediately. More often than not, they will get an answer quickly, but they should be encouraged to complete the timed session for other possible experiences. It has been my experience that such answers are often rapid, but more important questions and perspectives will continue once the client has found a mind frequency for reception. For example, I had one executive who was worried about what to do with some possibly inflammatory statements he had made in confidence being made public, and the potential threat to his job. His favorite path into the transpersonal space was imaging his father (deceased) walking him through a garden and conversing with him. In his imagery his father came to him and his immediate response was, "You are taking yourself way too seriously."

In this man's imagery, their walk began and his continued session contained smells of the flowers and a powerful sense of awe about the universe. When we communicated about his experience, he admitted that he laughed at himself and immediately understood how minor his issues were and that they all related to fear. The flowers gave off a peaceful aroma and the message became a blessing.

As a person experiences his or her imagery, whether it is visual, olfactory, auditory, or other, it always has layers of symbolic meaning to the individual. It is the understanding not only of the symbols themselves, but the multiple layers and their interactions that provides the most powerful perspective and helps develop an action plan.

There is a caution not to interpret the symbol *for* the person, but *with* the person. There are too many complex secrets that no therapist would know or could guess, and too often counselors can do more harm than good with ready answers. That is the value of writing via chat. However, that does not mean that some guesses can't be made to open up possibilities. I have used the statement, "I don't know if this relates to your experience, but if I had this imagery, I would think it would mean for me . . ." I have used my knowledge of cultural anthropology. For example, if a person has an owl come into his or her imagery, I might explain that cultures have used this symbol for many interpretations. In some Native-American cultures, the vision of an owl means mystery and new life, to others, it means good luck, in others it means life transitions or transformations. However, the client usually has some story about personal experiences relating to the imaged symbol, and meaning is derived from those.

In general, the approach is based on three phases—separation from ordinary reality to transpersonal space, receiving the symbolic images, and returning back to understand their meaning and integration. This is a very rich experience that has true life-changing elements, and not only does the medium of online work present no obstacles, it enhances this process.

Q: How would you approach the client's emotions over the Internet?

Lawlis: Transpersonal medicine has the mission of helping a person deal with his or her resources, both within and beyond the individual. A person's emotions can be helped if the person knows some avenues for addressing them from a higher, wiser plan. I would recommend a suitable direction, based on the person's perspective of life. It might be to take a three-day journey in the desert or listen to drum beats, focusing on their breathing for 24 hours. It might be a special music or walking the path of meditation. Some people have found answers in sexual relationships with their partners.

These approaches are as easily done online as face-to-face because they are basically homework assignments. I prepare diaries and rating forms so that the client can report back about the experiences. Like so many of the rituals of rebirth, these experiences become more important when they are written and preserved as well as better understood through the writing process.

Q: Do you have any legal and ethical considerations about online therapy?

Lawlis: Because transpersonal medicine is a personal journey and does not demand a dialogue, per se, no extraordinary legal or ethical considerations apply. In many ways, online therapy offers more legal protection to both client and therapist in this process. In face-to-face therapy there is the tendency to break boundaries because of the blurring of reality at times. In online work the computer serves as a terrific boundary because of the preserved objectivity of the therapist and the freedom for the client to go into secret realms.

Q: Do you have any concerns about online therapy being conducted nationally and internationally across borders?

Lawlis: The excellent quality about transpersonal counseling is that instead of using a cultural model unique to the United States, you are dealing with universal symbols. I have taught around the world, and the therapeutic process remains constant. Symbols surpass languaging with all the underlying facets for a person's life. The answer is no, I have no concerns, and yes, there are tremendous advantages.

Q: How would you terminate with a client online?

Lawlis: By determining whether the client has received the answer which he or she needed, in the same way a face-to-face therapy process would terminate. In transpersonal counseling, these answers often come more quickly because there is little need to confront behavior or become involved with the dynamics between therapist and client. The client is looking for answers, and once the answers are received, the course of action is implicit to the client. However, the door is always open to the client to explore other realms.

CONCLUSION

Therapists use a variety of theoretical orientations to experiment with and adapt interventions successfully to online therapy. Fenichel stated that "Regardless of where Cyberspace may 'be', when a mental health practitioner is 'meeting in session' with a client, whether asynchronously or in real-time (face-to-face [f2f] video, chat or phone), in order to experience 'being connected' to the person on the other end there is a continued need just as in days of yore, to understand the client's experience of *here and now*" (2002).

Online therapy styles and orientation demonstrate commonality regardless of the theory used. Therapists have been using the online modality as they blend a variety of other theoretical approaches, such as client-focused, cognitive–behavioral, family systems therapy, Gestalt, imago relationship therapy, narrative therapy, psychoanalytic, object relations, solution-focused therapy, and transpersonal therapy. Many eclectic therapists utilize different interventions from different theories and orientations, as they see fit, with online clients.

The relationship between therapist and client, regardless of the theoretical orientation, depends on how their communication creates a profound impact on the client so that he or she feels warmth, empathy, and genuineness. These essential factors are based on the work of Carl Rogers and other therapy process researchers. The entire course of treatment is dependent upon the communication and the extent to which dialogue is experienced as being synchronous communication versus **asynchronous communication.**

It is obvious that with the 21st century, communication between people around the world will be as simple as a click away on the computer. It is inevitable that increasingly, therapists will practice their theory and interventions online. As technology grows and continues to become a way of living, online therapy will become as natural as face-to face-therapy. As the masters in the field of psychotherapy have made clear, it is possible to utilize almost the same theory and interventions that would be used in face-to-face therapy, with an obvious adaptation to the means and the technology of online therapy.

CHAPTER **2**

Common Questions about Online Therapy

Despite its growing popularity, some mental health profession-als continue to have concerns about online therapy. Some con-cerns are valid, but others are based upon misconceptions about online therapy. During the early years of online therapy, some mental health professionals observed problems and is-sues that led to serious misconceptions about this method of delivering psychotherapy services. None of these individuals were wrong in their observations. These observations allowed for appropriate scrutiny and evaluation, which continue to en-sure that all **telecommunication** therapy methods remain legit-imate, credible, ethical, and effective. Continuing evaluation resulted in a long list of reasons to appreciate the benefits and successes of online therapy. These successes prompted a look at the validity of the negative perceptions surrounding online therapy. There were doubts regarding its effectiveness, pur-pose, benefits, the nature of its possible client base, and con-cerns about ethical issues. The main misconceptions that continue to fuel the controversy surrounding online therapy are: (1) that it is impossible to practice; (2) it replaces traditional therapy; (3) it is very different from traditional therapy; (4) it can only be done via e-mail; (5) it does not allow for the human experience to occur (i.e., the therapeutic alliance); (6) it is not effective for serious disorders; (7) it can only be practiced in the state in which the therapist is licensed.

Many professional associations, once skeptical of the practice of all telecommunication therapy, have now developed policies and issued guidelines specific for these methods (see Appendix C). The American Psychological Association (APA) is in the process of developing an online policy, thus opening the door for legitimizing this form of therapy for its members and the numerous clients they serve. The APA's initiative in developing guidelines for online therapy lends much credibility to the field. According to Burgower, a clinical psychologist currently helping the APA develop its online policy,

> Within ten years, computers will become so embedded in our lives, we won't even think of this as **telehealth**. The housebound patient will be able to receive care on a regular basis. Therapy will be conducted (via e-mail or **chat rooms**) with remote or extended family members located thousands of miles from each other. (Burgower, 2001)

Other associations in various stages of developing policies and guidelines for online therapy include the American Association of Marriage and Family Therapists (AAMFT), American Psychiatric Association, California Association of Marriage and Family Therapists (CAMFT), National Association of Social Workers (NASW), International Society for Mental Health Online (ISMHO), and the American Counseling Association (ACA).

As online therapy grows, so does the attention from prominent leaders in the therapy field. See Chapter 1 for interviews with theorists offering feedback and suggestions for applying their specialties to online therapy. The expansion of online therapy is bringing with it greater understanding, acceptance, and willingness to let go of the misconceptions.

IS ONLINE THERAPY POSSIBLE?

The first concern is in regard to the identity of the client; how can it be verified? The identity and legitimacy of the therapist may also be in doubt if there is no way to ensure that the therapist is legitimately licensed. The second concern is that privacy and confidentiality cannot be guaranteed.

Verifying Identity

In the early days of online therapy, people primarily met in chat rooms, and therapy was informally conducted in those public (or even private) chat rooms and also via e-mail. There was no procedure used to verify any type of information, because these relationships were based upon the assertions made by the people involved.

With the advent of **online clinics**, procedures and systems were put in place to protect clients from individuals fraudulently claiming to be therapists. Additionally, the commercialization of online therapy brought structures into play that allowed for the payment of services. Typically, clients pay by credit card, electronic check, and in the near future possibly as a part of their health plan. All of these methodologies ensure that accurate and detailed information regarding the identity and location of the client is known. In fact, it can be argued that clients online must provide more accurate information than those who visit clinicians in person. Therapists generally never ask for identification from their clients, and if a client self-pays for therapeutic services, he or she may easily provide completely fictitious information regarding identity and location.

With respect to the legitimacy of the practitioner, therapists offering services from **personal Web sites** should post their license and malpractice information for potential clients. Reputable online therapy clinics should also conduct background checks on therapists prior to listing them. (See Appendix B for a partial list of online therapy clinics.)

With proper authorization, authorities can trace the exact location of the computer user through the **Internet protocol** (IP) address. But in addition to this, when online, a client usually has entered a credit card number or an insurance plan account number, so therapists actually have more accurate, up-to-date, and accessible information on the client's location than they would in face-to-face practice. In fact, some e-clinics actually provide a mechanism that will instantly put therapists in touch with police, hospital, and emergency services close to the client's location.

Without question, the identity and whereabouts of a client are important pieces of information to have available in case of a crisis.

Privacy and Confidentiality

Guaranteeing privacy and confidentiality in the online medium may not be possible, but an acceptable level of privacy and confidentiality can be achieved. In fact, guaranteeing privacy and confidentiality is just as difficult in a traditional face-to-face practice. For instance, someone can easily be seen walking into a therapist's office by anyone in the vicinity as well as those who are in the waiting room. For those therapists who share an office suite with multiple practitioners, it is possible that someone could listen at a door. Realistically, it is much more plausible that someone seeking therapy in person could have their privacy compromised than someone who seeks therapy online. The reason for this is that in the online environment, no "casual" breaches occur just because someone is in the vicinity.

Online, the issue of privacy revolves around using technologies that best deflect the efforts of computer **hackers**. Typically, hackers focus on data that can be sold (such as banking information) and on creating computer system disturbances that affect the flow of data and commerce. In order to protect client information from hackers, those who run online therapy services (the actual software that powers online therapy) have a variety of tools and options that can be used to protect such information.

It is commonly conceded that if hackers are determined to break into a system, they will do so. However, it is possible to minimize the chance of this through use of the proper security protocols that are typically run by both individual and online therapy clinics. Other than possible credit card information, there is little to appeal to hackers at online therapy sites. Credible online therapy Web sites run protocols that not only protect clients' credit card information as effectively as financial institutions do, but also separate financial information, identity, and communications. Therefore, a hacker would need to hack at least two of three systems in order to make sense of the information attained, and would be discovered, at the latest, after breaching one system. Once a breach is detected, the other systems are placed on **alert** and the effort thwarted.

The second way that privacy and confidentiality can be jeopardized is by using tools that do not provide any security. Some of the communication tools to be wary of are: **public message boards**, chat rooms, e-mail, and instant messaging. A public message board is software used by a support group. Chat rooms are located on Web sites that contain individual pages (rooms) where you can chat with random **surfers** or arrange a meeting. The chat takes the form of inputting lines of text, often with the option of complementary emotion signifiers (e.g., **emoticons**), and waiting for a typed response. There are also free instant messaging programs. These are services that alert users when friends or colleagues are online and allows them to communicate with each other in real time through private online chat areas, such as those provided by AOL Messenger, Yahoo Messenger, or MSN Messenger. These are third-party companies that own and manage the **servers** through which these communications are supplied. This also applies to free e-mail services such as Hotmail and even paid e-mail services such as AOL. The problem arises from these companies not having any responsibility to maintain the necessary privacy of psychotherapeutic communications. Not only are therapist–client communications capable of being viewed by other users of the services, these communications may also be viewed by any number of company employees who are not bound by confidentiality. Secure e-mail is sometimes used with the thought that messages remain private, but there are two issues that work against that premise. First, the security used in secure e-mail programs can be penetrated, and second, once the e-mail is downloaded to the user's computer, anyone who has access to the computer may also gain access to the decrypted e-mail.

From a legal standpoint, the current **telemedicine** laws (see Chapter 8) and HIPAA guidelines ensure privacy and confidentiality. Online therapists, properly trained, understand the privacy laws and equip their Web sites with secure tools and technology. Web sites are ethically managed, provide communication via secure chat rooms and **videoconferencing,** and utilize **encrypted e-mail,** secure **passwords,** and **digital signatures.** To ensure the highest security, online therapy Web sites must also have the most current **antivirus protection.**

WILL ONLINE THERAPY REPLACE TRADITIONAL THERAPY?

Online therapy is thought by many professionals to have been conceived to replace traditional therapy. There are two perspectives from which to look at this idea. At the time of writing, with the current state of technology, online therapy is mostly understood to mean chat-room style therapy and e-mail therapy. The use of video and audio is not a widespread practice due to the limitations of the current technologies available. Therefore, if face-to-face therapy is determined to be appropriate by the therapist, online therapy is typically ruled out as an effective treatment medium. However, the future will make available full-size video displays and other technologies that work together to make possible face-to-face meetings using the Internet. For the moment, clinicians who are well versed in the state of online therapy will mostly affirm that currently it is meant to enhance, not replace, traditional face-to-face therapy. Some clients will always be better suited to face-to-face therapy, while for others online therapy will be a helpful adjunct to face-to-face therapy. Still others will benefit from online therapy alone.

Appropriateness of Online Therapy

In most cases, simple logic provides the answer to the ever-present concern of how therapists may best serve their clients. There are clear situations when online therapy is not the best treatment alternative; for example, in cases in which the therapist must be present and interact with the client in a way that cannot be done using Web-based tools. Just the same, there are also clear situations when online therapy does provide an equal or better alternative to face-to-face therapy. We suggest that therapists use their judgment and trust their training. It is best to have the most current training and education (see Appendix D) with regard to the practice of online therapy. In addition, it is advisable for all practitioners to be educated with regard to the most current law and ethics regarding online therapy and all therapy telecommunication methods (see Chapter 8). Only by having that knowledge are therapists able to make well-informed decisions as to when it is advisable or inadvisable to integrate online therapy into their practices.

IS ONLINE THERAPY VERY DIFFERENT FROM TRADITIONAL THERAPY?

Those who contend that online therapy is very different from traditional therapy cite the use of typing as the determining factor.

However, those who have had significant experience using on-line therapy cite the end result as being the same as traditional therapy, and therefore determine that online therapy is not fundamentally very different from traditional face-to-face therapy.

Ways in Which Online Therapy Differs from Traditional Therapy

In terms of therapeutic interaction, goals, and ability to help people, online therapy is no different from traditional therapy. The differences between online therapy and face-to-face therapy are some of the unique factors that make online therapy a good choice. Clients who have difficulty scheduling weekly face-to-face sessions benefit from the online method more than traditional therapy. Online therapy can accommodate people's illnesses, frequent traveling, schedule changes due to personal and work issues, and time zone changes. People with disabilities often embrace the different options online therapy offers. For example, hearing impaired clients are often better able to express themselves using text communication and appreciate not having to depend on an interpreter.

In an effort to study the efficacy of online therapy, the International Society for Mental Health Online (ISMHO) sponsors a clinical case study group. The ISMHO Clinical Case Study Group (2000) includes transcripts from therapists using chat to demonstrate how therapeutic relationships may be established "with such poignancy and immediacy that a review of the case session transcripts was, to our amazement, quite difficult to imagine as having taken place via the Internet rather than face-to-face (or on the couch)" (ISMHO, 2000b).

The ISMHO has continued to explore some of the many ways in which online mental health professionals engage in clinical online practices, either as the primary treatment modality or in combination with traditional face-to-face office practice. The cases reviewed point to numerous similarities between traditional and online therapy with regard to the use of various therapy techniques.

Among the many useful techniques which were demonstrated and validated through our case studies, powerful therapeutic relationships were recognized and clarified, replete with transference and countertransference, deep and immediate emotions expressed by the client, and the possibility of long-term engagement even with an ambivalent client. We often observed how this was facilitated by establishing the benefits of true synchronicity through the chat medium—especially with good technology and two fast typists—and then marveled at the similarity between a text-based transcript and a comparable office session, as well as the expressiveness and depth of text-based communication. (Fenichel et al., 2004)

Despite the numerous applications, benefits, and growing popularity of online therapy, there continue to be some professionals who disregard the fundamental rules of therapy when practicing over the Internet. It is imperative for all mental health professionals expanding their practices with online therapy or any method of telecommunication to remember that the basic issues surrounding standards of care, legal and ethical responsibilities, and confidentiality remain the same for either in-person or online therapy.

CAN ONLINE THERAPY BE PRACTICED ONLY VIA E-MAIL?

Online therapy can use a multitude of communications tools to facilitate therapy sessions. These include online presentations (slide shows, Web sites, documents, etc.), chat, instant messaging, e-mail, and **online journaling**.

Combining all the telecommunication methods enables online therapists to have a broader and more synergistic approach when communicating with their clients. Clients have a greater variety of ways to express themselves and are able to disclose more aspects of their identity, emotions, and issues. The use of real-time chat offers text-based, synchronous communication that allows therapy to be in the here-and-now. Online therapists also find it helpful to develop treatment plans specifically designed for the different methods of communication, whether with voice, text, or visuals.

Online group therapy combining videoconferencing, real-time chat, and **message boards** can be just as effective as face-to-face sessions. Therapists use synchronous chat sessions, videoconferencing, and web-based message boards to communicate with a group of their clients. As with traditional therapy, clients benefit from therapists and other group members sharing information and support for common problems and issues. In addition, clients are also instantly provided with access to online sources through **hypertext links** (URLs).

Data gathered by MyTherapyNet.com indicated how a group of working mothers, who were dealing with time management issues combined phone and online sessions. They found it profitable to spend time in a chat room rather than having to go to an office. The working mothers reported liking the convenience, the ease in using the chat rooms, and the direct approach to their therapy. This group also reported that it was helpful not to have to go through the usual adjustment of getting to know their therapist ahead of time. The chat room allowed the focus to be on the issues. When they integrated a phone session with the chat room, the therapeutic relationship was additionally enhanced.

A case reviewed by ISMHO (Fenichel et al., 2004) also demonstrated the value of integrating face-to-face therapy with several online therapy methods using a weight management group. The group members specifically benefited from real-time chat rooms and message boards that offered continuous access to other group members and experts in the field of nutrition and mental health. The group members could also share their experiences, assignments, and associated dydactic information through the secure message board.

Audio- and videoconferencing are in their infancy as Internet tools. Although there are those who use **audioconferencing,** the vast majority of Internet users have never done so. Yet, every indication shows that using the Internet to speak to others is a reality in the near future for the masses, and is already in use by early adopters of the technology.

The latest online therapy method involves using a virtual environment to simulate a face-to-face meeting. Therapists and clients create visual representations of themselves, called **avatars.** This multimedia approach provides an opportunity to apply techniques that involve fantasy, imagination, and role-playing to online therapy.

CAN TEXT BE USED TO CREATE THERAPEUTIC ALLIANCE?

Online therapy does currently rely primarily upon text communications. Some opponents to online therapy claim that the subtleties of human experience cannot be relayed solely by the use of written words. Our knowledge, experience, and research findings dispute this claim.

Using Text to Communicate

One of the most common issues discussed with respect to this new medium is the viability of conducting psychotherapy in a purely written environment. To take the example of family therapy, older children and adolescents are comfortable with the online environment. Their experience with using chat and instant messaging is generally fully integrated into regular communications with friends and family. Moreover, the experiences related by both therapists and clients seem to indicate that there are some unique and positive effects that derive from these written communications (MyTherapyNet, 2004). Writing succinctly to accommodate both the timeframe of the therapy as well as the impetus to disclose effectively, often brings issues to the table more rapidly than in the case of traditional therapy. Some clients have reported that **text messaging** gives them time to collect their thoughts prior to typing a response. The alleviation of a perceived need to immediately respond allows additional time for reflection, which can be quite beneficial. Issues may be discussed candidly, without fear of judgment. The slightest nonverbal nuance that a therapist may unconsciously portray, such as the lifting of an eyebrow or a passing frown can cause some, though by no means all, clients to feel self-conscious about their disclosures. In a traditional session, the client at times tends to sugarcoat the issue, to explain and rationalize behavior rather than to focus on disclosure and solution.

Precedence for Text Having the Capacity to Relay Complex Emotions, Thoughts, and Concepts

The use of the written word to express great depth of emotion has been considered highly effective for centuries. The advent of the Internet reawakened the pleasures of writing for millions of people worldwide, as they found the advantages of instant messaging, chat rooms, e-mail, and electronic message boards. In fact, putting deep emotions into words has a very powerful effect, and that process in and of itself is highly therapeutic. Interventions specifically rely upon "awakening" the individual into recognizing harmful patterns. When an individual sees in print what they have been harboring inside, self-realization is very likely to be expedited.

IS IT POSSIBLE TO CREATE A THERAPEUTIC RELATIONSHIP ONLINE?

It is often argued that therapeutic relationships must have a visual component. Two examples clearly illuminate why this is not always the case. In the case of the visually impaired therapist, there is no question that a therapeutic relationship is created in their work. In fact, many utilize other senses which can result in a sharpening of their clinical skills. The second example is telephone therapy. In most cases, the first contact between client and therapist is by telephone. At this time, the client makes a decision whether or not to enlist the services of the therapist based on an assessment of how well he or she is suited to the therapist. The client feels a connection over the telephone, and connection is the foundation to the therapeutic relationship. Many renowned therapists and theorists use online and telephone therapy as a means of establishing relationships in cases where there are logistical obstacles, as well as a manner of enhancing the ongoing therapeutic relationship.

Online Therapeutic Relationships

The numerous barriers to finding mental health services create the need for people to go online. Many turn to the Internet when traditional resources are too difficult to access. E-therapy is very effective. Clients and therapists report that the online therapeutic relationship is often comparable to the face-to-face therapeutic relationship. Those who communicate online with ease and comfort experience more comfort in creating a therapeutic relationship based on words rather than visual cues. Our clients report that healing occurs through the therapeutic alliance based on the relationship itself, regardless of the psychotherapeutic techniques. Deep and meaningful relationships are constantly being formed using text-based correspondence alone, without visual cues.

Visual Cues

Online therapy does not, by nature, exclude the ability to have access to visual cues: **Webcams** allow users to both see and speak to each other. Computers that only have a microphone are able to connect for audio conversations. Audio-only mental health services have been successful for many years, as evidenced by the effective use of suicide prevention telephone hotlines.

The real question becomes whether chat room therapy is effective for crisis intervention and suicide prevention. Again, if a user seems in dire need, the therapist can easily check his or her location and take appropriate action. Short of that, is text messaging effective between someone in crisis or contemplating suicide and his or her therapist? In the majority of cases, after considering all the anecdotal evidence available on this topic, we may agree that it is indeed effective.

Therapists must always use discretion in therapy, and recommending a modality may become part of a treatment plan. For example, a therapist might recommend that a face-to-face client have some sessions online. This would be particularly appropriate in the case of an agoraphobic whose ability to regularly attend therapy is disrupted by the disorder.

The issue of whether visual cues can occur in strictly text communication is debatable, but there are instances in which it is fairly clear that a type of visual clue does exist in that medium. For one, people can use **emoticons** to express their feelings when writing instant messages or e-mails. These emoticons can be happy faces, sad faces, representations of such emotions, or representations created by characters on the computer **keyboard**, such as ;) for *wink*, :) for *smile*, :(for *sad*. There are also codes for other behaviors and emotions, such as *lol* for laughing out loud, *xoxo* for hugs and kisses, *rofl* for rolling on the floor laughing. Additionally, if one studies the manner in which the client is typing, insights into his or her behaviors can prove highly instructive.

IS ONLINE THERAPY EFFECTIVE FOR SERIOUS DISORDERS?

Online therapy can be used as a bridge to encourage resistant clients with serious disorders to get help. Some clients may simply be too depressed or otherwise adversely affected by their disorder to actually set and keep face-to-face appointments, and seeking therapy and online therapy can offer a first step to receiving help.

CAN I PRACTICE ONLINE IN MY STATE?

The geographical relation between therapist and client is the most debated issue surrounding online therapy. There remain, at the time of writing, diverging points of view on this subject. There are no national laws forbidding a therapist to treat someone outside of his or her state of licensure, though some state boards have taken a stand on where the therapy takes place. For more information on the out-of-state issue, please refer to Chapter 8, and also the guidelines in Appendix C.

CONCLUSION

Through the description and discussion of the most popular misconceptions, it is apparent that many are genuinely unfounded and do not apply to online therapy. This does not remove the fact that there are valid issues for concern when trying something as new and innovative as online therapy. Again, many of the concerns result from caution in regard to a new therapeutic approach. It is important to make sure that the profession of psychotherapy maintains its professional standing, but it is also important to explore new opportunities, whether they be in technology or any other aspect that can applies to the field, and provides increased opportunity to help those in need.

CHAPTER 3

Clinical Guidelines and Approaches

Online therapy is an extension of face-to-face therapy. Therapists draw upon their personal and professional tools and abilities when they conduct online therapy. All the basic principles of psychotherapy remain the same, and only some additional principles should be considered for online therapy. What differs is the medium in which therapy is conducted and the adjustment of the therapeutic approach for each phase of therapy to suit this medium. The phases of online therapy are divided into: (1) initial contact; (2) first session; (3) early sessions and therapeutic alliance; (4) early sessions and identifying issues; (5) middle stage sessions; (6) termination. For many practical and bureaucratic matters (e.g., billing online) that are specific to online therapy, please see Chapters 6 and 7.

INITIAL CONTACT

Traditionally, clients select a therapist via a referral from a friend, colleague, or physician. They may also choose from individual therapists' Web sites, **e-clinics**, print ads, or the Yellow Pages. In an online setting, the client may use any of the above mentioned methods or find a therapist by using an online **search engine** or a specialized Web site. Both individual therapist Web sites and online therapy clinics can actually provide clients with enhanced features, in addition to license and educational qualifications. These features may include therapist's pictures, therapist's profiles, and a variety of therapy options.

In a traditional setting, therapists normally have a chance to speak with their clients on the phone prior to the commencement of therapy. In online therapy, many times the first contact with clients can actually become a full session. The therapy session can range from a single contact to a lengthy course of treatment. The conversation can vary from assessment, referral, or simple problem solving to short- or long-term treatment. Clients may decide to make the first contact by sending an e-mail to the therapist. This e-mail may contain a question that needs a rapid response. If the e-mail question indicates that the client actually needs more than a rapid response, the therapist can reply with some recommendations for treatment.

Clients often need to ask many questions regarding how the therapy is conducted before they decide to engage in online therapy. Some online therapy Web sites allow clients a session to evaluate the appropriateness of this therapy method as well as the fit with the therapist. Other Web sites offer 15- or 25-minute sessions for the initial contact, which often is fee for service. When clients pay for the initial contact time online, defining the purpose of the session is very important. The following are some questions therapists should ask themselves to prepare for the initial contact.

Is the client at the research stage in terms of finding a therapist and thus interviewing the therapist throughout a 15-minute session as opposed to using the time for therapy?

Has the client previously been in traditional or online therapy?

Is this an experiment on the potential client's part, or is the client already committed to the process of therapy?

Does the client want a one-time educational and counseling session?

Is the client interested in the reduction of symptoms or in long-term therapy?

THE FIRST SESSION

The first session, the most important, is the time for the therapeutic alliance to begin forming between online client and therapist. This session is when the client meets the therapist, a bond is created, and the client assesses whether the therapist is to be trusted and if the therapist's style of therapy fits well with the client's needs. In the course of the first session, the therapist assesses the client's diagnosis and whether he or she has the competency to treat the client. This session is also where therapist and client assess whether online therapy is appropriate for this particular client. The ability to communicate empathy effectively and to use prompts and probes are the primary therapy skills needed in this initial stage of assessment and exploration.

Defining the purpose of the online session is very important within the first session. Regardless of whether they are providing a 15-, 25-, or 50-minute session, online therapists should collaborate with their clients to define the clients' needs. These needs or expectations could be a single session consultation, crisis intervention, psychoeducational, motivational, or short-term therapy. Many Internet users explore the Internet for quick and easy answers and may not want to engage in a therapeutic relationship. They might be open to a therapeutic relationship but not know that the therapeutic relation is available to them. Some might expect a very brief "Dear Abby" style response. Through the assessment, the client's needs become more apparent. The therapist then has the opportunity to educate the client about the process of online therapy.

As with traditional therapy, an intake form can be used by online therapists to gather information for assessment and diagnosis. Online therapists e-mail an intake assessment form to their clients so they can write a list of their presenting issues and answer questions related to psychosocial issues. Clients e-mail the assessment back to their therapist for review prior to the next session. Some interactive therapy Web sites allow clients to fill out the assessment form online at the Web site.

Another helpful way to view the first session is in stages. According to *The Helping Interview* (Benjamin, 1987), the three main stages of an interview are: initiation, development, and closing.

Initiation or Statement of Purpose

This stage is comprised of (1) a choice of online therapy mode (i.e., e-mail, chat, audio, video) and (2) assessment. Therapist and client confirm the location where the client resides, where the therapist practices, and the state in which the therapist is licensed to practice (see Chapter 8 and Appendix C). This stage is generally completed when both the therapist and client agree on the client's symptoms, the purpose, and the issues to be discussed during the therapy.

Development or Exploration

The client's purpose for seeking therapy is further explored. Assessments of the clinical issues are pursued, a provisional diagnosis is formed, and a preliminary treatment plan is discussed. In this phase therapists should ask themselves the following questions:

- Did I clearly explain online therapy?
- Have I explored online therapy's benefits vs. limitations?
- Did I create a space for a therapeutic alliance?

- Did I communicate my empathy and presence to the client?
- Does the client communicate effectively online?
- Is the client comfortable with all the technological aspects of online therapy?
- Was the client able to look at things the way they appear to her or him rather than the way they seem to me or to someone else?
- Did I perceive the client accurately or did I misunderstand the words without the visual cues?
- Did my attitude prevent the client from exploring his or her own life or enable him or her to move about in it, unhampered by external influences?
- How did I transfer my warmth through my words?
- Did I help the client move from an external to an internal frame of reference?
- Did I help the client to come closer to him- or herself?
- Do I have the minimum amount of information to form a diagnostic impression?

The assessment and information gathering can be done through direct or open-ended questioning, depending on the therapist's style. Online clients often feel comfortable responding to an assessment form or a series of questions online without being in the presence of the therapist. Their anxiety is often less because they are not facing their therapist and do not feel the risk of being judged. On the other hand, some online clients may not trust people they have not met and cannot see in person, and they may resist responding or disclosing. At the onset of online therapy, it is beneficial to discuss the client's impression of the therapist after he or she has seen a picture or read about the therapist on the Web. For some clients, the absence of physical presence might minimize the feeling of intimacy and trust and might also minimize their commitment to therapy. If chat or e-mail therapy is chosen, the text may create a sense of formality and represent distance and separateness. On the other hand, some clients may drop the social rituals quickly and dive right into their most intimate feelings. In chat therapy, they may enjoy the space and the silence in between communications, using such time to gather their thoughts. With the absence of face-to-face distractions, the client may be able to connect to the essence of therapy more quickly and with more ease. It is important to be aware of the differences between online therapy and a traditional setting in order to successfully discuss and explore the client's issues. Standard questions for therapists to ask themselves are:

- Do I have all the needed information for crisis management?
- Do I know the city, state, and country where this client resides?
- Have I assessed ethical and legal issues in case a crisis occurs?
- Have I assessed for the variety of possible disorders?
- Do I have enough information about events in the client's life from birth to the present, and the sequence of symptoms from when they first occurred?
- Have I gathered appropriate information regarding the client's family history?
- Do I have information regarding recent life stressors?
- Have I assessed for the function of each symptom?
- Have I identified, in collaboration with the client, what are the most clinically significant, acute, disabling, and critical symptoms?
- Do I think online therapy will be beneficial for this client?
- Could online therapy not be beneficial in any way for this client?

- If not, what kind of referral would be beneficial for this client?

In addition to the standard assessment questions, it is useful for therapists to know the following about these clients: accessibility to a computer and Internet; level of comfort with the computer and the Internet; familiarity with instant messaging and chat; ease in writing about their thoughts and feelings; and level of typing skills.

Closing

Both client and therapist need to be aware of and accept the fact that closing is taking place. During the closing, no new material should be introduced. It is at this time that the client and the therapist agree on future goals and commitment to therapy. The therapist could initiate the closing by saying:

> "We have five minutes until our session ends. Tell me how you feel about online therapy."
>
> Or, "Let's discuss some of the goals for your therapy."
>
> Or, "Let's plan how you may utilize what we have talked about today, in your day-to-day life."

As with traditional therapy, online therapists can wrap up the clinical findings and help their clients define a goal. In closing, therapists may want to point out issues that were mentioned but not discussed due to lack of time. The number of sessions necessary to meet the agreed upon goals should be determined, depending on what the goals are. Short- and long-term goals should be defined and the client can be asked to give a commitment to short-term goals.

Contracting with the client about the extent of the therapy sessions is more important in online therapy than in traditional face-to-face therapy, because clients may not return as readily in online therapy as they would in face-to-face therapy. Some therapists require a 6- to 8-week commitment to achieve stated goals. Other therapists talk throughout their sessions about renewing contracts. As new issues emerge during the course of therapy, new goals must be set along with a new time commitment. Agreements about scheduling, fees, intersession communications via e-mail, and technical interruptions can be made. Different modes of therapy can also be discussed. In the course of therapy, a combination of chat, e-mail, telephone therapy, and face-to-face therapy can be scheduled. A discussion of what is beneficial to the client is important.

When using online chat therapy, it is important for therapists to talk about the speed of typing and what is comfortable for both the client and the therapist. It is also important to explore how the client felt about waiting to receive the therapist's response. People use that silent time in different ways and have different feelings about the waiting period. It is also important to clarify future expectations and potential misunderstandings related to timing. For example, would the client prefer the therapist to use short sentences or to type an entire thought before sending it? Assigning words or symbols to indicate that statements being made have ended (i.e., end, done) is helpful.

Online therapists using text communication rely on their skills with the written word to develop therapeutic alliances with their clients. Therapy that uses written communication still conveys the depth and breadth of the human experience. More proficient e-mailers use a variety of keyboard techniques to enhance their communication. They express emotions using capital letters, asterisks, different fonts, colors, graphics, **embedded images**, and words such as *sigh*. As the therapeutic relationship develops, these cues, expressions, and accentuations are fine-tuned and understood more clearly. Over time, therapists working with text communication learn to appreciate the nuances and subtleties of their clients' written expressions and individual style. Clarifying and agreeing upon the use of emoticons and **online slang** (e.g., LOL, "laughing out loud," BRB, "be right back") is very important.

INFORMED CONSENT

As with traditional therapy, it is beneficial, ethical, and a safe practice to have an informed consent form for the client to read and sign. This form can be digitally provided in various forms, including e-mail, fax, or **uploade**d to a virtual office in an e-clinic. Information that may be included in the informed consent form are:

- Therapist's name
- Therapist's license number
- Therapist's scope of practice
- Therapist's address (Web and office)
- Therapist's telephone/fax numbers
- Fee
- Confidentiality laws and exceptions to the confidentiality based on the state in which the therapist is licensed (e.g., child abuse, elder abuse, harm toward self or others, third-party payment, collection of fees)
- Cancellation or rescheduling guidelines, communication modes, session length (chat, audio, video, vs. e-mail), and fees
- Alternate colleague whom the client can call or contact in case of an emergency
- Therapist's therapeutic orientation and its specific benefits and limitations
- Overall benefits and limitations of online therapy
- Intersession communication—e-mails between sessions
- Alternative plan of communication regarding sessions in case of technical difficulties
- Termination guidelines

This form can be e-mailed or **downloaded** from the online therapy Web site by clients and signed and faxed back to the therapist before the onset of therapy. Some e-clinics also offer digital signatures, allowing the clients to "sign" the form via the Internet, utilizing protocols that meet the legal definition of a digital signature. These protocols do not require specialized software and are Internet **browser**-based, requiring no download on the part of the client or therapist. This type of digital signature complies with the telemedicine law.

EARLY SESSIONS AND THE THERAPEUTIC ALLIANCE

Whether therapists are treating clients face-to-face or online, the therapeutic alliance is initiated in the first session. It is more firmly established during subsequent sessions and then progresses in stages. Research indicates that developing a therapeutic alliance is critical to treatment outcome. In *Negotiating the Therapeutic Alliance* (Safran & Muran, 2000) the authors identified the following with regard to the importance of the therapeutic alliance:

- Patient's participation within the first three therapy sessions is predictive of the pattern and the treatment outcome.
- The therapeutic relationship's quality, such as the bond between the client and the therapist, and the therapist's empathic understanding and the degree of agreement between the patient and the therapist on goals and tasks of treatment, is predictive of outcome.
- A therapeutic alliance is created when the client views the therapist as compassionate, warm, kind, friendly, trustworthy, respectful, nonjudgmental,

empathic, and understanding of the client's perspective. As a result, the patient feels listened to, understood, and respected.

- The client's rating of the therapeutic alliance is a more important assessment than the therapist's rating of the alliance. It is important for the therapist to monitor and be aware of the client's assessment of the therapeutic alliance in order to be most effective with the client. It is the client's rating of the therapeutic alliance that provides a more relevant view of the relationship, as it is the client's session and experience.

Online therapy differs from face-to-face therapy in the manner that the alliance is established and maintained. In traditional therapy, therapists tend to establish a level of safety and create a therapeutic alliance with their clients through their presence, a friendly face, a warm smile, and a soothing tone of voice. The goal when using online therapy is to create a similar therapeutic alliance through the use of written words.

In traditional therapy, therapists rely on the visual observation of their clients' nonverbal communications to give them information beyond their clients' words. They feel the essence and emotions of their clients by virtue of sitting in the room with them. So what happens when these tools are taken away and when therapy consists of chatting with the client online?

Online therapists must rely on enhancing their other senses and skills, because the client is not in the room. Online therapy sharpens therapists' clinical skills for the very reason that they are not in a room with their clients. When using text only, it is important for therapists to relay compassion, caring, collaboration, and a nonjudgmental acceptance through written words. Without the physical cues of face-to-face therapy, therapists learn the most effective use of questioning or communicating to give and receive information:

It is possible that the quality of one's writing interacts with the quality of the relationship with the other. As a text relationship deepens and trust develops, people may open up to more expressive writing. They become more willing to experiment, take risks—not just in what specific thoughts or emotions they express, but also in the words and composition used. Composition can advance when people feel safe to explore; it regresses when they feel threatened, hurt, or angry. Those changes reflect the developmental changes in the relationship. Writing isn't just a tool for developing the text relationship. Writing affects the relationship and the relationship affects the quality of the writing. The therapist can modify the writing techniques—even basic elements of grammar and composition—to interact more effectively and empathically with the client. (Suler, Kraus, Zack, & Stricker, 2003, p. 21)

How can a therapeutic relationship be developed using only text? Gary Stofle wrote about *presence*, a concept that helps to clarify this process:

Presence is the perception that a video- or computer-mediated experience is not actually mediated. During a chat session, the therapist and the client each may feel as though the other is physically present. That feeling of presence is created as a result of the unique way each individual presents themselves in the chat room in every moment of time. This presentation may include the person's screen or chat name, font style, typing speed, interaction tempo, verbosity, use of colloquialisms and emoticons, and use of spelling and grammar. Another term for this might be non-textual; that is, everything other than the words themselves. Although not all of these factors are specifically evaluated while online, many can be assessed through a review of the transcript, and they all add to the feeling of presence. (2002, p. 94)

EARLY SESSIONS AND IDENTIFYING ISSUES

As with face-to-face therapy, the role of online therapists is to help clients define, clarify, and explore their problem situations in terms of their particular experiences and feelings. If therapists are aware of and able to accurately perceive their clients' experiences, then it is possible to accurately assess and respond to feelings, concerns, and the most salient aspects of the presenting problems. It is also important for online therapists to assess clients' ability to deal with deep, emotionally laden issues. Online therapy may not be appropriate for clients lacking appropriate coping skills for managing intense emotions. Clients unable to manage their emotions effectively might become harmful to themselves or others and are more appropriate for face-to-face therapy. The following standard therapy skills are used to move clients through the online therapeutic process.

Inviting the Client

Allowing clients to begin their sessions is ideal but does not typically occur when therapists are doing online therapy. Clients often wait for therapists to start the process and may need prompting to begin exploring their current issues. Using chat in online therapy requires that therapists be efficient with the use of words. Appropriate utilization of questions facilitates a smoother communication while addressing the major treatment issues. As with traditional therapy, it is important for online therapists to practice formulating questions to explore their clients' most important and relevant thoughts, beliefs, fears, and expectations. The following sample online session may help online therapists through the beginning phase of therapy.

Therapist: Hello.
Client: Hi, I saw your picture and bio on the Web site and decided to have a session with you.
T: Great, what would you like to talk about today? (*validating the client and utilizing an inviting question*)
C: Well, I have been depressed for a while now, and I don't have any motivation.

For several reasons, once clients and therapists have begun to establish a therapeutic alliance, online clients often get to deeper issues more quickly than in traditional therapy. For one, many clients have experience using online chat for socializing and creating intimate relationships. The act of writing allows clients to process material directly and by-pass tendencies toward circular thinking. Writing also aids the growth of new relationships by encouraging the exchange of complete thoughts and concepts without conversational interruptions, while eliminating instant visual feedback that may have an affect on the course of disclosure. The therapeutic intervention of journaling, which makes use of this phenomenon, is an inherent component of online therapy; as a result, online therapy possesses a recognized and exceptionally effective intervention as its fundamental structure.

Developing Empathy

Empathy involves the therapist's ability to see the client's world from his or her perspective, to actually get a feeling for what it is like to be this person, and then to be able to communicate this understanding to the client. In online therapy, it is very important to provide and demonstrate empathy through the careful and appropriate use of words, so that clients feel understood and cared for while looking at a computer **monitor** instead of into the eyes of the therapist. The following demonstrates empathetic online responses:

Therapist: Hmmm. Sorry to hear that. How long have you been depressed (*empathizing with the client and moving toward information gathering*)

Client: Oh, about five months now.

T: Did something change in your life five months ago?

C: Yep. I broke up with my boyfriend seven months ago and I was just fine, and then suddenly after a couple of months it hit me.

T: Breakups can be very hard, tell me more. (*empathizing with the client and inviting her to talk more about her life*)

By giving one's full attention to what the client is saying, listening is the fundamental way to express empathy. Online therapists using text focus on the written words. It is therefore important to make frequent but brief responses that are flexible and tentative enough so that clients feel free to either confirm or correct the response. Online therapists also may need to probe their clients' feelings more frequently because they lack visual and voice clues. If therapists fail to attend or listen well (for chat, a therapist may fail to perceive well), empathy may be adequately conveyed.

The tendency to slip into paraphrasing or to mimic what clients have said may be even more detrimental when communicating only with the written word. This can act as a barrier to the accurate expression of empathy and building rapport. Online clients respond best when therapists attend to their feelings and when they believe therapists understand the essence of their communication. The following are some brief supportive statements that let clients know that therapists are paying attention and are showing understanding and empathy.

Client: Yes, it was hard, I thought I was ugly, fat, disgusting, and no one wanted me.

Therapist: Ouch! ugly, fat, disgusting, that must have really hurt. (*mirroring back some of the words that the client has used to create an alliance, and empathizing*)

C: Yes, I am still hurting. The pain was so much that I just wanted to stay home and not be seen by any one. I could not concentrate and lost my job. I feel horrible.

T: Horrible. It must be very difficult for you to have lost your relationship and your job.

Exploration

As with traditional therapy, it is important for online therapists not to move their clients too quickly out of their experiences, into interpretations and solutions. Therefore, attending, observing, and listening are the initial techniques online therapists use to build and establish a genuine working relationship with clients and identify the issues to work on. Statements and questions that encourage further clarification and definition of feelings, experiences, or behaviors give clients the opportunity to become clearer and to see their issues with greater definition. Examples of exploring questions include:

Client: Sigh . . . I miss him very much

Therapist: How long were you in this relationship?

C: For two years. We spent all of our free hours together. Every minute I thought about being with him.

T: How did the relationship change?

C: He became cold toward me and started to be angry constantly.

T: Angry, hmmm, because . . . ?

C: Oh, I don't know, he came up with any excuse to be angry.

T: At you, or in general?

C: He was angry most of the time and then he would pick on me.

T: How was it for you to be picked on?

C: I hated it. I felt that I was walking on an eggshell, like something bad would happen.

T: Did it?

C:	(*client states that she is crying*). He would get so angry that he would break everything in the living room or the dining room.
T:	Did he ever hit you or hurt you physically?
C:	No, but I thought that I would be next. I was so scared of him. I would go hide in the bedroom or the bathroom and lock the door until he left the house. He usually would leave the house after he broke stuff.

Summarizing, Clarifying, and Reflecting

Summarizing, clarifying, and reflecting are important skills to move online therapy through the exploration stage to problem identification. As with traditional therapy, online therapists should check the accuracy of their perceptions and ask for clarification when lost or confused. Therapists using chat need to constantly check for accuracy because they do not have the luxury of witnessing or hearing nonverbal messages. Therapists doing therapy via audio have more information through the voice, thus resembling telephone therapy. Videoconferencing therapy is the method closest to having clients in the therapy office because therapists can experience their clients' verbal and nonverbal messages. Suggested statements and questions for summarizing include:

Therapist:	So, you tried to hide from him when he would go into these enraged modes. (*summarizing*)
Client:	Yes, I am still shaking when I talk about it.
T:	I am sorry that you had to go through that. (*Empathizing*) What did you do when he came back? (*Exploring*)
C:	I tried to calm him down by feeding him, caressing him, and saying nice words to him.
T:	Did it work?
C:	Sometimes, but not really, that is when he would attack me verbally.

T: Correct me if I am wrong. What I hear from you is that you have tried to calm him by feeding him and loving him when he is angry; in turn, he breaks everything in your home and attacks you verbally. (*clarifying and summarizing*)

C: Yes, most of the time.

T: I get the impression that you loved him more than you love yourself at times. (*clarifying and summarizing*)

C: Wow, yes, it seems like that, doesn't it?

T: So, what ended the relationship?

C: One day, after he trashed my home and left, he did not come back.

T: How was that for you?

C: Shocking. I felt that I did something wrong; that I could not keep him.

T: You wanted to do everything to keep him. (*reflecting the content*)

C: Yep. I would've done everything.

T: You would have taken the fear, the pain, the humiliation, the cost of broken items to keep him so that you wouldn't have to face the pain of him leaving. (*reflecting the process*)

Collaboration and Goal Setting

As with traditional therapy, online clients move toward goal setting when they believe that their therapist authentically collaborates with them. It is essential that the work conveys the goal of authentic collaboration. Goal setting may feel more concrete and real to clients when they actually write down the goals. Here are some examples that demonstrate the collaboration and goal-setting process:

Client: Oh, absolutely.

Therapist: Now you have decided to take care of yourself and let go of your depression. I am glad that you are

	taking care of yourself this way. As we both know, the more that you begin to like yourself and do loving acts for yourself, the less you'll have feelings of fear and anger toward yourself, and so your depression will begin to lift.
C:	Wow, I would like that.
T:	Let's take things one step at a time. What do you think is the first step you would like to take? Where should we begin our work?
C:	Ah, I feel very lonely and down most of the time.
T:	OK, what state of emotions would you like to live with in the future?
C:	Well, I would like to be happy and move on with my life.
T:	Great. If you were completely successful in accomplishing what you want, what would be changed?
C:	I would like to have a good job and be in a good relationship.
T:	Wonderful. What things might get in the way of your being able to follow through on this?
C:	LOL, trying to hold onto his memory as if he was the last man on earth.
T:	Great. Now that we know this, when this thought comes up, what will you think about instead?
C:	That I deserve to be with someone who loves me.

The early stage of online therapy can be completed with goal setting and referrals for the client to other professionals or appropriate groups. The search for referrals can be done online by the therapist either for other online professionals and groups or to obtain information regarding finding professionals and groups where the client resides. If the therapist and the client are in different geographical locations or even different countries, the search for referrals can be given as homework to the client, then explored and talked about in the following sessions. At this time, there can be a transition into the middle stage, where the therapeutic process goes deeper into the client's issues.

After-Session Documentation of Client Notes

Text-based chat communications can be cut and pasted into word processing software and saved on the **hard drive** or to a **disk** to be stored in a locked filing cabinet. The therapist's session notes are legal documents to be preserved as part of the written record to remain available for rereading and reinterpreting. Most states have made it a legal requirement for therapists to keep notes (refer to individual state laws) in consideration of possible legal ramifications or actions.

Bear in mind, these communications may have to be disclosed pursuant to court order. It is significant that a transcript of an online session is no longer an interpretation of the session, as such a transcript would be a word-for-word documentation of the session. Although no legal precedent has yet been set, it is conceivable that there could be discrepancies between the actual session as it transpired and the transcript saved to the document. This is due to the capability that one has to edit that transcript prior to saving the document to a **file**.

MIDDLE STAGE SESSIONS

This phase of online therapy is similar to traditional therapy, with regard to how the therapist utilizes the interventions suited for the client, based on the therapist's theoretical orientation, and the treatment plan for the client's diagnosis. By this time, the therapeutic alliance has been established and therapy addresses deeper issues. As the following example demonstrates, it is at this phase that the therapy deals with the client's core beliefs and deep emotions.

Client: I feel very lonely.
Therapist: Lonely, tell me more.

C: I feel that I have to have him in my life. If I don't, I will not exist. I don't know who I am without him.

T: You only knew him for two years, who were you before him?

C: An insecure woman who only wanted to be in a relationship.

T: So, you don't exist if you are not in a relationship. And a relationship gives you . . .

C: . . . a purpose to live, a purpose to wake up in the morning.

T: Your purpose in life has been to be in a relationship. It makes sense why then you would take breaking of household items and verbal attacks toward you, just so that he would remain and fulfill your purpose.

C: (*crying*) . . . that is so sad.

T: Yes. It is sad . . . stay with your feeling and talk from your sadness . . .

C: I am an empty shell, with nothing inside, lonely, with the hope that someone would come and fill the inside of the shell.

T: Fill it with . . .

C: . . . some substance, life, joy, passion.

T: Has it ever been filled before?

C: Yeah, when I was a little girl, before my parents got their divorce (*crying*).

T: What changed?

C: My life. I moved with my mom. She was usually busy with work. I was alone most of the day (*sobbing*). That is when I got molested by different people. I had no one to protect me. I learned to leave my body and only take care of the men so that they would not harm me more.

T: How old were you?

C: About 6, but I only had them. So I wanted to keep them. If not, I would be left alone again.

T: Wow, what an important decision at such a young age. And that has become your life story.

C: Yes, it certainly has.

There is a misconception that in-depth emotional therapy cannot be done online. This online therapy example demonstrates how the presence of the therapist, through written words, can contain the healing space necessary for the emotional release and healing to take place and to become complete. The following conversation happened between the therapist and client during the eleventh session. See how online therapy is working through the following issues of childhood molestations, expectations, beliefs, and stories:

Client: I am getting a promotion at my job.

Therapist: Wow. Congratulations. You just got hired a month ago!!

C: Yup, the person is leaving and they like me, and said that I was doing a very good job so they want me to move to this new position.

T: I am so proud of you, what do you think they see in you?

C: Oh, she said I was smiling most of the time, a happy face, and I am detail oriented and my coworkers like me. LOL, yeah, I do feel good when I am at my work.

T: What about after work, when you come home?

C: Well, you know I have started dating. I also plan to do some activities with my friends. I've signed up for classes and have made myself very busy.

T: You had mentioned early on about feeling like an empty shell. Do you remember that analogy?

C: Yes, I feel half full. I think I am still waiting for a man to fill the rest of it. It just seems to me that life can only be *somewhat* joyous without a man in my life.

T: Well, I am glad that you feel half full and dating. So the prospect of becoming full is right around the corner. I still think that it would be great to be independently self-generating joy and passion and feel full. From there, share your fullness with the man in your life. It transforms relationships toward giving rather than needing.

C: I like that, let's go for that.

As the client achieves her goals in online therapy, similar to that of traditional therapy, the therapeutic process naturally moves toward the termination phase.

TERMINATION

When clients reach their goals and are consistently using their new coping skills in everyday life, it is time for termination. It is important for online therapists to have many resources available for their clients, both online as well as accessible from their clients' homes and workplaces.

For those clients who may experience anxiety saying goodbye, termination from online therapy is sometimes easier than with traditional face-to-face therapy. On the other hand, the bond that is created via online therapy is very often as solid as face-to-face therapy and requires a similar mourning process when it ends. Termination is most effective when client sessions are slowly reduced, say, by reducing weekly online sessions to every two weeks, then to monthly sessions, and eventually terminating when the client is ready.

Premature Termination

Unplanned termination might occur when the client terminates before reaching his or her goal. Therapy may be terminated for the following reasons: If the therapy is not being effective after four to six sessions; if the therapeutic alliance has not been created; if the financial situation has changed and the client needs to be referred to a sliding scale agency; or if there is a significant transference or countertransference that cannot be worked through.

To prevent premature termination it is important to educate the client about the importance of closure. Together, therapist and client should create an agreement to complete the course of treatment and commit to a termination session. An invitation for a follow-up session can be made so that the client would be able to return for a brief consultation or treatment for other issues.

WHAT TO EMPHASIZE AND WHAT TO AVOID

Many aspects of the clinical work used in traditional face-to-face therapy are similar for online therapy. However, it is important for therapists to know what they need to emphasize and what they need to avoid when using online therapy.

Emphasize

It is important for therapists to emphasize those aspects of the therapeutic process conducive to the online therapy session.

- Create a therapeutic alliance with the client via chat, audio- or videoconferencing. This will be sure to sharpen your clinical skills.
- Make sure that the client feels comfortable with the medium that he or she has chosen to connect with you.
- Clarify content, process, emotions, and symbols. An example of this is the use of emoticons (happy faces, sad faces, etc.). Some clients may not want to see a facial expression at all. A facial expression may mean some sort of judgment. Ask the client if the use of emoticons is comfortable for him or her.

- Utilize interventions and techniques that are more suitable for online therapy (e.g., cognitive interventions).
- Be the best therapist you can be for your client. Utilize all of the appropriate tools and interventions. Be careful if online therapy is new to you. Remember, with continuous use, this process will also become natural.

Avoid

Consider the client's needs, abilities, and knowledge before using some therapeutic interventions and interpretations online.

- Avoid thinking that you need to be different because you are in a different therapeutic setting. You can modify your approach based on receiving additional education or training (see Appendix D). However, avoid changing who you are as a therapist.
- Avoid assuming the content or a client's meaning of certain words and symbols. Ask clients to clarify. Ask additional questions that can help elicit further discussion and lead to more clarification.
- Unless clients use them first, refrain from using abbreviations such as LOL, BRB. Your clients might not know what they mean and might feel uncomfortable asking you to explain.
- Keep away from excessive typographical changes, such as caps or italics in the middle of a sentence, and excessive use of exclamation points and question marks without first clarifying with clients how they perceive those symbols.

SPECIFIC CLIENTS

As with traditional therapy, online therapists need to make appropriate decisions with regard to the type of clients they choose to treat online. Clients' issues and problems need to be assessed carefully at the onset of therapy. Based on their presenting problems and history, clients may need more personal care than can be offered using online therapy. These clients should be referred to a local therapist or a mental health agency for traditional face-to-face therapy.

Adolescents

Adolescents provide a therapist with a whole different feeling when conducting therapy online. Adolescents tend to be extremely active, expressive, and engaging during their sessions. Most adolescents are used to engaging in friendships by the use of text messaging and chatting online. Many resistant adolescents who would prefer not to come into therapy, find online therapy acceptable. Adolescents tend to write letters, poems, or songs in order to express their feelings to their friends and family. As a result of their choice of communication in their daily lives, online therapy is a form of therapy that they can benefit from and relate to quite readily.

Confidentiality is also important for teenagers. In using online therapy, teens do not worry that their friends might find out that they are going for therapy.

Keep in mind that grammar and spelling errors are prevalent in chat sessions, especially with adolescents.

Sample Online Adolescent Session
Therapist: Hello
Client: hi
C: so . . . my day has been going pretty well
C: there is a slight chance that Tom and mom will get back together
C: they are thinking of therapy
C: i spoke to my mom and Tom and they both encour-

age me to be active with Tom's family, even if they aren't together

C: cause i really do love their family

T: Go on.

C: i mean . . . like . . . obviously it will be a little more challenging to like . . . be with them, they both say that i should

T: So far that sounds great.

T: That is hard to do, but I am glad that they are taking your needs into consideration.

C: and like, i was talking to Pat [Tom's son] last night on the phone, and he still wants to like, keep in touch and stuff, and that means a lot to me . . . he and i were really close, and it meant a lot to me that he even said that

T: I know that was a concern that you had.

C: yeah

C: but still, i want more than anything for them to get back together, cause i know that they were happy together. i mean, i have never seen my mother smile like that in a long time

T: Did you and your mom have a talk?

T: Did you tell her that? It is a great point.

C: no . . . not really. i dont feel at this time that i want to talk to her too much

C: yes, i havw old her that

T: Good

C: rrr, i hate this keyboard, lol

T: Tell me more about why you don't want to talk to her.

T: ☺ ☺

C: i feel like too hurt right now to like, talk to her, but later in the week i probably will, like, maybe saturday.

T Good. It is important that you tell her your feelings.

T: When people break up ... sometimes they don't re-
        alize how many people will get affected by the
        breakup.

T: They only see their own pain and frustration.

C: exactly .... and it sucks that i am the one greatly af-
        fected

C: like, Pat [Mom's boyfriend's son] and i are kinda the
        same people in some ways, but he never was as at-
        tached to my mom as i was with Tom, and Pat still
        thinks it sux and all, but i am hurt a lot more than he
        is ...

C: imean, i thought, and still think Tom is the person
        for this family

T: You're right.

T: Pat may not have been through as many breakups
        as you have.

T: Also, his pain may be deeper.

C: and i like that they are still talking and stuff, and
        thinking about therapy and so forth, but sometimes
        i feel that it "takes two to tango" and my mom isn't
        dancing. i feel sometimes that Tom is doing a lot of
        the work, but she isnt trying to help the situation.

T: Meaning hidden.

T: You may totally be right ...

C: michael [her brother] has trouble trusting people.
        ... and he never felt he could trust my mom, so
        he never got attached. there are only three people
        in this world he trusts, and i am one of them ... i
        felt we had a bond. and now (if they completely
        break it off) Pat and i wont be able to have nights
        and stuff.

T: Do you also think that maybe you are more angry
        towards your mother because of everything that you
        have been through?

C: he wont drive out to Pasadena, especially not when

he has a life out there. i wanted to be in that life so bad, move there, start fresh . . . but i feel i am always restrained because of my mom.

C: ye . . . that too

T: You may still be able to get together if your mom and "Tom" can handle it

C: i have resentment towards her, but i still feel that she doesn't help situations . . .

T: I see that you have resentments toward her.

C: an i think they can. . . . but like. . . . it would still be so different.

C: an loosng that life i so badley wanted hurts more than anything.

T: I know.

T: You had so many plans.

T: I think more importantly, you are tired of all of the letdowns with your mom's past relationships.

Couples Therapy

Online therapy is a great tool for couples therapy. Couples can create a safe space and communicate directly and effectively with each other with the guidance of a professional therapist. Online therapy allows partners to type whatever they want to say and then view their own words and thoughts as a way of becoming more aware of how they are presenting themselves to one another. This helps each of the partners to take more responsibility for their words and actions. Using chat, each partner has a chance to be heard, because he or she has to wait for the other person to finish before responding. This minimizes cross-talking and interruption and allows space for the couple to be attentive to each other's expressions, thoughts, and needs.

Two of the most common ways to conduct online couples therapy are: (1) each partner is at a separate **terminal** while involved in a private chat therapy session, or (2) both partners can use the same terminal and take turns using the keyboard.

Either option provides an opportunity for each participant to fully read the other's comments while having time to formulate his or her thoughts prior to responding.

Audio- and videoconferencing are also great tools for online couples therapy. With audioconferencing, the therapist will draw upon such nonverbal cues as the vocal tone, volume, and inflection of the voice. In videoconferencing, therapists receive yet another range of nonverbal cues from the partners, including how they sit together, their body language toward each other, as well as their facial expressions while they are talking about emotional issues.

One of the suggested methods for using online therapy for couples is to have the clients in the same room for the first two sessions, so that they can gather information and observe their dynamics together. The couple can use text, audio/videotherapy, or chat therapy to **interface** with the therapist. After a few initial sessions with the couple in the same room, therapists move the couple to separate computers (home/office, office/office, home/friend's home). Interacting from separate physical locations provides a safe space for each partner to vent emotions while allowing each to speak freely about issues without being interrupted and needing to censor him- or herself. Having this combined form of "separate" yet "connected" therapy helps create a safety zone for the couple's communications. Once the partners have been able to release the anger, frustration, and resentment they have carried over time, the therapist brings them back together to the same computer terminal.

When using online therapy as an addition to traditional, face-to-face therapy, we recommend that the couple e-mail each other or chat (e.g., MSN, Yahoo!) to communicate feelings, thoughts, and desires between sessions. Frequent online communication between sessions is helpful when they see a roadblock with respect to communicating face-to-face. This allows the couple a safe time and space to express themselves. It also encourages them to be vulnerable without feeling threatened, judged, or interrupted. The partners usually feel complete freedom of expression because they can communicate without interruption. This also minimizes reactions to each other's reactions when they are involved in face-to-face conversation, where partners often react to each other's nonverbal rather than verbal messages. Whether through e-mail, chat, audio- or videoconferencing, or face-to-face, the couple can practice communicating with the goal of becoming intimate again. Practicing healthy communication and intimate gestures online can help create a safe transition to effective in-person communications.

Family Therapy

As with couple's therapy, family therapy can be done online via e-mail, chat, and audio- or videoconferencing. Family therapy via chat can be limiting, due to the number of family members involved. Online therapy via audio- or videoconferencing can be a much better medium for family therapy. In using audio- or videoconferencing, therapists can obtain additional information about family dynamics because they are able to observe voice patterns, nonverbal behavior, and how the family interacts and communicates with one another.

Online therapy is a great tool for weekly family meetings. The concept of family meetings is introduced to the family by the therapist. The boundaries and parameters are set for the family with the guidance of the family therapist. The family can choose to continue weekly family meetings on their own via chat from other browsers (e.g., MSN, Yahoo!). Family therapy can also be conveniently done when family members are at work and the teen is at home, or even when one family member is out of town. Online family meetings should not take the place of face-to-face family meetings. However, they can be a great addition to regular weekly sessions.

As we noted earlier, teenagers feel comfortable communicating online. With online therapy, the teen in the family can feel that he or she has space to talk and share experiences with family members without being talked over, judged, or discounted.

The Suicidal Client

One of the most frequently asked questions about online therapy is how to deal with suicidal clients. As with phone therapy and crisis hotlines, it is helpful to find out identifying information, such as a zip code, telephone area code, home address, and a friend or a family member's telephone number. Online therapists should attempt to keep clients online as long as possible while waiting for the psychiatric emergency team (PET), police officer, or members of the person's family to reach them.

Therapists often feel powerless and anxious when they are chatting with a suicidal client. They have to realize that even if they try to obtain all identifying information, a person who is intent on suicide could call from an undisclosed location with an undisclosed telephone number. This also could happen in traditional therapy.

One case that highlights the clinical challenges with suicidal clients comes from a supervisor. The supervisor recalled how one of her profound moments, both as a therapist and a human being, occurred when she worked for a suicide prevention hotline. Clients would call in and not disclose any information. In some cases, these clients would call after already having taken pills or cut their wrists, and just wanting to talk to someone until they died. The supervisor attempted to heal and validate these clients until there was no longer communication from the other end of the telephone. An online therapist could provide that service, using chat or audio, even if clients choose not to reveal their whereabouts but want to have someone with them during this transition.

Many professionals have concerns regarding the assessment of risk and initiation of appropriate suicide intervention addressed via the Internet. Some conclude it is impossible to do without seeing clients face-to-face and benefiting from visual and other verbal and nonverbal cues to assess their state of mind. No doubt there were similar critics when telephone hotlines were first established. Today, we consider phone communication the norm and a necessary part of crisis intervention with teens, runaways, and victims of domestic violence, rape, and other human tragedies. The reality is that, just like phone counseling, online counseling is needed and can be very effective for suicide and crisis intervention.

Gay, Lesbian, and Bisexual Clients

There are many places around the world where the gay, lesbian, and bisexual population do not have access to community resources, therapists and clinics that specialize in their specific needs. An example of a state that has fairly comprehensive outreach programs, therapists, and community centers is the state of California. Even in communities where help is accessible, there are people in this group who desire anonymity due to work, family, or individual personal preference.

There is a need for anonymity in the process of "coming out of the closet" to themselves, environment, community, and their friends and family around them. Usually people begin to identify their confusion about their sexual orientation during their adolescent years. For these young people, going to a gay and lesbian center, school counselor, or speaking to their parents about getting a therapist is not a viable option because of fear surrounding being exposed prior to discovering for themselves what their orientation is.

It is important to keep in mind that there are certain parts of the United States or the world where "coming out" does not seem to be an option. Seeking a therapist about this issue within their community would be fear producing and possibly detrimental to their career and home life.

Online therapy is not only conducive to the anonymity that this group desires, it is also convenient for them to connect with a therapist who specializes in their area of need.

There are many gays, lesbians, and bisexuals who have desired and worked very hard at creating a family for themselves. This includes having children through adoption, artificial insemination, and the use of surrogates. Going through this process can be time consuming, frustrating, and emotional regardless of sexual orientation. However, it could be more diffi-cult for this population when family or community support is not available.

Gay, lesbian, and bisexual families with children may face dealing with their sexual orientation on a regular basis as a re-sult of the concerns of their children interacting with other children, teachers, neighbors, and their own families. It re-quires a tremendous amount of strength, courage, and clarity to deal with these issues, especially when they come on a daily basis.

Online therapy is an option that offers the anonymity, con-venience, and support that are so necessary in aiding in the success of these families.

Other Sexual Identity Groups

These specific groups, which, among others, include transgen-der and cross-dressing individuals, often experience difficul-ties relating to people in their work, home, and communities, due to possible feelings of shame and confusion. At times these individuals are viewed by their community and their families as deviant and ill, as opposed to individuals who are struggling with their identity. The privacy and convenience of online therapy facilitates this group in working with their indi-vidual issues.

Multicultural/Multilingual Clients

People from many multicultural groups such as African Amer-ican, Hispanic, Native Americans, Asians, Middle Eastern, and Jewish often do not seek therapy because they are not able to find a therapist in their community who also shares their back-ground. Serious issues such as immigration, acculturation, family values, change of gender and family role, racial profil-ing, and acts of racism are some additional issues that these in-dividuals may experience.

Clients may choose a therapist who is from the same culture

or speaks the same language because they feel more comfortable and assured that the therapist will understand them. The clients know that they do not have to explain their culture and that the therapist knows the standards, taboos, rituals, and values of the common culture. A British client who lives in the United States can meet a British therapist in England, or anywhere else in the world, for that matter. A German therapist can be available for online therapy with a German client, regardless of where therapist or client lives.

A therapist can connect with a client online by chance and find out that the client is from another culture. It is important for the therapist to be aware of his or her own cultural influences, biases, prejudices, and limited understanding about the client's cultural role in the experience of physical or mental illness. Due to her culture, the client may have certain expectations about therapists that she might project onto the therapist. The client may also fear not being understood and being judged by the therapist. The client may feel that the therapist can only give limited help due to ignorance of the client's culture. There could also be linguistic misunderstandings that need to be constantly clarified.

At times, it is beneficial for the client to have therapy with a therapist who is not from the same culture. A therapist who does not subscribe to the cultural values, standards, rituals, and taboos may assess the issue from a more objective perspective.

With Web sites available in every language, there are simple ways of conducting therapy via e-mail in the client's primary language. These Web sites provide chat rooms and/or e-mail in the primary language without the need for translation. This is accomplished by the Web site providing users with instructions that demonstrate how to use their own standard keyboard to write in the characters of their own language. For example, each letter on the keyboard represents a particular alphabet or symbol from their specific language. Below is an example of text between a Farsi speaking client and therapist:

دکتر ....
من یک زن سی و پنج ساله هستم که یک سال قبل همسر مراطی یک حادثهٔ اتومبیل از دست دادم
و در حال حاضر با دختر شش ساله ام زندگی می کنم. از حدود شش ماه قبل احساس غم و تنهایی
در من بیشتر شده و اکثر اوقات احساس افسردگی می کنم. به آینده امیدی ندارم و تا بحال چندبار
به فکر خودکشی افتاده ام و اگر بخاطر دخترم نبود شاید این فکر را عملی کرده بودم. خواهش می کنم
به من کمک کنید.

(Translation: "Doctor, I am a 35-year-old woman, I have lost my husband one year ago to an automobile accident and I am living with my 6 year old daughter in the present time. Since 6 months ago my feeling of sadness and aloneness has worsened and I feel very depressed. I have no hope for the future and I have thought about suicide couple of times and if it wasn't for my daughter I would have acted on my thought. Please help me.")

Below is another example of writing an e-mail in Farsi using the English alphabet. This e-mail is a representation of the client needing help and the client not allowing the lack of accessibility to the chat room in her own language to stop her. She writes her question and asks for help in her primary language with the English alphabet. In this e-mail, the client has seen the therapist's article on a Web site and wants help:

salam,doctor,man Afsaneh 26 sale az tehran be ko-mak shoma shdeedan neeyaz daram man ta be hal az heech doktoree moshavere nagereftam, valy az shoma kheily khosham amad,omeedvaram man ro rah namaee koneed ke rahamo peyda konam.

(Translation: "Hello, Doctor, I am Afsaneh, 26 years old from Tehran, I need your help very much. I have never gotten help from any one before, but I liked you so I hope that you can help me find my way".)

This is another example which represents a client typing in Spanish while communicating with a Spanish-speaking therapist. With languages that utilize the same alphabet, this task is much easily established.

Soy una joven de 26 anos.

Tengo un problema. Mi problema es que no tengo buenas relaciones con mis companeros de trabajo. Me da mucho coraje con todos. Me afectan todas las cosas muy personalmente. Por favor ayudeme encontrar un modo que pueda quedarme aqui. No quiero perder este trabajo tambien. Gracias.

Culture is an important factor to be considered in online therapy. Awareness of differences, constant clarification, and education about the client's culture are all important factors to be considered by the online therapist. When the geographical boundaries are opened vastly, so are the factors to be considered in clinical settings.

TRANSFERENCE AND COUNTERTRANSFERENCE

Online therapy can bring to the surface transference and countertransference issues that face-to-face therapy may not uncover or may take longer to uncover. The online chat often triggers these issues and offers an opportunity for therapists to follow up using both online and face-to-face therapy. A clinical case group (CSG; ISMHO, 2000a) demonstrates how to handle transference and countertransference issues both online and offline.

the client became jealous of the attention her therapist gave to other members, which led to a deeper exploration of those feelings in f2f (face-to-face) therapy. The therapist experienced countertransference when she felt hurt by a few angry messages that her client posted about her in the public forum. Because the client's words were posted online, the therapist was able to copy and paste the post verbatim and send to the CSG's e-list to receive collegial feedback and support almost immediately, before responding.

As mentioned at the beginning of this chapter, many clinical aspects of an online therapy practice are similar to a traditional face-to-face practice. However, additional issues can surface, as a result of the lack of face-to-face interaction, including boundaries, timing, and depth of clinical work, different meanings applied to words by clients and therapists, and projection.

Boundaries

Boundaries are one of the most important issues that might be affected in an online therapy session. When therapists are sitting face-to-face with their clients, they are trained to separate themselves from their reactions to the client's stated issues. They attempt to keep their reactions to a minimum in the room so that they do not disturb the client's process.

When sitting in front of a monitor instead of the client, therapists need to be very cautious not to allow their reactions to surface. They may think, "I don't have to hide my feelings because she isn't watching, nor is she sitting in front of me." It is important to be fully aware that the same transference and countertransference issues that therapists encounter when face-to-face with their clients may also occur during online therapy.

Therapists working from home may encounter additional triggers and challenges with boundaries. Consider this scenario: A therapist is sitting at home in his or her pajamas, watching a nice movie or a show that he or she is eager to watch, when suddenly a message is received that there is an emergency with an online client. It is so easy to keep the TV on while conducting online therapy. While the therapist is waiting for the client to type in her message, he or she can watch TV, eat popcorn, and drink soda. It does not sound harmful, does it? The problem is that the therapist's presence and focus are no longer with the client. Multitasking therapists might miss their clients' feelings, the meanings of their thoughts, or the dynamic of their process. In online therapy, therapists need to have an acute sense of timing to be able to respond in a manner that reveals their attentiveness to the material being presented.

On the other hand, a similar lack of focus is often experienced by therapists who sit in front of clients. Perhaps they did not have enough sleep, or maybe they are not feeling very well, or they're preoccupied with some life issue (taxes, financial, relationships, etc.). In online chat therapy, it is fortunate that the therapists have the text of their sessions, and may go back to read them, in case their attention was compromised. As with traditional therapy, online therapists who divide their attention run the risk of not being attentive to the process that the client is experiencing and thus reduce the quality of their clinical work.

It is also important for online therapists who are not working in a therapy office, or a room with a closed door, to keep interruptions to a minimum. Family members walking in and out of the room, the phone ringing, and the dog barking all contribute to inattention and lack of focus. It is also important to keep confidentiality. Therapists need to make sure that no one in their home or office is able to see or hear identifiable information about their clients. Clients who are at home while having an online therapy session also may be interrupted constantly and might not be able to fully "open up" emotionally. Therefore, it is very important for both therapist and client to find a safe, quiet, convenient time and place to have their sessions. It is important for client and therapist to communicate clearly with family and friends to ensure they have the needed time and space for uninterrupted therapy sessions.

Another aspect of maintaining boundaries is the therapist's disclosure of personal information. Some therapists who have an individual private office have stated that they feel very lonely, unseen, and unheard most of the day. These therapists are trained to keep their personal lives out of the therapy room and be there only for the client. Online therapists may experience even greater feelings of loneliness. The feeling of being unseen and unheard might increase due to the fact that when working online, therapists are literally not being seen or heard. Therapists subconsciously might start giving personal information to feel close and useful to their client. Personal disclosure is useful at times. However, it needs to be done for the benefit of the client and not because of the therapist's countertransference issues.

Timing and Depth of Clinical Work

In traditional therapy, many sessions are needed for the client to learn to trust and bond with the therapist. The therapist also needs to have enough knowledge of the client's overall history and patterns to begin working on deep childhood issues, such as childhood abuse, and any issue that holds a high emotional charge for the client. In online chat therapy clients will often get to their deep issues much more rapidly than face-to-face in the therapeutic office. In response to some of our questionnaires, clients have stated that not having to be worried about the therapist's disapproval of them and not having to deal with the therapist face-to-face has made it easier for them to be free with their expressions, thoughts, and feelings.

In some cases, clients might have strong trust/nontrust issues and in a face-to-face therapy setting, the therapist might help them gain trust more quickly. In online therapy via chat, the client does not see the therapist's face or feel the therapist's presence. Clients often need to test the therapist in many different ways to finally allow themselves to trust and go deeper into past emotionally charged issues. These tests could be in a format of questions about the therapist's personal beliefs, ideas, and life issues. Or, they could bring up a dramatic issue that they are not ready to talk about, yet they want the therapist's reaction on that issue.

It is very important for the therapist not to delve into deeper issues before assessing if the client is ready to discuss the deeper issues. In traditional face-to-face therapy, although clients might talk about their childhood sexual abuse, they may show discomfort through facial expressions or physical gestures. A client's resistance might be more on the surface and apparent for the therapist to see, respect, and work through. In online chat therapy, it is important for therapists to complete their assessment and know that their client has the appropriate coping skills before delving into deep painful issues.

Conducting clinical work involving trauma, grief, and loss issues via online chat therapy needs the therapist's full attention and focus. The timing is of the utmost importance when working with deeper and more intense feelings. The client may become very vulnerable and may feel alone and unprotected in his or her own home, without the presence of the therapist. Because online therapy keeps the client physically separated from the therapist, it is very important for the therapist to ensure that the client has the appropriate ego strength to enable him or her to avoid resistance to revisiting emotionally painful past issues. Also, the therapist needs to make sure that the client has a healthy support system in case of crisis management.

Different Meanings

In online therapy, clarification of written words is particularly important because therapists do not have the client's nonverbal cues. An example of this is when a therapist is using face-to-face therapy to confront a client with a very important issue and the client experiences the therapist as safe, kind, and caring because of the visual and verbal cues. The client is able to face the confrontation well and see it as a process. In online chat therapy, clients do not have the therapist's physical presence and might experience a critical inner dialogue while going through the confrontation process.

Therapists must consistently and frequently verify what they perceive from the client's words they are reading. Using capital letters might mean different things to different people. In one reported case, a therapist accidentally pressed the "caps lock" **button** on the keyboard, and suddenly the text was all in capital letters. The client wrote back, "Why are you yelling at me? Are you angry at me?" With further clarification, it was discovered that the client and her friends had created this rule for chat rooms. It is very important to practice using chat rooms. Only through practice can therapists learn chat room etiquette. Many clients may already be familiar with these rules. It is important for therapists and clients to review the chat rules or guidelines together, to ensure they have a common language. After becoming familiar with the client and clarifying what the meanings of different symbols are for them, therapists usually may use the symbols that the client is using.

Projection

Projection is a vital part of every second of our perception and life. Clients project onto therapists what they want them to be. They may create a parent transference and project many of their parent's qualities upon their therapist. They may project their fears, fantasies, or sexual desires onto the therapist.

Many times in the therapy office, a client may project the therapist's kind, empathic, caring attitude and words as romantic love and sexual feelings. The client may act on those projections and behave accordingly or present nonverbal cues. The therapist needs to be aware of the projection and attempt to clarify and set appropriate boundaries. It is possible that the therapist may also experience countertransference attraction issues toward a client.

It may be more difficult to understand and clarify sexual projections in the online therapy medium. The therapist must be cautious because of the absence of nonverbal cues. If the issue is not clarified soon enough, the client may continue to be involved with the sexual projection, which will then affect the outcome of therapy. The client is not in front of the therapist, so therapists will not see the physical cues of the sexual transference and possibly allow looser boundaries. As they become aware of the issue, it is important for therapists to explore possible countertransference issues with a respected colleague.

This may not only affect the outcome of therapy, but also could lead to an illegal and unethical sexual relationship.

CONCLUSION

As the therapist begins clinical work online, the majority of skills that are used in a traditional setting can be transferred to an online setting. As an adjunct to face-to-face therapy, or as it is utilized as the only medium of therapy with a certain client, online therapy will enhance the skills of the therapist. The therapeutic alliance manifests itself in a very different way from face-to-face therapy. Through the use of text and therapeutic techniques—inviting the client, developing empathy, exploration, summarizing, clarification, reflection, collaboration, validation, and being present to the client—a very deep and trustworthy relationship can flourish.

Online therapy requires more of a focused attention from the therapist toward the written word, clarification of words, symbols, transference, countertransference, boundaries, and crisis management issues.

Online therapy is a successful medium for conducting therapy and engaging an adolescent in distress. This medium can also be utilized with couples and families with separate monitors in different locations, or with the members of the family being in the same room sharing their issues with the therapist via chat, audio- or videoconferencing.

CHAPTER 4

The Effectiveness of Different Modes of Online Therapy

Clinicians and researchers of computer-mediated mental health and online therapy began addressing its efficacy in the 1990s. Although comparative empirical studies with regard to psychological treatment via the telephone have been increasingly performed in recent years, similar studies using the Internet have been sparse (Rabasca, 2000). Most studies on telehealth, including Internet-mediated therapy, have focused on patient and provider satisfaction with the technology rather than the effectiveness of the technology in delivering services. These studies primarily have small sample sizes and few use randomized clinical trials. So far, most of the studies have involved computer-guided self-help (psychoeducation) followed by treatment through e-mail (Lange et al., 2003). A study by Lange and colleagues (2003) demonstrated how the use of an Internet treatment involving psychoeducation without e-mail may be effective in treating clients with posttraumatic stress. Although the treatment takes place through a **database** implemented on the Internet, the results indicate further research using e-mail and chat is merited.

Much of the early research is based on findings from the International Society for Mental Health Online's (ISMHO) Clinical Case Study Group (CSG). ISMHO (2000b) provides professionals and consumers who have an interest in online mental health an opportunity to work together on issues such as:

- research
- psychotherapy online (e-therapy)
- group communication
- education
- computer-assisted communication in the work of mental health

The first CSG was formed in the late 1990s out of the need for more in-depth study of online therapy. The primary organizers and facilitators of the CSG, John Suler and Michael Fenichel, saw this as an opportunity to use real clinical cases to generate a systematic investigation of online therapy's efficacy. Online therapy cases from November 1999 to mid-April 2000 included:

- Face-to-face therapy cases in which contact with the client via the Internet played a significant role (e.g., e-mail between sessions, the use of Web sites as resources).
- Short- and long-term clinical encounters with clientele that occurred primarily via the Internet (e.g., therapy via e-mail or chat).
- Online groups and communities in which the mental health professional acts as an organizer, facilitator, or consultant.
- Supervision via the Internet (e.g., via e-mail or message boards).

Research is mixed as to whether online therapy is even an effective modality for certain disorders (Fenichel, 2000; Laszlo,

Esterman, & Zabko, 1999). Fenichel (2000) noted that when people communicate using asynchronous technology, such as e-mail, this can be more thoughtful and focused (given enough time) than speech. On the other hand, writing can also reduce spontaneity and create more impulsivity. There may be temptation to attempt to replicate the quickness and casualness of verbal conversation in the written conversation, potentially resulting in a serious misunderstanding. The impulsiveness can be compounded by the anonymity of the online environment, which tends to have a disinhibiting effect on behavior.

Under "Assessing a Person's Suitability for Online Therapy" on the ISMHO Web site (http://www.ismho.org/) there are guidelines developed by the CSG that delineate possible concerns about using this treatment modality.

Initial findings of the ISMHO research and several other online therapy research studies point to numerous advantages and some concerns with using this treatment modality for various client populations and diagnoses. Primarily the findings point to evidence that many people turn to the Internet because of the existing barriers to appropriate mental health services offline. The mental health care service delivery system in America is so complex and fragmented that it is difficult for people to get the care they need.

More recently, CSG explored some of the many ways in which online mental health professionals engage in clinical online practices, either as the primary treatment modality or in combination with traditional face-to-face office practice. The cases reviewed point to numerous similarities between traditional and online therapy with regard to the use of various therapy techniques. Although these results are not rigorous scientific findings, they might be indicators with potentially important implications for the future.

The following summary points out several issues with regard to usefulness of using chat and online text communication (e.g., Fenichel, 2000).

- Lacking face-to-face cues, text communication may disinhibit clients, encouraging them to be more open and honest than usual, or encouraging them to act out.
- Writing may in itself be therapeutic by encouraging self-expression, self-reflection, and cognitive restructuring.
- Clients with a history of chaotic relationships may experience text communication with the therapist as predictable and safe.
- A client's ambivalence about intimacy may be expressed and can be therapeutically addressed in text communication, which is a paradoxical blend of allowing people to be honest and feel close while also maintaining their distance.
- Clients struggling with issues about shame or guilt may be drawn to text-based therapy in which they cannot be "seen."
- Clients who have been physically traumatized may be attracted to the silence and nontactile quality of text communication.
- Text communications may be a steady, ongoing effort to restructure a client's cognitions.
- Lacking face-to-face cues, text communication can be ambiguous and an easy target for misunderstanding and projection.

With regard to clients' therapeutic responses to e-mail or chat, the cases reviewed by the ISMHO (Fenichel, 2000) found that:

- The psychological meaning that clients associate with "writing" will affect how they experience text communication with the therapist.
- The therapist's e-mail can be a steady, supportive,

reality-testing, ego-building voice "inside" the client's head—a benign internalization or introject.

- Text communications (e.g., e-mail) can be a steady, ongoing effort to restructure a client's cognitions.
- A client's ambivalence about intimacy may be expressed and can be therapeutically addressed in text communication, which is a paradoxical blend of allowing people to be honest and feel close, while also maintaining their distance.
- People struggling with issues about shame or guilt may be drawn to text-based therapy in which they cannot be "seen."

Fenichel's extensive work on consumer satisfaction and the Internet demonstrates how the Internet has made therapy available to many people who otherwise might not have received help. In May 1999, out of 619 total responses to his survey, 307 (68%) said that they had never been in therapy before contacting a therapist on the Internet (Fenichel, 2000).

Yager (2001, cited in Winzelberg and colleagues, 2000) conducted research that illustrated how e-mail can be used as an adjunct to face-to face when treating anorexia nervosa. The results indicated that clients who communicated via e-mail several times a week reported high levels of satisfaction and demonstrated increased adherence to treatment.

FORMING A THERAPEUTIC ALLIANCE

Research indicates that many therapists are concerned about whether therapy can take place merely via writing and reading (Glueckauf, Pickett, Ketterson, Loomis, & Rozensky, 2003). The mean level of ability for reading and writing skills in the United States is approximately 8th grade. Illiteracy is still widespread, worldwide, as well as in the United States, which may diminish widespread appeal for using text-based communication (Fenichel, 2000).

Anecdotal case studies and a few empirical studies demonstrate that interpersonal closeness is possible through online therapy. A phenomenon called *disinhibition* has been reported by clients who may feel insecure about revealing their identity or problems in face-to-face therapy, but feel less inhibited about revealing themselves online (Maheu & Gordon, 2000; Ritterband et al., 2003). Specific studies with intravenous drug abusers at risk for HIV demonstrated that these participants revealed more personal information with a computer-administered interview than with a face-to-face interview (Joinson, 1998, cited in Liss, Glueckaf, & Eckland-Johnson, 2002).

Consistent with telehealth research on clinical interviews (e.g., Schopp, Johnstone, & Merrell, 2000) Glueckauf, Whitton, and Nickelson (2002) found that the therapeutic alliance was shown to be moderately high across all modalities of telehealth, including using the Internet. The therapeutic alliance was found to vary significantly with the type of telehealth modality and the family member participating. Further research is needed to evaluate the potential interactions among modality attributes, client characteristics, and situational factors influencing the quality of the therapeutic relationship.

Self-Disclosure

Some experts argue that online therapy does not foster self-disclosure because of the lack of face-to-face cues. Others report that online therapy creates a sense of liberation for individuals to say things that they would not normally talk about in a face-to-face session, resulting in more uninhibited text. Studies with regard to filling out psychological assessments online point to the privacy of online therapy as a key factor in providing safety for self-disclosure (Buchanan, 2002). Richman, Kiesler, Wiesband, and Drasgow (1999) reported similar findings from a 25-year meta-analysis on the role of computers in personal self-disclosure. The results showed that individuals offered more accurate and complete information about themselves when filling out questionnaires while using a computer than when completing the same form on paper or through a face-to-face interview. In addition, the differences were increased when the information was more personally sensitive.

Another concern of some professional organizations such as the American Psychological Association (APA) is that there is room for distortion or overreaction to a written text message when therapists do not experience clients' tone of voice or body language. At the APA's Year 2000 Town Hall Meeting, APA's Executive Director Russ Newman described a Harvard study that found that in interpersonal negotiations, e-mail communication was more likely to lead to misperception and lack of accommodation than either face-to-face or telephone discussion (Fenichel, 2000).

Research has demonstrated that text-based **computer-mediated counseling** (CMC) offers online privacy that can lessen social risks, expectations, restraints, and inhibition (Liss Glueckauf, & Eckland-Johnson, 2002). Liss Glueckauf, and Eckland-Johnson (2002) reviewed empirical studies demonstrating that CMC allows people to express controversial and hidden thoughts or feelings without fear of real-life judgment, rejection, or confrontation. The lack of regulating feedback (e.g., eye contact, tone of voice, and other nonverbal expressions), the diminished impact of status and prestige cues, as well as delay of communication allow people who feel isolated, excluded, or lonely to present a more enhanced self-image through the relative safety of a computer screen (Liss Glueckauf, & Eckland-Johnson 2002).

TELECOMMUNICATION-MEDIATED SERVICES

Ritterband and colleagues (2003) reviewed empirically tested Internet healthcare interventions and provided an overview of the issues in developing and/or using them in a clinical practice. This review points to the efficacy of telehealth (Internet and/or phone) with regard to such settings as hospitals, community mental health centers, long-term care facilities, school, prisons, and rural health centers. Many of the health care interventions provided these organizations with positive outcomes.

Maheu, Whitten, and Allen (2001) noted that the telecommunication-mediated services offered by healthcare organizations involve almost every aspect of traditional face-to-face health care delivery. Review of the services that successfully adapt to the Internet include brief screening interviews; psychological assessment; neuropsychological evaluations; consultation; and counseling with individuals, groups, and families. Other research demonstrates effectively managing cases with remote biofeedback; education; patient and family support; preadmission and discharge planning; court commitment hearings; and case conferences (Glueckauf, Pickett et al., 2003; Ritterband et al., 2003). Other healthcare applications noted include **virtual reality** applications of exposure-based treatment of phobias and anxiety disorders (Riva, 2003) and Web-based psychoeducation (Glueckauf, Whitton, & Nickelson, 2002). Early studies to determine the efficacy of these applications found that they had an impact on patient behaviors by reducing negative physical and psychological symptoms (Glueckauf, & Eckland-Johnson, 2002, Riva, 2003).

Comparing Online Therapy with Computer-Guided Therapy

Online therapy differs from **computer-guided therapy**, where the computer program itself both determines the nature of the problem and provides feedback to the client (Liss Glueckauf, Eckland-Johnson, 2002). In a comparative study (Jacobs et al., 2000 cited in Liss Glueckauf, Eckland-Johnson, 2002) of traditional face-to-face therapy versus computer-assisted therapy for short-term interventions, the computer-based method was favorable, though in certain areas the traditional method out-performed the computer-assisted method.

Web-Based Treatment Interventions

Some researchers are beginning to test the feasibility and effectiveness of delivering **Web-based treatment interventions (WBTIs)** as a form of stand-alone treatment or in conjunction with face-to-face and/or online therapy. Studies testing the effectiveness of WBTIs reported positive outcomes for body image (Celio et al., 2000; Winzelberg et al., 2000), posttraumatic stress, pathological grief (Lange et al., 2003), and diabetes management (McKay, Glasgow, Feil, Boles, & Barrera, 2002).

Computer-Assisted Health Education

There is evidence that computer-assisted health education (CAHE) programs may be helpful adjuncts to the therapy process. Research points to the usefulness of CAHE with regard to low cost, convenience, and frequency with which clients can repeat the programs as part of their homework assignments (Winzelberg, 2000). Winzelberg has demonstrated success with using CAHE with eating disorders.

Virtual Reality

Virtual reality (VR) is a technology, a communication interface, and an artificial experience that can be used for integrating and enhancing actual therapeutic approaches (Riva, 2003). Virtual reality is being used by mental health practitioners primarily in the treatment of phobias. VR exposure therapy (VRE) is being used as a new medium for exposure therapy (Riva, Wiederhold, & Molinari, 1998) that is safer, less embarrassing, and less costly than reproducing real-world situations. Clients are active participants within a computer-generated, 3-D virtual world. In VRE, the patient learns to manipulate problematic situations related to his or her problem. The immersive nature of VRE provides a real-life experience that reduces the anxiety through the processes of habituation and extinction.

VRE can be administered in traditional therapeutic settings, making it more convenient, controlled, and cost effective than in vivo exposure. Studies indicated that VRE can isolate fear components more efficiently than in vivo exposure.

For instance, in treating fear of flying, if landing is the most fearful part of the experience, landing can be repeated as often as necessary without having to wait for the airplane to take off. Rothbaum and colleagues (Rothbaum, Hodges, Watson, Kessler, & Opdyke, 1996) and North and colleagues (North, North, & Coble, 1997) evaluated the use of a virtual reality (VR) airplane for exposure therapy in the treatment of fear of flying for a 42-year-old woman. Treatment included six sessions of graded exposure to flying in a virtual airplane. Positive outcomes included symptom reduction with a successful post-treatment flight. Subsequent studies repeated similar results, and consistent treatment gains were maintained up to a year after treatment. (Rothbaum, Hodges, Anderson, Price, & Smith, 2002). These positive outcomes point to further research to understand the best combination of therapy techniques, including combining VR with online therapy.

Information Web Sites

Health-related information Web sites for patients are found to be helpful adjuncts to online therapy (Glueckauf, Pickett et al., 2003; Liss et al., 2002; Riva, 2001). Most of the available studies examining the efficacy of combining Web-based information (bibliotherapy) with online therapy have shown that this treatment approach is, at the very least, feasible (Glueckauf, 2002; Liss et al., 2002; Riva, 2001). Further studies are needed to determine how best to use these adjunct services either alone, with self-help groups, or with online therapy or medical consultations (Glueckauf et al., 2003).

Psychological Assessment Tests

Although online therapists report using online psychological assessment tests, studies determining how well traditional assessment tests adapt online are limited. Buchanan (2002) noted that although assessment is an integral part of online diagnosis and case management, how well traditional tests adapt online is questionable. Maheu and Gordon (2000) suggested that online therapists frequently adapted traditional psychological assessments, which they termed, *web-based psychological assessment* (2000, p. 487), to their online practices. They reported that 68% of 56 mental health practitioners surveyed provided behavioral health assessments via the Internet (Maheu & Gordon, 2000).

Internet-mediated psychological assessment procedures can play an important role in online therapy, but their use is not unproblematic. Some empirical evaluations of Web-based personality tests indicate that they can be reliable and valid, while other evaluations suggest potential difficulties with measurement of some constructs (particularly negative affect), as well as ethical considerations (Buchanan, 2002; Maheu & Gordon, 2000). While offering great potential, online tests need to be scrutinized for the possibility of interactions between the construct being tested and the medium used to test it. Based on the following preliminary research, Buchanan (2002) suggests that further studies are needed to determine if assessment tests done online need special considerations.

Anecdotal evidence with our online clients point to increasing use of psychological tests. Evaluations of online tests also indicate that adapting traditional tests online may not be an adequate measure of the same constructs. Buchanan (2002) pointed to possible computer anxiety affecting participants' responses.

Tseng, Tiplady, Macleod, and Wright (1998, cited in Buchanan, 2002) demonstrated that levels of computer anxiety could affect participants' responses. Davis (1999, cited in Buchanan, 2002) demonstrated that online respondents tend to report higher levels of negative affect than participants filling out paper-and-pencil questionnaires.

Evaluations of online tests also indicate that using traditional tests online may not produce the same results as the same test taken with pen and paper. Buchanan (2002) suggested further evaluation of the efficacy and usefulness of online psychological tests, especially with regard to the before mentioned practical and psychometric issues.

THERAPEUTIC APPROACHES

Anecdotal case studies suggest that face-to-face interventions are effective when adopted to an online therapy practice. The therapists at MyTherapyNet.com have reported successfully applying many traditional therapy skills, therapeutic approaches, and theories with their online therapy clients using text e-mail and real-time chat. Although these therapists report that most theories can be adapted to online use, the most widely used interventions are based in the solution-focused, cognitive behavioral, family brief therapy, imago relationship therapy, and client-centered theories. Other suggested interventions include journal writing, self-help therapies/support, and aspects of psychoanalytic models of treatment (Lange et al., 2003; Laszlo et al., 1999; Maheu & Gordon, 2000; Ritterband et al., 2003). The narrative approach is very well suited for online therapy due to the emphasis on writing as the main intervention (see Chapter 1).

Although Chapter 1 reviews anecdotal case studies demonstrating the successful use of many of these therapeutic approaches, empirical evidence is limited. Anecdotal evidence points to many of the cognitive-based and brief therapies as working best with online therapy. The following review offers a basis for further comparative studies needed to explore the effectiveness of these approaches.

Psychoanalysis

Colon stated: "I use psychoanalytic psychotherapeutic models in my work [online]. It has been a challenge to take what I know and apply it to this other medium . . . [but] repetition, recollection, transference, resistance, conflict, and acting out are all there" (1999, pp. 80–81). Online therapy can help surface transference and countertransference issues that face-to-face therapy may not uncover. The online chat often triggers these issues and offers an opportunity for therapists to follow up using both online and face-to-face therapy.

Fenichel (2000) noted that the ISMHO case study demonstrated an effective handling of transference and countertransferance issues. Synchronous chat allows for the emergence of the deep and immediate emotions necessary for the psychoanalytic approach. The case study demonstrated similar text-based transcripts and transcripts of face-to-face sessions (Fenichel, 2000).

Cognitive–Behavioral Approaches

Anecdotal evidence suggests that many of the cognitive-based theories work well with online therapy (see Chapter 1). Much of the research on interventions based on cognitive–behavioral therapy principles has been with cases combining online therapy with computer-mediated or guided self-help programs. These combined therapeutic and self-help approaches have demonstrated positive outcomes. Self-directed cognitive–behavioral body image therapy used with some face-to-face therapy has been found to improve body satisfaction (Winzelberg et al., 2000). Using interactive multimedia computer programs, several studies by Winzelberg and colleagues (2000) demonstrated symptom reduction for eating disorder clients. These results point to the need for further research to determine the efficacy of combining therapy and computer-mediated or guided cognitive–behavioral techniques. Empirical studies are also needed to compare online and face-to-face therapy as a component of this integrated approach.

Similar studies using a computerized interactive program demonstrated that cognitive–behavioral therapy (CBT) may be effectively used with anxiety and depression (see Chapter 1).

Other research further demonstrates the feasibility and effectiveness of delivering other types of computer-mediated or guided programs of Web-based treatment interventions (WBTIs) as a form of stand-alone treatment or in conjunction with face-to-face and/or online therapy. According to Ritterband and colleagues (2003), studies testing the effectiveness of WBTIs involved both cognitive and behavioral techniques, which were tailored to each member of a therapy group based on an in-person individual assessment.

This assessment allowed the therapist to tailor cognitive–behavioral intervention strategies to each client's goals, needs, knowledge, and skills. The assessment involved setting goals; reviewing knowledge and beliefs about social relationships, behavior, and emotions (including cognitive distortions and automatic thoughts); reviewing social skills; reviewing self-presentation skills; reviewing thoughts; reviewing self-management skills in decreasing loneliness; reviewing access competencies; and reviewing affect management skills.

All participants received basic social skills training, while other interventions were tailored to the specific needs of each client based on the assessment results. Examples included treating anxiety in social situations through hierarchical exposure and cognitive modification interventions. Group members who isolated themselves in the group were helped through the sharing and provision of potential resources. These clients also had many opportunities to explore negative or distorted cognitions and automatic thoughts pertaining to social situations. Positive outcomes were reported; group members found it especially helpful to practice applying techniques to modify these cognitions (Ritterband et al., 2003).

A study by Hopps, Pépin, and Boisvert (2003) demonstrated how people with physical disabilities were effectively treated using group goal-oriented cognitive–behavioral therapy for chronic loneliness, via text-based computer-mediated counseling (CMC). There was statistically and clinically significant improvement in reported feelings of loneliness and the acceptance of disability and social difficulties in handicapped situations among the participants. Although this study used a group moderator rather than a therapist, the results point to further application of group goal-oriented cognitive–behavioral computer-mediated counseling interventions with online therapy.

Cognitive–behavioral interventions are effectively used with a text-based medium because they rely heavily on conscious processes and thinking. Gabriel and Holden (1999) suggested looking for emergent thought patterns in a text, such as over-generalization (where the individual frequently uses such terms as *always, never*, or *good/bad, right/wrong*), excessive responsibility ("I should have done this, I must do that"), predicting without sufficient evidence, making self-referential statements minimizing or maximizing the significance of the behavior ("Anyone could've done it"), or catastrophizing situations and only focusing on the negatives ("World will fall apart if I don't do it"). Online text therapy easily allows therapists to question such statements, which serves to begin restructuring these thought processes and to foster change. Suggested uses of this approach can be found in Chapter 1.

Narrative Therapy and Solution-Focused Therapy

Although not validated through empirical studies, narrative therapy (White & Epston, 1990) and solution-focused approaches (de Shazer, 1985) have been reported to be effective when used with online therapy. The writing process and viewing issues, in print, on their computer screen enhance the externalization of problems and thereby promote therapeutic change (Murphy & Mitchell, 1998). Clients often see the contradictions they hold in their beliefs, without the need for the therapist to indicate them.

Transpersonal

The only research found so far on the effectiveness of the transpersonal approach to online therapy is an electronic interview with G. Frank Lawlis (see Chapter 1), where Lawlis discusses about the applications of transpersonal counseling online.

TREATING SPECIFIC COMPLAINTS

Although there is evidence that online therapy is effective, how its effectiveness differs among the different client populations and diagnoses has not yet been empirically determined. According to Fenichel's extensive work on consumer satisfaction, 73% of survey respondents had tried online therapy and 92% said that it had helped them (Fenichel, 2000). Yet there is a scarcity of empirical studies comparing online with face-to-face therapy and among these different client groups and diagnoses. This review reflects some of the online mental health interventions that are being developed and evaluated for use with several client populations. It also reviews the empirical research representing different client populations with regard to the effectiveness of online therapy and/or other computer-mediated/guided or mental health services.

Many of the clients that are seen by MyTherapyNet.com therapists include teenagers, people living in rural areas, parents at home with a newborn, busy executives, victims of domestic violence, people with disabilities or recovering from an illness, and people who want personal growth and fulfillment. Empirical research is limited but it is beginning to explore specific client populations treated using online therapy alone or in conjunction with computer-mediated or guided programs. This includes people with posttraumatic stress disorders, eating disorders, addictions (and their families), phobias, anxiety, suicidal thoughts, disabilities, and health related issues (HIV, diabetes, and insomnia). Other client groups studied are couples, families, gays, veterans, and inmates.

Included in this review are studies that combine computer-guided programs with face-to-face and/or online therapy. By including this research the authors hope to offer a better understanding of the effectiveness of these combined therapy approaches. The results suggest effective adjunct use of computed-guided programs with *online therapy*, but only with extensive empirical research will this concept be tested.

Ritterband and colleagues (2003) reviewed many interventions including computer-based health information and support systems for patients with life-threatening illnesses, phobias, and marital problems. Although most of the studies reviewed pointed to positive outcomes, Ritterband and associates (2003) suggested that additional treatments need to be developed and examined for their efficacy. Specific studies with positive outcomes included treating patients who are HIV positive (Gustafson, Hawkins, Boberg, Pingree, Serlin, Graziano, & Chan, 1999), patients with breast cancer (Gustafson, Hawkins, Pingree, McTavish, Arora, & Mendenhall, 2001), and patients with fear of public speaking (Botella, Banos, Villa, Perpina, & Gracia-Palacios, 2000).

Some of this research may be used as a starting point for further studies to determine efficacy and the best course of treatment. One point to keep in mind is that as online therapy continues to grow, and more therapists continue to gain experience in providing online therapy, the list of people who are helped by online therapy will expand. It is imperative that the psychological community continues to evaluate how to best serve the people receiving this mode of therapy.

Literature reviewing online interventions for all health care offers a basis for understanding the usefulness and efficacy of online mental health interventions. Ritterband and colleagues (2003) reviewed empirically tested Internet healthcare interventions and provide an overview of the issues in developing and/or using them in a clinical practice.

Other healthcare applications noted include virtual reality applications of exposure-based treatment of phobias and anxiety disorders (Riva, 2003) and Web-based psychoeducation and support for family caregivers (Glueckauf, Whitton, & Nickelson, 2002). Early studies to determine the efficacy of these applications found that they impact patients by reducing negative physical and psychological symptoms (Glueckauf, 2002; Liss et al., 2002; Riva, 2003).

Postraumatic Stress Disorder

Studies by Lange and colleagues (Lange, Van de Ven, Schruken, & Emmelkamp, 2001; Lange, Rietdijk et al., 2003) demonstrated significant improvement in posttraumatic stress (PTS) symptoms using a type of computer-mediated therapy that includes psychoeducation, structured writing assignments, and a protocol-driven (self-guided) treatment via the Internet. Although this treatment did not involve e-mail and thus was not a comparative study with this mode of online therapy, the results suggest that Internet-driven treatment for posttraumatic stress disorder (PTSD) is effective. This study also demonstrated the effectiveness of using the Internet for cognitive reappraisal of thoughts related to the trauma. The writing assignments and other interactive computer-mediated activities helped the participants challenge their dysfunctional automatic thoughts about the traumatic event and create a new symbolic meaning concerning the experience (Lange et al., 1999; Lange, Van de Ven et al., 2001).

Virtual reality (VR) has also been successful in reducing PTSD symptoms. Studies by Riva (2001, 2003) demonstrated how to combine VR with traditional therapy when treating Vietnam veterans with posttraumatic stress disorder. Therapy included exposing vets to two virtual environments replicating their war experience and following up with extinction techniques.

Drug Addicts and Alcoholics and Their Adult Children

Drug addicts and alcoholics and their family members often find online therapy safer than traditional therapy. Due to the shame that is involved with addiction, the privacy of online therapy can open the space for addicts to begin working on their underlying issues. Addicts and adult children of alcoholics (ACOAs) effectively use online therapy to deal with feelings of shame, low self-esteem, lack of self-care skills, problems with trust and intimacy, and unawareness of their own needs. Cognitive–behavioral interventions and homework, such as narrative therapy (see Chapter 1) assignments and journaling, work well with individual and group online therapy for ACOAs and addicts.

Body Image Issues and Eating Disorders

Therapists report that clients with anorexia nervosa and bulimia nervosa benefit from beginning their therapy online. It is much easier to convince these clients to start therapy on the computer than for them to commit to face-to-face traditional therapy. Therapists report that many of their clients feel less fearful of being judged and less ashamed of how they look when they can't be seen by the therapist.

Much of the research demonstrates that psychoeducational and computer-guided programs are effective components of a comprehensive treatment plan for treating eating disorders (Celio et al, 2000; Winzelberg, Eppstein et al., 2000). Research by Winzelberg et al. (2000) suggests that an Internet-driven (computer-guided) intervention, combined with some face-to-face contact, was more effective in improving body image and reducing disordered attitudes and behaviors than a purely face-to-face intervention. Internet-delivered interventions also have been found to have a significant impact on reducing risk factors for eating disorders (Winzelberg, Eppstein et al., 2000). Luce, Winzelberg, Osborne, & Zabinski (2003) suggested replicating these studies with a larger number of participants and for a longer duration of time. If the positive outcomes are replicated, then such Internet-driven interventions combined with online therapy could also be studied to determine efficacy and even prevention with high-risk clients.

Celio and associates (2000) demonstrated similar results with college-age women and suggested that by using the computer as a medium to collect adherence/participation data, participants stayed more accountable to the treatment. In addition, this study showed the usefulness of using moderators to monitor the content of both the discussion group messages and the personal body image journals for indications that participants needed help beyond what was provided by the program.

Riva and colleagues (Riva, Bacchetta, Baruffi, Rinaldi, & Molinari, 1998; Riva, Bacchetta, Cesa, Conto, & Molinari, 2001 cited in Riva, 2003) proposed experiential cognitive therapy, an integrated approach combining cognitive–behavioral therapy with virtual reality (VR) in the treatment of eating disorders and obesity (Riva, 2003). In a case study, a 22-year-old female university student diagnosed with anorexia nervosa was treated as an inpatient with experiential cognitive therapy to modify body image perceptions (Riva, Baccehetta, Baruffi, Rinaldi, & Molinari, 1998). The positive outcomes included increased bodily awareness, a reduction in level of body dissatisfaction, and a high degree of motivation to change.

Riva and colleagues expanded these results with two different inpatient clinical trials, one with 25 patients suffering from binge-eating disorder, and the other with 18 patients who were obese (Riva, Bacchetta, Baruffi, Cirillo, & Molinari, 2000; Riva, Bacchetta, Baruffi, Cirillo, & Molinari, 2001, cited in Riva, 2003). The positive results for both samples included modified body awareness associated with a reduction in problematic eating and social behaviors (Riva, 2003).

Anxiety Disorders and Phobias

Clients who cannot leave their home and be involved in the world, such as those who have agoraphobia, anxiety disorders, panic attacks, or social phobias, are effectively treated via online therapy. At times online therapy may be the only medium these clients want to use to begin therapy, because they need to remain in the safety and comfort of their own homes. It is much easier for clients with these types of diagnoses to disclose to another person via a computer screen than it is to disclose in front of a live person. Over time, as the online relationship between the mental health professional and the client strengthens, the client's relationships in the outside world also strengthen.

According to the ISMHO case studies:

> There is *growing anecdotal evidence* that use of cognitive assignments and online treatment have been effective at addressing social anxiety. Great success stories abound about improved relationships, self-awareness, and the value of support in making it through a stressful time, or crisis. Married couples have reported successes, while group dynamics in chat rooms and message boards are said to have infinitely improved people's awareness and social skills. (Fenichel, 2000)

Suicidal Clients

The Internet can be used specifically to offer support for people in crisis and those who are considering suicide, through direct, synchronous communication as well as closely watched asynchronous communication devices. Internet chat and instant messaging are similar to telephone hotlines in that they enable direct and immediate communication between people. The Internet has been a helpful method for many suicidal people to receive help. According to the ISMHO case studies:

> The use of online support groups is known to have significant impact on people in various types of distress, including medical diseases, depression, relationship problems, or other kinds of personal difficulties. As such, online support groups—easy to approach, with no threat of identity exposure—are efficient means of crisis intervention and prevention of suicide. In combination of these measures, SA-HAR, the Israeli online crisis service (http://www.sahar.org.il), has proven that suicide can effectively be

prevented and people in crisis and severe distress be helped through entirely online activity. In its 15 months of operation, SAHAR has provided online support to thousands of Israelis, and helped in preventing the suicide death of many of them, sometimes in last-moment detection of people who delivered farewell notices. Not only has SAHAR thus proven the value of such a program for the suicidal client with Web access, but also an additional benefit has developed, in that Israelis who reside abroad contact SAHAR regularly for personal support. Internet-based support is borderless, and synchronicity allows convenient interaction from a distance. (Fenichel, 2000)

Medical Issues

Treating the psychological component of health issues has been successfully done by online therapists at MyTherapyNet.com. However, empirical evidence of efficacy of providing mental health services to clients with medical issues is limited. Research with regard to online therapy alone is needed. Several research studies suggest that Internet-based technologies appear to be a promising new vehicle for providing health care education and support to individuals with chronic medical problems.

Research offers preliminary support for the efficacy of Internet-based interventions with insomnia, diabetes, and HIV. Studies of people with HIV and diabetes found positive results using a combination of group chat and stand-alone information modules (Gustafson, Hawkins, Boberg et al., 1999; McKay, Glasgow, Feil, Boles, & Barrera, 2002). Specifically, the findings demonstrated self-reported improvements in health quality of life and a reduction in the need for healthcare services.

Insomnia

Ström, Petterson, and Anderson (2004) investigated the effects of an Internet-based intervention for insomnia. One hundred nine participants were randomly assigned to either a cognitive–behavioral self-help treatment or a waiting list control condition. Participants used a sleep diary to measure symptom changes during five weeks of interventions consisting of sleep restriction, stimulus control, and cognitive restructuring. Results showed statistically significant improvements on many outcome measures, including total sleep time, total wake time in bed, and sleep efficiency.

Weight Management Group

A case reviewed by ISMHO (Fenichel, 2000) demonstrated the value of integrating face-to-face therapy with several online therapy methods using a weight management group. The group members specifically benefited from real-time chat rooms and message boards that offered continuous access to other group members and experts in the fields of nutrition and mental health. The group members also shared their experiences, assignments, and associated didactic information through the secure message board.

Another advantage of this multimedia approach was the increased feelings of safety and extra personal attention clients received through check-in e-mails and the supportive group chats offered in between face-to-face sessions. Clients reported feeling that their individual needs were met and their progress was managed in a safe, private environment. The members noted that not being face-to-face all the time gave them a greater feeling of safety "to share more openly with each other online than in f2f (face-to-face) meetings due to feelings of shame, fear of rejection, and avoidance of intimacy or emotional expression in person (all of which was made easier online)" (Fenichel, 2000).

Inmates

Almost one quarter of the 1.8 million incarcerated individuals in the United States today (Office of Justice Programs, 1999) are seriously mentally ill. Correctional psychologists are being asked to help mentally ill inmates by using behavioral tele-health, telecommunications, online therapy, and information technology (Magaletta, Fagan, & Peyrot, 2000). According to Magaletta, Fagan, and Peyrot (2000), behavioral telehealth offers substantial benefits for inmates, correctional adminis-trators, institutions, and the communities in which the institu-tions are located. Inmates have greater access to physical and mental health services, thus offering them a quality of care that may not otherwise be available.

Magaletta and colleagues' (2000) study of 75 inmates deter-mined that the majority of the inmates had initial satisfaction with the telehealth consultation process, more comfort with the process over time, and a willingness to return for follow-up. Although inmates with thought disorders and inmates with mood disorders were satisfied with telehealth, they became frustrated and angry. Future studies using technological up-grades and allowing more time for preparing inmates for con-sultation are needed (Magaletta et al., 2000). Further research may also help delineate which inmates respond best to this mode of service delivery and under what conditions.

Online Support Groups

The Internet can facilitate the provision of peer support groups to underserved populations. Peer support is more convenient and accessible through the Internet than through traditional in-person groups, and the Internet may be useful in providing support groups for persons with illnesses or disabilities that prevent them from accessing in-person groups. Peer support groups can also be formed to address disorders for which in-person groups may not be applicable because the infrequency of the disorder prohibits the gathering of sufficient members to form an in-person support group. Members of an ISMHO case study group (Fenichel, 2000) indicated that they were able to integrate ongoing therapy and peer support by using e-mails and message boards to communicate among group members during vacation times. They successfully maintained continuity and cohesion through the informal contact with one another.

TRAINING AND SUPERVISION

The Internet provides mental health practitioners with increasing opportunities both to supervise psychological services and to obtain supervision when needed. This is especially good news for practitioners who have little or no access to adequate supervision. However, even though the benefits of this medium exist, it is necessary to consider computer technology, ethical issues, and how online supervision might occur.

Kanz (2001) suggested that although the Internet has potential as an important tool for supervision, there are several ethical and relationship concerns. There are practical and ethical issues such as confidentiality, client's informed consent (see Chapter 8), licensing, and relationship.

Training online is an increasingly popular adjunct to the mental health practitioner's required supervision and education. Continuing education is essential and often beneficial when done online. Recognizing that therapists may encounter clients or issues for which they have not received adequate training, multicultural training in issues is now required in all American Psychological Association (APA)-accredited professional psychology programs. Therefore, for therapists to provide multiculturally appropriate services, some form of clinical supervision is necessary.

Computer technology can help individuals transcend geographical barriers and therefore may be particularly well suited to overcoming some of the obstacles in developing a professional community. The growth of the Internet has given rise to speculation that communities can be developed without the need for frequent face-to-face contact among members. In computer-mediated discussion groups, members "converse" by posting e-mail messages to be read by the other group members, who in turn can respond or post their own messages.

Another interactive training program presented in the case study group of ISMHO incorporates students working across modalities, creating an online Web project and utilizing a variety of online resources in a guided "quest" of self-exploring a psychosocial topic. Increasingly, not only in the training of mental health professionals but in higher education generally, use of forums, "whiteboards," **bulletin boards, blogs,** and so forth is proving to be a useful and motivational supplement to conventional classroom lectures.

The work of the CSG itself is a testament to the power of peer support and supervision. It dramatically illustrates the power of such an endeavor to stimulate a steep learning curves and promote enhancement of technical skills, cross-cultural awareness, and familiarity with the many new issues that have arisen in ethical and professional practice. Rapid sharing of references and resources through hyperlinks and instant access to peers have also been of great value for the members of this group. In terms of advanced clinical training, the value of online peer group supervision has proven itself to be tremendous (ISMHO, 2000b).

Another case was presented where there was a very serious call for help via e-mail, and the group shared online resources, suggestions, support, and personal experiences with various treatment providers local to the client. It might be noted that during these case presentations, there was almost always one or another colleague present, online, for consultation or assistance with any urgent situation. This turned out to be tremendously helpful in a number of cases. Several effective, rapid, and knowledgeable interventions would not have been possible were it not for the opportunity to utilize both synchronous and asynchronous communication channels to consult with respected peers, around the clock, and in some cases around the planet (Fenichel, 2000).

Other issues discussed by ISHMO CSG members include being delayed in response by several hours and issues around cultural diversity. Here is the experience of a group member in the United Kingdom:

> Working with someone from a completely different culture, time zone, and social system can clearly be problematic, and this is something to consider before concluding that "anyone can practice worldwide" in any circumstance. On the other hand, long-distance, cross-cultural training and practice are being conducted and some very exciting opportunities are emerging due to our ability to shift time and still be able to focus effectively and respond to another person as if in a shared "here and now" (Fenichel, 2000).

CONCLUSION

Although not all studies reviewed had positive outcomes based on rigorous scientific research methods, some of the findings might be indicators with potentially important implications for the future. Several studies had encouraging results with various populations, including groups with HIV, eating disorders, posttraumatic stress disorders, anxiety disorders, phobias, disabilities, and insomnia.

Some of these studies were not based on evaluating online therapy alone, but were studying online therapy combined with computer-mediated and -guided programs. The review of studies evaluating online therapy alone demonstrates very few randomized clinical trials on Internet-delivered interventions for any mental health disorder.

Further research may help delineate the potential benefits and understand which clients respond best to online therapy and under what conditions. Future studies should also compare interventions and expand the scope of conditions to include gender, ages, and ethnic groups. By empirically determining the interventions best suited for each population and diagnosis, online mental health services can be tailored to meet each client's needs. The samples used should also be representative of the population that could effectively receive and participate in the online therapy and/or computer mediated services.

Research will help guide mental health professionals in choosing interventions and therapeutic approaches appropriate for their clients. Future studies will help therapists determine if an intervention is empirically reliable and valid and if it is at least as effective when used online as it is offline. By demonstrating that online interventions provide equivalent results and outcomes as face-to-face therapy, they can be used with certainty.

Research such as this will be useful in determining whether online therapy is a viable, cost-efficient, and effective medium for providing mental health services. It is important that this information then be provided to potential clients so that they can make informed decisions about the value and potential benefits of using these services.

PART II

Setting Up an Online Practice: Business, Legal, and Ethical Issues

CHAPTER 5

Is It Time to Go Online?

There are many questions to be asked and answered before making the final decision to practice therapy online. In this chapter we raise some of the issues that must be considered. When a therapist first begins to consider online therapy options, it is important to remember that there is an interface between the personal, business, and clinical issues.

ADVANTAGES AND DISADVANTAGES

The decision to do online therapy can bring with it many major business, lifestyle, and clinical changes, and each one has to be considered very carefully. We emphasize that this is not a decision to be made in haste. To rush into doing online therapy without considering all of the many factors involved can lead to personal and professional disappointment, unforeseen expenses, possible damage to one's professional reputation, and worst of all, inadequate or inconsistent treatment of clients. The main categories that must be considered are these: How will adding online therapy to an existing face-to-face practice impact the therapist's lifestyle? How will the decision affect the therapist from a business perspective? What will be the impact of the decision on the therapist's existing client base? If a therapist is just setting up his or her practice, should the decision be made to include both face-to-face and online, or to go to online therapy alone?

Do I Want to Increase My Client Base?

There are several factors to consider when deciding to increase your client base. Becoming informed about the benefits and limitations of increasing your client load is recommended.

Lifestyle.
Time is the big consideration: You must consider how you spend your time daily, weekly, monthly, and throughout the year. Sit down with a paper and pencil and figure out how you spend your time in terms of professional commitments (clients, further education, attending meetings, networking, reading professional journals); personal commitments (household tasks, yard, reading, time spent with family and friends); relaxation, hobbies/avocations, entertainment/enrichment (participating in sports, visiting museums, art galleries, theater, movies, travel). If your life is already overscheduled, you aren't going to be happy if you decide to take on more clients online, thinking you can "always drop" your favorite activity—whatever it is, you'll miss it, and your health and happiness, and that of your family and close friends, will suffer.

Number of clients.
Are you professionally and personally comfortable with the number of clients you are treating face-to-face? Why would you want to increase that number, whether face-to-face or online? If you did decide to increase your client base, could you do so without either working excessively long hours or walking yourself into a case of early burnout while also disrupting

family and other personal relationships in the process? How many clients is too many? How many hours a week are you working now? How many more hours a week could you comfortably work? If you increase your client base and find you are working too many hours a week for comfort, it may not be possible to reduce your hours immediately.

Do you need to make more money (kids off to college, the house needs a new roof)? Should this be a factor in your decision to add to your client base by doing online therapy in addition to your present caseload? For example, you might choose to solve this problem by teaching a college course or doing more supervision.

Greater Diversity of Clients with an Increased Client Base

Will providing online therapy mean that you have the opportunity to treat a greater diversity of clients, with regard to their mental health problems and their racial and cultural types, than is now the case? Are there racial or ethnic groups you have always felt you could treat, and would be accessible online, but are not now part of your client population? Perhaps you have skills in a second language that you would like to use but find few opportunities to do so in face-to-face therapy, given the demographics of your location. Perhaps you were not born in the United States and would like to do online therapy with people from your country of birth. Online therapy could certainly help you achieve these ends.

Would you need further professional training if you were to expand into treating different types of clients? How much time would you need to commit to further education and what would be the costs?

Treating Homebound or Therapist-Shy Clients

Perhaps there are types of clients you haven't treated because they aren't accessible geographically, because they have physical disabilities, suffer from conditions such as agoraphobia, which keep them housebound, or are simply fearful of walking into a therapist's office in case someone sees them and thinks they're "crazy." Certainly, online therapy could provide the kind of outreach that could help these categories of people.

Client Privacy, Client Shame

Some clients can open up more rapidly if they have the perceived privacy of "talking" online without having to look at a therapist in person. For example, an adult who was sexually abused as a child, and still erroneously believes the abuse was his or her "fault," might be better able to overcome immobilizing feelings of shame online and talk about the situation. Are there those among your present client base who might be helped by augmenting face-to-face therapy with online therapy?

Children and Adolescents

If your client base includes children and adolescents, you will find them naturally adept at online therapy. They grew up with computers, and whether in combination with face-to-face, or on its own, online therapy would certainly be of great value to this group. Perhaps you would like to extend your client base to include children and adolescents; online therapy would certainly be helpful in doing that. Would you need to undertake further education before treating youngsters?

Communicating with Your Clients Online

If you have clients who live or work in a different location from your office, then it is worth considering the advantages of being able to communicate with them online, either between sessions or as an alternative to face-to-face sessions.

Having Sessions When Either
You or the Client is Out of Town

Perhaps you teach a course or courses at colleges in other towns as well as maintaining your therapy practice. Perhaps you have clients who also commute to other locations or must travel in the course of their work. In the age of laptops, you and your clients can meet online wherever you and they happen to be.

Perhaps Your Spouse or Partner has a Job Offer That Involves Relocation

If a family move is inevitable, online therapy will enable you to continue treating many of your current clients. Some will prefer face-to-face and will find another therapist, but many will be glad of the continuity provided by switching to online therapy. In some cases where a client prefers face-to-face therapy, you can use online therapy as a termination device so that the change to another therapist is less abrupt.

Ability to Offer Therapy from both Home and Office

Having this flexibility can cut back on no-shows and cancellations. Clients with work-related scheduling problems will find it convenient not to have to leave their workplace, and this can enable them to maintain continuity in their therapy sessions. From the therapist's point of view, more daytime sessions can be scheduled, reducing the need for either very early morning or evening sessions. In this respect, even though the client base may increase, the availability of online therapy can make it possible for the therapist to manage time more efficiently.

BUSINESS ISSUES

You need to examine the business issues as closely as the lifestyle issues in determining whether or not to set up an online therapy practice. We suggest you do some serious research: Contact therapists who have added online therapy to their practice. Networking with colleagues is essential in order to identify the significant issues. Contact your professional organization and read articles about online therapy (e.g., several

American Psychological Association journals have articles on the subject [http://www.apa.org] and the International Society for Mental Health Online [http://www.ismho.org] is also a useful source).

Contact your accountant well in advance of making the decision to go online; he or she may have some helpful suggestions.

Computer Skills

How good are your computer skills? Will you need to take a computer course before providing online therapy? You certainly need to be very comfortable with the main lines of communication before treating a client: e-mail, chat, instant messaging. It is essential to know what you don't know so that you can take steps to obtain the necessary information. For example, if you do group therapy, how is that handled online?

Legal, Ethical, and Therapist Skills Concerns

Have you considered such issues as where the online therapy takes place in legal terms? At the time of writing, among the professional organizations, there is no agreement as to where the therapy takes place. Have you considered the ethical issues involved in treating a suicidal client online, who is either not located in the same state as the therapist or not located near the therapist's office? Or consider the situation of a client who tells you about behavior that it is mandatory for you to report to the police in your state but not in the client's state; for example, elder abuse? It is imperative for all mental health professionals who plan to expand their practices with online therapy and the use of any method of telecommunication to remember that while the basic issues surrounding standards of care, legal and ethical responsibilities, and confidentiality remain the same for either face-to-face or online therapy, there will be additional questions to ask and answer with online therapy—the examples of a suicidal patient and an elder abuser both raise such questions.

Additional Therapist Skills in Online Therapy

Do you understand that you may need to sharpen your clinical skills when receiving information from a client in typed form during a session, with none of the nuances and information provided in a face-to-face situation? Seventy percent of communication is said to take place nonverbally, so don't underestimate how much you learn in a face-to-face situation from nonverbal signs.

Will Online Therapy Fit Well with Your Lifestyle?

Do you really see yourself doing therapy while you're on vacation, at home, on a business trip, or would you rather keep your therapeutic interactions with clients in one place within predetermined hours/days? Will online therapy open up opportunities that you welcome, or would it spread you too thin? Given that online therapy sessions can range from 10 to 50 minutes, you might well be doing therapy with more people every day. How would that affect you? Are you more comfortable with the schedule and client load you have now?

AN INDEPENDENT WEB SITE OR AN ESTABLISHED E-CLINIC?

Whether you decide on an independent Web site or join an e-clinic, it is important to be sure that your clients' personal information regarding name, address, credit card information, and so on, is clearly separated from clinical communications. Additional risks to confidentiality exist with the use of message boards, discussion groups, and **public chats**. Although they are very effective for use by online support groups, they are not private and are not bound by the law and ethics that govern the psychotherapy profession.

An Independent Web Site

Here again, networking with colleagues can be very helpful. Before approaching a Web designer (and you need to look at the work of several designers who have created Web sites specifically for independent therapists both as to style and cost), you need to develop some basic knowledge about the process of building a Web site so that you acquire at least a basic vocabulary and have some idea of the basic questions that need to be asked.

Whether you hire a Web site designer or are able to design your own Web site, you need to consider the following: How will you protect your clients' confidentiality? You will need to set up a system for contacting emergency services in other states and have it in place from the onset in case of a suicidal client or other emergency. You will need the tools for billing, accounting, and scheduling. The Web site will have to include your license number and information on your education and qualifications. You will need to contact third-party payers. Perhaps you now work through an HMO as one of its preferred therapy providers. What is the HMO's position on online therapy?

An Online e-Clinic

What should you look for when checking online e-clinics? How does a clinic protect client confidentiality? What does the clinic provide in terms of billing, accounting, scheduling, and other services? Is there a reliable "wall" between billing information and clinical material? Will the clinic be cost effective for you? If you want to expand your client base, will the clinic's publicity and promotional activities enable you to do so? Will you be comfortable being listed with the other therapists who use the site?

Cost Effectiveness of Independent vs. e-Clinic

Have you discussed the lifestyle, business, and clinical logistics of online therapy with colleagues, both those who have independent Web sites and those who have joined e-clinics? What are their problems and solutions? Does your state professional organization provide any guidance to members who are considering online in addition to, or instead of, face-to-face therapy?

CLINICAL ISSUES RELATING TO ONLINE THERAPY

As with face-to-face therapy, online therapists need to consider which types of clients are appropriate for this mode of therapy. As noted earlier, online therapy is particularly suited for homebound clients who would not otherwise have access to therapy, such as those who suffer from panic attacks, agoraphobia, social phobia, or physical disabilities. However, we urge therapists to network with colleagues and contact their professional associations to establish, in their own minds, the significant issues. For example, a therapist treating clients online will still need to find sources for supervision; and he or she will need to be sure that the psychological tests used with face-to-face clients are as effective online.

Unsuitable Diagnoses
Acutely suicidal clients who require ongoing monitoring or homicidal clients are not good candidates for online therapy. Clients with disturbed thought disorders, such as paranoia, schizophrenia, and delusions, are not appropriate for online therapy; neither are clients who need support in order to function at a basic level outside of a hospital.

Unsuitable Theoretical Applications
Many therapeutic theories and interventions are very effective for online therapy, while others are not applicable. Interventions such as hypnosis, eye movement desensitization and reprocessing (EMDR), thought-field therapy, many of the Gestalt interventions, psychodrama, and many types of body work

therapies cannot be utilized online using text-based communications.

Limitations and Disadvantages

Online therapy restricts therapists' abilities to assess clients' appearance and self-care skills. Visual communication is needed for therapists to determine how well clients take care of themselves. Clients using only text communication often hide their inability to take care of themselves and limit therapists' abilities to accurately assess areas of hygiene, dishevelment, and physical disabilities requiring medical intervention.

Diagnosis may not be straightforward online. Crisis management, especially with a client in another state, may also pose additional problems, miscommunication can arise, particularly if the client isn't skilled at expressing him- or herself in writing.

Therapy Choices

The most successful online therapists understand the distinctions among online, telecommunication, and offline therapy choices and make well-informed decisions regarding their clients' treatment plans. They know which clients are best suited for online therapy alone or combined with face-to-face therapy. We recommend that therapists understand how to apply their traditional clinical skills to online therapy.

Seasoned online therapists claim that they experience their clients in other and often deeper ways using online therapy. They create a safe therapeutic alliance, even when they do not have the benefit of being physically in the room with their clients and even when visual or verbal communication is not available.

Therapeutic Benefits

The following are specific therapeutic benefits that pertain to online therapy:

- More rapid self-disclosure, greater opportunities for reflection, and more succinct expression of feelings than with traditional therapy may occur.
- Clients who are uncomfortable talking find it easier to express themselves in writing when they do not have to be confronted by the therapist in person.
- Feeling less inhibited and safer behind the keyboard, many clients accept suggestions and move to solutions more rapidly than in face-to-face therapy. Writing becomes the tool for uncovering deep emotions and truths that many clients find difficult or impossible to express in face-to-face therapy.

Combined Face-to-Face and Online Therapy

There are advantages when therapists use a combination of face-to-face sessions, written text, videoconferencing, and Internet phone. All of these therapy methods enhance the traditional therapeutic experience. Experienced online therapists match their clients' individual communication abilities and styles with the appropriate therapy delivery method. (They may not use online therapy to replace traditional therapy, but they definitely view it as an appropriate addition to face-to-face therapy as well as sometimes even an advantage over the face-to-face experience, depending, of course, on client needs.) It will be important to consider how best to move a suitable client from face-to-face to online therapy.

Good Research Will Protect the Therapist

Careful and well-organized research into online therapy, its benefits and hazards, effects on the therapist's lifestyle, business benefits or disadvantages, clinical benefits (when applied to the right set of problems and the right client), will protect the therapist from making a bad decision—either to plunge into online therapy with insufficient information to make a good decision, or to avoid online therapy when it might well have benefits for a therapist as well as his or her clients.

CONCLUSION

We have discussed some of the personal, business, and clinical issues that must be addressed when a therapist considers extending his or her practice with the use of online therapy. The need for careful research—networking with colleagues, reading journal articles, and contacting professional organizations—has been stressed; all of which should be taken into consideration before a therapist makes the decision to either set up his or her own Web site or join an e-clinic.

CHAPTER 6

Going Digital

Once therapists have decided to provide their services online, they need to make a number of choices to determine the best path for their online practice. In this chapter, we will assist therapists in making the right choices. The first decision is to determine whether to set up an independent online practice or to join a large online clinic.

The first option, conducting an independent online practice, allows therapists to operate their own Web site. They control the content of the site and decide how to operate it.

The other option, joining an established online clinic, allows therapists to join an organization that will set up their online practice for them, as well as maintain and market it. There are advantages and disadvantages to using either method.

INDEPENDENT ONLINE PRACTICE

There are some advantages to maintaining an independent online practice via a personal Web site. A Web site may either be built by the therapist, or the services of a Web site designer may be enlisted. Building one's own Web site can sometimes be less costly than having it designed by a Web site designer. Cost factors are directly related to the complexity of the Web site desired.

Web Site Building

The online therapy practice requires a Web site that includes three primary areas of functionality: billing, **calendaring,** and communicating. Beyond these fundamental elements are a myriad of functions that further assist therapists in their online practice. There are also many functions that provide clients with an enhanced online therapy experience. Unlike a "static" Web site, which is purely informational and does not incorporate any functionality, online therapy requires functions that involve a more advanced knowledge of computer code, databases, and logic structures. Whether one enlists the services of a professional Web site developer or designs the site on his or her own, it is imperative to begin with a clear idea of the functional flow and logic structure which will become the Web site's database. It is extremely important for therapists to know precisely what functionality they desire in their Web site before the work is begun. Otherwise, what may seem like a "simple" add-on could very easily require a substantial change to the database, which most often has a domino effect on other aspects of functionality. Therefore, it is also important to decide what functionality may be desired in the future. This way the Web site developer can build the database in a way that allows for the future functionality without creating the need to rebuild the database from scratch once that functionality is implemented.

The therapist will likely have to weigh the advantages of having some functions available upon launch as opposed to becoming available in the future. In the case of planning for future functionality, some of these functions may be quite easily allowed for and may not cause initial additional expense. Other future functions may be quite complex, and even just leaving "holes" in the database for the function may be a time-consuming task and cause considerable additional expense. This expense is measured in time and the cost of lost opportunity for therapists building their own site. This is of course measured in dollars for therapists using the services of a Web site developer. For some, it may make much more sense to consider the building of their online practice in stages. The first stage may be a basic online therapy practice that allows for the primary functions—i.e., billing, calendaring, and communicating. Once the practice is fruitful, the therapist may decide to engage a second phase that incorporates more detailed functionality and the ability to expand. This second phase would likely be a completely new development project, but would be funded from the success of the first phase.

Whatever choice therapists make should be based upon the scope of their needs, from a business perspective. "Build it and they will come" is fine if the volume of clientele needed to offset the cost of construction is weighted favorably in terms of the therapist's bottom line.

An alternative to building a custom Web site is to piece together the various elements required from **third-party software** sources. Although there are some products that exist in the marketplace from which an online practice Web site could be assembled, there are two considerations that must be addressed very seriously before deciding upon this course of action. The first issue revolves around automation and inte-gration. When piecing together a Web site using third-party software, these programs will not interface (or work well) with one another. Opportunity for automation, efficiencies, and synergies are thereby lost. Second, there are the much more pressing issues surrounding patient care in the area of confidentiality. Web-based third-party software will generally run on third-party servers, and the information therein is subject to viewing by any number of individuals not bound by confidentiality. Moreover, clients information would be accessible to each company whose products are used.

Therefore, although it may seem an attractive course to take, piecing together an online therapy Web site in this fashion is likely fraught with peril.

Choosing a Domain Name.
The domain name is the Web site's address (e.g., www.my therapywebsite.com). Web site names ending in ".com" are preferable to any others because most people are used to the ".com" suffix. Second, keep the name as short as possible to help prevent clients from mistyping the name or forgetting it. Also, try to choose a name that is easy to spell, as misspellings will take the clients to error pages and create stress and frustration in their online therapy experience. Therapists should stay away from using homonyms, and if they must, then it is advisable to purchase both versions of the domain name.

There are many companies that sell domain names. Prices vary from company to company. Do an Internet search for "domain names" to find a suitable company.

Choosing a Hosting Company.
Once therapists have decided upon a domain name, many are tempted to immediately purchase space on a Webserver (or server). The Webserver is a computer that is connected to the Internet which "serves" the pages of the therapist's Web site to their clients. Although therapists could conceivably host their own Web site on their own Webserver, the server would require a continual connection to the Internet and must run specific software. Only those therapists with significant computer knowledge should attempt hosting their own Web site, as it is critical that their online practice not be compromised by inconsistent Internet connections and reduced capacity. Therapists should consider that the well-being of their clients requires effortless accessibility. Therapists should also consider that the details of hosting a Web site (as well as maintaining a Web site) are quite numerous and time-consuming, which will likely take them away from the actual practice of psychotherapy.

If a therapist decides to host his or her Web site with an established **hosting company**, there are many options available which have a direct relationship to the type of Web sites that are hosted. Before signing a lengthy contract with a hosting company, it is advisable to complete the "on paper" design of the Web site so that the therapist or his or her developer can decide exactly what services will be required from the hosting company. If the therapist desires to have an immediate presence on the Web (perhaps a welcome page with contact information and no functionality), there are many inexpensive Web hosting companies to choose from which will suffice in the interim.

Overall Design.
Therapists must first decide upon the functions they desire to have in place upon going **live**. This means getting specific—i.e., "I want my clients to arrive at a page that describes my services, a place for them to click to register. There will be a link for my terms and conditions. I will have a log-in box for clients to get to their online session, etc." Every detail must be articulated. The therapist should create detailed (not artistic) sketches of each page with all of the desired links and functions, even writing descriptions, as shown above.

After completing the Web site design is the perfect time to meet with a few professional Web site developers. It is important to meet with a high-end developer as well as some lower cost developers. Therapists should bring their rudimentary design to these meetings and discuss the plans with the developers. In this way, therapists will receive the benefit of having professionals review their plan and offer suggestions. Therapists may then decide to update their plan with what they learn from these professionals. At that time, they may wish to make their final decision as to either building the Web site themselves or hiring a professional to build it. If a therapist decides to hire a professional, he or she should be absolutely certain to ask for references and speak to the person's other clients. Therapists should also be completely clear in the contract as to what functionality will be provided and how long the project will take to complete. Check with references specifically on the subject of schedule—a developer who is late in producing the work can cost the therapist money in addition to causing an enormous amount of frustration.

Database Structure.
If a Web site is compared to the human being, the Web site's database is its DNA. Everything is built around the database, so it is imperative to have a firm understanding of the overall scope of the project before undertaking the construction of the Web site. If a Web presence is desired immediately, a one- or two-page simple Web site can be used to welcome visitors and inform them of the work in progress.

Resources.
There are many books on the market that speak in detail to the various aspects of Web site design. In general, the Web developer will need varying degrees of knowledge and proficiency in the following areas: html programming (**hypertext mark-up language**—used for Web-pages that only require display functionality), database configuration (a Microsoft Access database is not robust enough to conduct a practice—knowledge of MySQL, MS SQL, or comparable is required), ASP programming (Active Server Pages **programming,** or equivalent, allows for dynamic functionality on a Web-page), and graphic design.

Finally, it is important to realize that an online presence is judged by customers very much the same way physical buildings are judged—i.e., by appearance. If the building looks "shabby" or unprofessional, people tend to form an impression about the product or service being offered. They may even avoid stopping to look further. Because of the speed by which advances are made on the Internet, taking the time to research how to make the best impression upon customers is a never-ending and mission-critical project for the online business-owner.

Advantages

A personal online therapy practice has the advantage that the Web site can be modified repeatedly. Therapists can control all aspects of the content of their Web site. They have an almost unlimited opportunity to post any information they wish; for example, articles, pictures, and links to other Web sites. The only constraints upon making such changes are the time and skills needed to do so. In addition, the layout can be completely customized. Therapists with a basic knowledge of the Internet may be able to make changes on their Web site themselves. Above all, the therapist is the only therapist featured on the Web site, so the focus of the site is solely on his or her practice. If desired, at some point other therapists may be added to the Web site; perhaps those whose specialties are in slightly different areas and add to the Web site's usefulness, but do not compete with the originating therapist.

Disadvantages

One of the downsides to conducting a private online therapy practice is that therapists will need to have the knowledge and expertise to build the Web site, or they will need to hire a professional to create a Web site for them. If therapists set out to create their own Web site, they will require a wide range of technical skills, including learning hypertext mark-up language (html), using a **text editor**, finding a hosting company to host their Web site on a server, and learning how to upload, publish, or use **file transfer protocol** (FTP) to move their site's Web pages to the hosting company's server. They will have to endure a learning curve that requires aptitude for computer programming of moderate difficulty and a willingness to spend dozens of hours studying and practicing to become proficient if they wish to build the Web site themselves.

Additionally, it is important to note that such highly specialized communications as calendaring and billing functionality may require a high degree of computer programming knowledge for which a professional will be required.

When Web site design and creation are outsourced to a third party, the process of updating a Web site can become more complex. It may be difficult to explain to the designer exactly what is desired. Ongoing Web site maintenance may be required, which is a fee-based service. Although the initial cost of a Web site can be significant, it is important to realize that the maintenance of that Web site also has a cost associated with it, and it is absolutely imperative that a good Web site be regularly updated.

Therapists are likely to discover that if they multiply the number of hours it takes to build and manage an online therapy Web site by the amount they estimate their time is worth, the process is likely to be more costly than if they provided their services through an online clinic. Also, if a therapist is contemplating building an individual Web site, it is important to consider how the end result will appear—Web sites are judged by their appearance and functionality. In contrast to paying a fee to practice from an online clinic, it can cost exponentially more to build and maintain a Web site that includes the very specific functionality that an online therapy practice demands.

If a therapist does decide to hire a professional to build a Web site, it is essential to very carefully research potential designers in order to select the best one for the job. For the task of building a Web site that supports online therapy, the Web builder must be more than a designer who produces a beautiful design. The Web builder must have an in-depth knowledge of computer software programming because the online therapy Web site is much more than simply an **online brochure**. There is functionality that must be built to very discerning standards, and such a task is suited only for those Web builders who have both design and programming knowledge.

Most often it is imperative to employ a Web-design firm that has programmers, designers, and project coordinators on staff. Such comprehensive services will be costly, but it is important to be wary of designers who bid very low—the time and resources necessary to program and design an appropriate online therapy Web site will necessarily carry a proportional price tag.

Another disadvantage to building an online therapy Web site is that unless the communication software is proprietary, the therapist will need to use third-party software, such as MSN, AOL, or Yahoo! Messenger, or use e-mail; neither option allows for the therapist to provide a reasonable guarantee of security and confidentiality. If indeed the therapist programs or his or her own communication software, it is also important to be sure that security cannot be compromised by a third party. If a Web-design firm programs the software, even if that firm is not used for maintenance, the firm may have built "back doors" into the software, allowing access to the site and any information contained therein. It is imperative to have the firm sign a confidentiality agreement.

If the therapist wishes to include other technologies in their own Web site, such as a message board, a calendar, or **automatic billing**, again, he or she will either need to learn how to build these functions or hire a professional to build them.

Finally, the therapist needs to give consideration to marketing. Once the Web site is complete, it will need to be listed on search engines and in directories. It does cost money and take specialized knowledge to achieve good **rankings** on a search engine. The term *ranking* refers to the position of a listing on a search engine. If a Web site is not optimized for search engines, it could be listed tens, even hundreds, of pages into the search result, and is unlikely to be viewed by a potential client.

ONLINE CLINICS

Large online clinics are national (or global) operations that provide therapists with virtual offices from which to practice therapy. They provide potential clients with access to hundreds, even thousands of therapists. Generally, online clinics do not employ therapists; instead, they verify therapist credentials and supply space, advertising, and other services that can be used by the therapist for a fee. These companies also provide content (e.g., news, self-tests, links, and games) on their Web sites for potential clients to peruse, much of which is very informative and usually provided free of charge to the client.

Web Site Content

The content of an online therapy Web site is what ultimately convinces a consumer to solicit the services offered. The information provided may be as basic as biographical information about the therapist or may include resources, health news, articles, and tools for visitors to utilize. Content keeps a visitor occupied on the Web site, increases the time spent on the Web site, and therefore increases the likelihood of the visitor purchasing therapy services.

Therapists should also explain the procedure to prospective clients. They may wish to inform their visitors about the billing process, whether they accept insurance, and if so, which ones and under what terms. If the client is to be billed by credit card prior to the session date, that information should be disclosed. Detailed disclosure should be included in the Web site's "terms and conditions" page, and broader, more market-friendly language should spell out the primary points very clearly and accessibly to the Web site visitor.

Advantages

The advantages for therapists conducting their practices via an established online clinic are numerous. The Web site and technologies used for conducting online therapy have already been built and implemented, and therapists are able to launch their online practice almost immediately. Maintenance is provided to the Web site by its operators.

Although the maintenance of the site is provided as part of the package, it is important for therapists to remain vigilant in their knowledge of the underlying processes in order to ascertain that their practice is compliant with their expectations. Therapists should be familiar with the Web site's billing practices and procedures, its content, security precautions, disclosures, and terms. Therapists should know how to update their personal biographical information, or, if done by the Web site's operators, what their process is for doing so. Also, from a business standpoint, it is important for therapists to be very familiar with the functionality and presence of the Web site so as to best put into play marketing strategies. By keeping a pulse on the Web site's infrastructure, therapists are more likely to be able to provide the most effective possible care for their clientele.

Online clinics will ordinarily have a marketing strategy in place. That allows therapists to make themselves available and leave the issue of marketing up to the online clinic. One thing to keep in mind, however, is that, as with any other business venture, it is always a good idea for therapists to continually market themselves and their online presence, independent of the marketing efforts of the online clinic. Refer to Chapter 7 for more information on marketing an online practice.

Disadvantages

The primary disadvantage to practicing from an established online clinic is that the individual therapist does not have control of site content. The operators of the site determine what material gets posted on the Web site as well as its visual design.

Therapists also have to share the site with other therapists from across the nation or world. When potential clients come to the Web site, they will oftentimes have a large number of therapists from which they may select. This could limit a therapist's potential client base. Some online clinics might charge a fee upon application; others might impose monthly or yearly fees for a listing.

Research is Essential.
If therapists decide to pursue practicing from an online clinic, the next step is to locate various online clinics and research them. A good place to start is the search engines. Using a comprehensive search engine such as Google, search for "online clinics" or "online therapy."

Check the therapists whose names are listed and contact a measurable percentage of them to find out how they feel about their listing with the clinic. How long have they been listed? Has it been cost effective for them? How have the site operators responded to complaints or requests? A group therapist would want to check with other group therapists to see how well a particular clinic functions.

WEB PAGE FEATURES AND TECHNOLOGIES

The technologies available for online therapy are able to greatly enhance the practices of many therapists. They can add dimensions to online therapy, and it is important to avail oneself of them.

Home Page for Would-Be Clients
Every online therapy Web site, whether it is an individual Web site or an established online clinic, will have a **home page**, the first page that people see when they reach the Web site. Depending on the intentions of the particular Web site, the information listed on this page will vary greatly.

The key to a successful home page is to have a clean look. Clients should be able to easily **navigate** around this page and be easily able to find the information they are looking for.

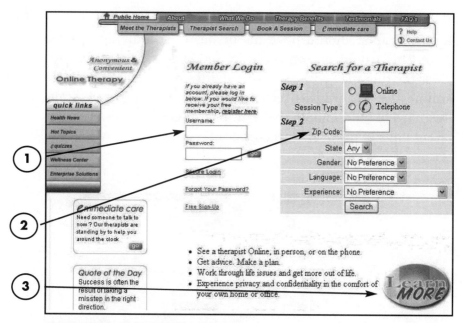

Figure 6.1a E-Clinic Home Page

1. Allows easy sign-in for both therapists and clients.

2. Allows clients to easily begin their search for the type of therapist they want—using criteria including gender, scope of practice, theoretical orientation, language spoken and availability.

3. Allows clients and therapists to find out more information about online therapy.

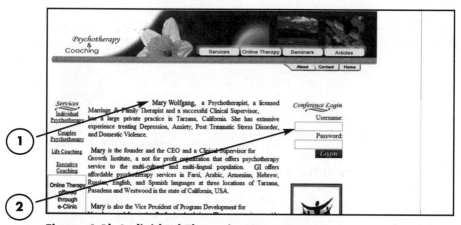

Figure 6.1b Individual Therapist Home Page

1. Allows clients to easily find information on the particular therapist who operates the Web site.

2. Allows easy sign-in for clients of this particular site.

Therapist Home Page

Each therapist should have his or her own individual home page. This would not be accessible to clients. This page provides the therapist with a starting point from which to navigate around their Therapist Account information. For an e-clinic, this page should enable the therapist to easily access the different links of his or her account.

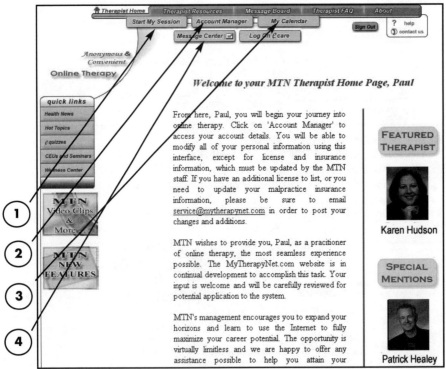

Therapists courtesy of MyTherapyNet

Figure 6.2a Therapist Home Page

1. This link allows therapists to begin their sessions.
2. This link allows therapists to access other information, including their biographical information, any photos posted of themselves, and other pertinent information.
3. This allows therapists to see their calendar at a glance and to see what sessions have been booked in the future.
4. Allows therapists to send and view e-mail messages.

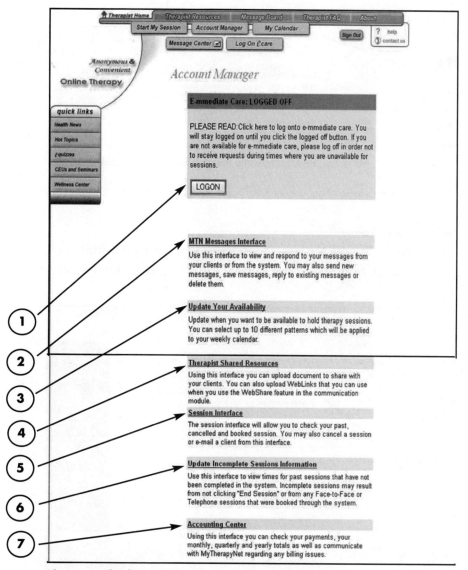

Figure 6.2b Therapist's Account Manager Page   (continued)
1. Allows therapists to log in and log out of the E-mmediate Care service.
2. Allows therapists to send and view messages.
3. Allows therapists to update their availability.
4. Allows therapists to upload documents and Web links they wish to share with their clients.
5. Allows therapists to check their past, canceled, and booked sessions.
6. Allows therapists to update their incomplete sessions, if any.
7. Allows therapists to view their accounting information.

Figure 6.2b (continued)

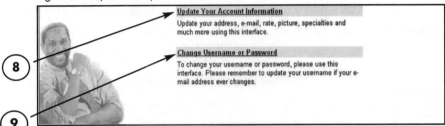

8. Allows therapists to update their account information, such as address, e-mail, picture, etc.

9. Allows therapists to change their user name and/or password.

What We Do

Every Web site, regardless of whether it is an individual Web site or a large online clinic, should include a page which details

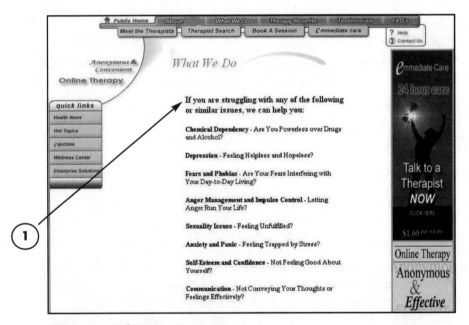

Figure 6.3 What We Do Page

1. This page includes some examples of the issues with which potential clients will be able to address by participating in online therapy. These issues can be shown as a list or as links which clients can access. Most people look for general conditions such as depression and delve into more detailed or specific issues at the time of their online therapy sessions.

information on what exactly the Web site provides, so that therapists and clients can determine what services are provided. There are numerous ways in which this information can be presented; Figure 6.3 shows a typical layout.

Frequently Asked Questions

Online therapy Web sites will likely include at least one page dedicated to answering some questions that therapists or clients might have in regard to the Web site and its services. This page can be known as *Frequently Asked Questions* (FAQs) or *Questions and Answers*. This page allows people to easily locate answers to commonly asked questions.

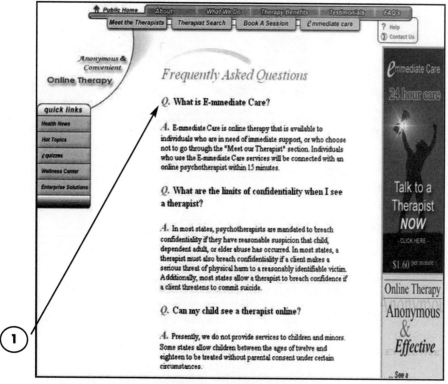

Figure 6.4 Frequently Asked Questions Page
1. These are some examples of the types of questions that can be found on an FAQ page.

For e-clinics, there can be two versions of this type of page: one for the clients who visit the site, the other for therapists who use the site.

Therapist Listings

Online clinics will provide pages dedicated to displaying individual therapists, their specialties, and other pertinent information. Individual online therapy sites will similarly list the qualifications of the therapist or therapists practicing from that site.

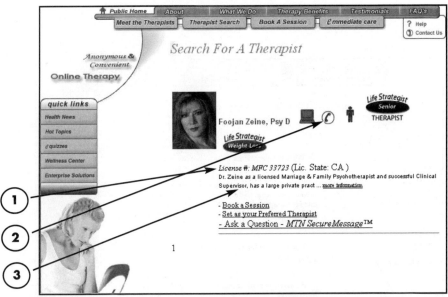

Therapist courtesy of MyTherapyNet

Figure 6.5 Therapist Listing Page

1. This provides the therapist's license number and state of issue.
2. These icons list the type of sessions this particular therapist may provide. In this case, the therapist is available for online sessions, telephone sessions, and face-to-face sessions. Some e-clinics allow their network of therapists to receive clients outside of the online modality. Clients are then able to receive services by telephone or in person.
3. This is the biographical information of the therapist; it allows the clients to get more information about the therapist, and it makes it easier for the clients to determine if this particular therapist is right for them. Included in the biography could be academic background and affiliations as well as relevant work-history.

Therapist Biography

Most online therapy Web sites will include a biography for each therapist. This provides an opportunity for potential clients to construct an impression of the therapist prior to booking services with them.

Log-In

All online therapy Web sites will have an area in which text may be entered that will allow people to log into their private accounts, whether it be as a client or as a therapist (see Figure 6.7).

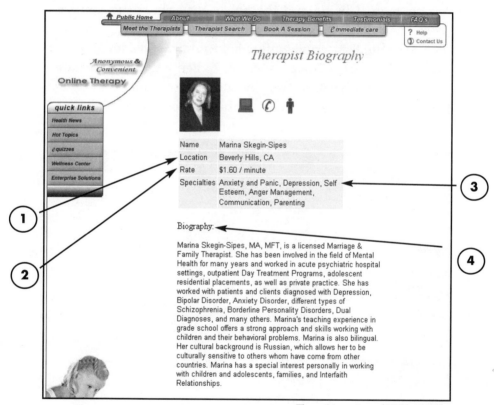

Therapist courtesy of MyTherapyNet

Figure 6.6 Biography Page

1. This shows the physical location of the therapist's office.
2. This shows the rate that the therapist is currently charging.
3. This shows the therapist's area of specialization.
4. This shows the therapist's biographical information.

Some Web sites even offer secure **log-on,** which encrypts their **username** and password. This allows for easy access to their personal information from most anywhere they may be on the Web site. The type of information that is generally accessed includes personal data, locality, credit card information, intake information and account history. Generally available to the user is access to change personal information as well as the opportunity to make changes to his or her log-in information (which includes changes to username and/or password). Generally, account information does not include text transcripts of previous sessions. Clients and therapists may choose to copy and paste their sessions into their own personal documents and files. Keeping transcripts online is generally considered a security risk, both from the perspective of keeping the information confidential and unattainable by outside users and from protection from court order directed at the online therapy e-clinic.

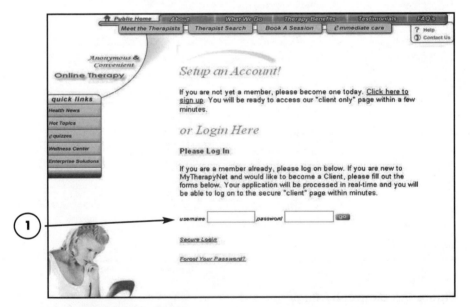

Figure 6.7 Log-in Page
1. This allows an easy sign-in for therapists and clients to access their information. Most sites have multiple ways in which clients and therapists can access their accounts.

Therapists' Resources

Some sites and online clinics will offer a therapist resources page. That allows therapists (but not clients) to access information on a variety of topics that will help them in their practice. An example is shown below, in which organizations dealing with eating disorders are listed for the therapist's use.

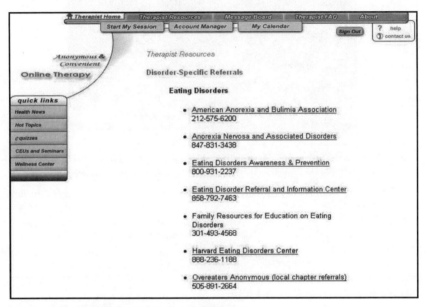

Figure 6.8 Therapist Resources Page

Waiting Room

In the process of starting an online therapy session, a client or therapist may need to wait until both arrive for the session (see Figure 6.9). In one form or another, all Web sites will employ a waiting room, which allows therapist or client to wait for the other to arrive. Once both parties are present, usually they are automatically taken to their chat session. A message will be shown letting therapist or client know that the other person has arrived, and the online session is ready to begin.

Figure 6.9 Waiting Room Page
1. The client waits for the therapist to arrive for their session in the waiting room, which also contains session information for the client. When the therapist arrives for their session, they go directly to the chat room.

Chat Room

This particular technology is the name given to a place or page on a Web site or an online clinic where people can chat with each other by typing messages, which are displayed in real time on the screens of others who are in the chat room.

For online therapy, this means that therapist and client are able to send instant messages to each other. One of the great advantages of using a chat room is the privacy. The therapist and the client are unable to see each other, which allows the client a greater ease in disclosing sensitive information to the therapist.

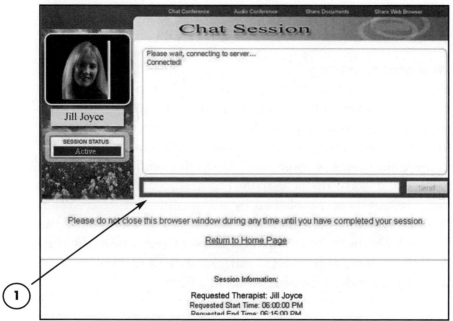

Therapist courtesy of MyTherapyNet

Figure 6.10 Chat Room Page
1. This allows therapists to type their messages here for the clients to see. The clients may then respond in their own time.

When using chat therapy for group sessions, multiple participants are able to meet at once in the chat room, similar in style to online chat rooms. Any attendee can voice thoughts at any time, and it is the therapist's responsibility to monitor, moderate, and lead the session. Online group therapy is especially effective because of the permanence of the messages sent—even the most offhand of comments is present throughout the session once it has been typed and therefore it may be referenced at any time during the session.

The sense of privacy afforded to the client is made possible by the clandestine nature of the meeting—no one is seen walking into the therapist's office. Although there is no anonymity in the true sense of the word (clients' identity, location, and billing information are usually mandated during the purchasing process), when the consumer is reasonably assured of the security of the Web site, this modality affords a reasonable approximation of true anonymity.

Audioconferencing

Some Web sites offer the opportunity for therapists and clients to communicate with each other through the chat room by using audio. This is similar to a telephone session, except that the speakers and microphones of their computers are used for communication. For those sites that offer audioconferencing, specialized software is usually required, and access to this functionality is accomplished by using controls that are often built directly into the chat room interface. Depending upon the particular software utilized, multiple people may be in the conference at once, although the current state of technology usually only provides for one speaker at a time.

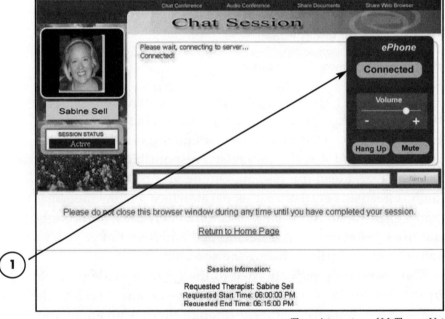

Therapist courtesy of MyTherapyNet

Figure 6.11 Audioconferencing Page
1. This allows therapists to connect with their clients using audio facilitated by the speakers and microphone on their computers.

Billing

Online billing allows therapists to collect payments from their clients, view past payment history, and keep track of their sessions. Clients use either a credit card or an electronic check. The nature of providing services online encourages payment for sessions when they are booked, prior to that session taking place. Generally, an industry standard of 24-hours notice is required for a refundable cancellation. Since sessions are paid for prior to occurring, the typical boundary issues regarding finances are no longer a dynamic of therapy, which is both a clinical as well as a business advantage to an online practice.

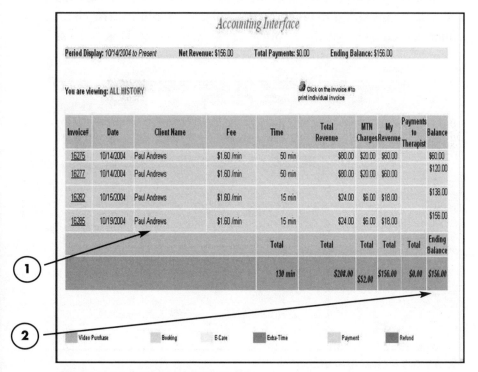

Figure 6.12 Online Billing Page

1. This allows the therapists to see the accounting information for recent sessions.
2. This shows the amount of money billed to date from sessions with a specific patient for the particular month.

Client and therapist are able to review their accounts and view a detailed description of all past and future sessions. Accounting reports can be printed to paper. Because the online practice is "virtual" and Web-based, clients and therapists may access their accounts from any Internet-connected computer, anywhere in the world.

Calendar

Using an online calendar allows a therapist to maintain his or her schedule on the Web site. This also allows any potential clients to see when a particular therapist is available. The client is able to research and schedule appointment times 24 hours a day, seven days a week.

Once the client is interested in seeing a particular therapist, a link will be provided to view the therapist's availability. The client chooses a convenient time and "books" the session. This process

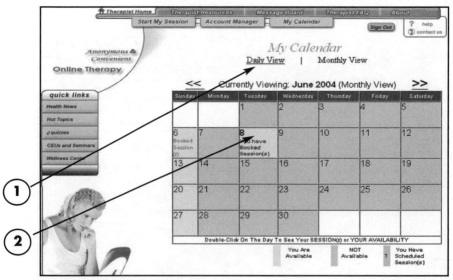

Figure 6.13 Calendar Page
1. This link allows therapists to see and modify their calendars on a "daily view" or "monthly view."
2. For this particular type of calendar, the therapists are able to double click on a particular date to view their sessions and/or update their availability.

usually encompasses selecting a date and time, confirming the date and time, and ultimately paying for the session. Once the session has been successfully booked, an appointment e-mail is sent to the therapist, as well as a text message, if the therapist has opted to receive such notification. The therapist's online calendar also immediately indicates the appointment information. A confirmation e-mail is also sent to the client.

Message Boards

A message board is a Web-based message center where users may post text communications for one another that are not

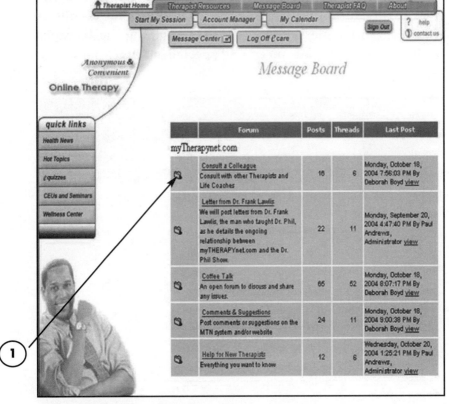

Figure 6.14 Message Board Page

1. This is an example of one of the headings in this particular message board that therapists are able to discuss with each other.

viewed in real time. Messages posted are converted into Web documents and may be viewed with browsing software. Message boards differ from e-mail the way a bulletin board at the supermarket differs from postal mail deliveries. In their most basic form, message boards must be visited to be read. However, some message boards do offer enhanced services to users, including the option of receiving e-mail notification of new postings, or even e-mail forwarding of the posted messages themselves. This technology allows therapists to post messages on a variety of topics.

Document Sharing

Some online clinics allow therapists to share documents with their clients during the course of an online session. This allows therapists to let clients view and read anything the therapist wishes to share. An advanced and specialized functionality for

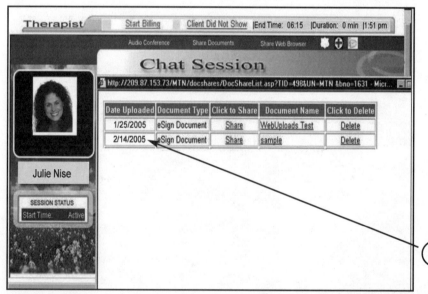

Therapist courtesy of MyTherapyNet

Figure 6.15 Document Sharing Page
1. This page shows all of the documents that the therapists are able to share with their clients.

the online psychotherapy practice is the process of **document sharing**. Documents may include resources, references, and even documents that can be electronically signed. Therapists who enter contracts with their clients or who wish to have an informed consent form signed may do so electronically, to standards that meet the legal definition of an electronic signature. Clients who wish to share personal documents that may aid in the therapeutic process are free to do so at will. Some clients will direct therapists to their personal Web site or a favorite Web site during a session to fully illustrate their thoughts and issues. Documents that can be shared may be web-pages, Word documents, pictures, PowerPoint presentations, and even video clips.

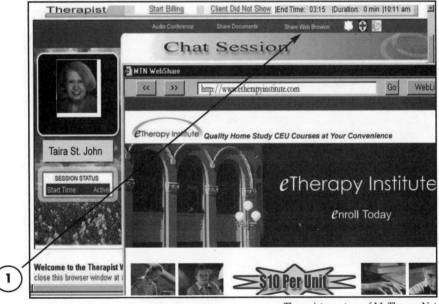

Therapist courtesy of MyTherapyNet

Figure 6.16 Web Site Sharing Page
1. This link allows therapists to easily share a Web page with their clients.

Web Site Sharing

Web site sharing is similar to document sharing, except therapists are able to share Web sites with their clients in real time (see Figure 6.16). For example, a therapist may be able to augment his or her point using a reference or resource from a Web page. Similarly, clients may direct their therapist to their personal Web site, their employer's Web site, or to a Web site of particular relevance to them at that time.

Electronic Signature Database

This feature allows therapists to view a database of client signatures from any document that they have shared with their clients and requested a digital signature. Commonly, therapists use this functionality to obtain a legal signature on their informed consent form. They can also use this functionality for

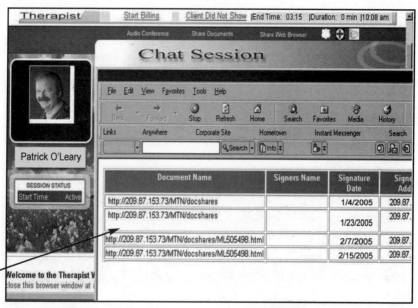

Therapist courtesy of MyTherapyNet

Figure 6.17 Electronic Signature Database Page
1. This shows a list of the documents that this particular therapist's clients have digitally signed.

court-ordered verification or even to enter into agreements with their clients, relevant to their course of therapy.

Local Police Locator

Some Web sites offer therapists the ability to locate the police station nearest to the client by using the client's zip code. This allows the therapist to quickly contact police by telephone if an emergency arises.

Therapist courtesy of MyTherapyNet

Figure 6.18 Local Police Locator Page
1. This button allows the therapist to locate the police station nearest to the client in this particular chat session.
2. This is a listing of the police stations nearest to this particular client.

Local Hospital Locator

This is similar to the local police feature, but allows the therapist to locate the hospital nearest to the client, in the case of an emergency (see Figure 6.19).

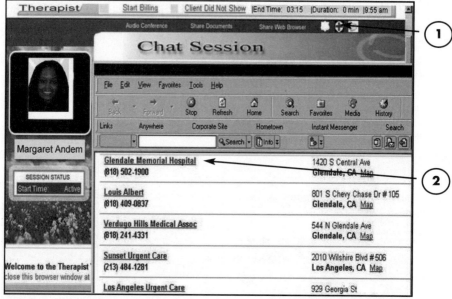

Therapist courtesy of MyTherapyNet

Figure 6.19 Local Hospital Locator Page
1. This button is used to allow the therapist to locate the hospitals nearest to the client in this particular chat session.
2. This is a listing of the hospitals nearest to this particular client.

Immediate Care

Online clinics will sometimes offer "walk-in" therapy services. This means that a client can go online and immediately be connected with a therapist without having to book a session in advance. The Web site below uses a pop-up box called an E-mmediate Care Coach™, which emits a sound when that particular therapist is being requested for an **E-mmediate Care** session.

Session Interface

This feature allows the therapist to keep track of any upcoming sessions that may have been scheduled or sessions they have had in the past (see Figure 6.21). This allows the therapist a quick, easy glance at session information.

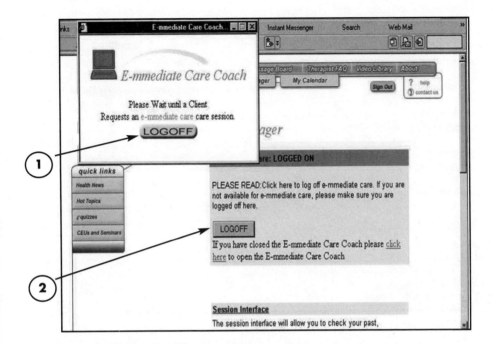

Figure 6.20 Immediate Care Page
1. For this particular online clinic, the *E-mmediate Care Coach* is used to notify the therapist of a "walk-in" session.
2. This allows therapists easy access to log on or log off the E-mmediate Care service, so that they may choose when they are available for "walk in" clients.

Articles

Some individual Web sites offer articles written by the therapist. Online clinics often offer articles written by the therapists listed on their Web site as well. Some offer links from the articles directly to the therapist who wrote the article so that a client may easily book a session with that therapist (see Figure 6.22).

Articles that deal with current health news can be included in the articles section, enabling both therapists and clients to keep up-to-date.

Books

Some Web sites feature books that pertain to the field of psychotherapy (see Figure 6.23). They may feature books and articles written by on-site therapists as well as other well-known authors.

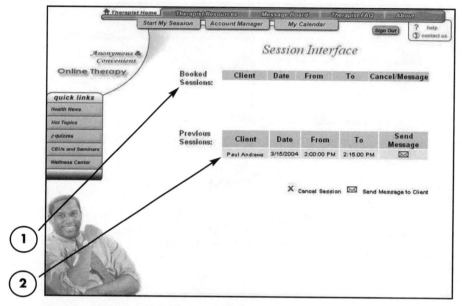

Figure 6.21 Session Interface Page
1. This shows sessions that have been booked for this particular therapist.
2. This shows sessions that this particular therapist recently conducted.

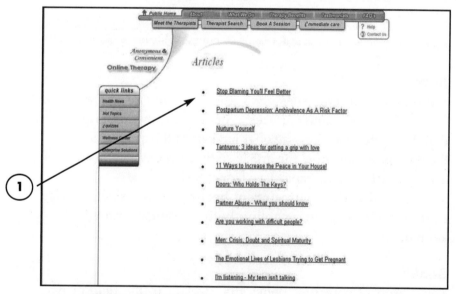

Figure 6.22 Articles Page
1. This page shows some of the articles posted by the therapists listed in this particular network.

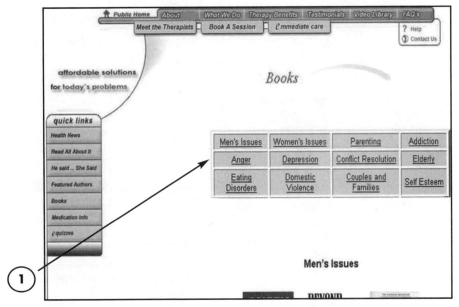

Figure 6.23 Books Page
1. This page shows books listed under various subject headings and from various authors that can be purchased by clients to help them deal with particular issues.

Featured Authors

In some cases, online therapy Web sites feature authors and the books they have written (see Figure 6.24).

Medication Information

Online therapy clinics sometimes offer medication information (see Figure 6.25). This will allow both therapists and clients to keep up-to-date in this area. The information is for educational purposes only. Medication can only be prescribed by a psychiatrist, and it is generally accepted that an in-person visit is required for medication to be prescribed. Therapists only reference this type of information as a resource for their clients. If a therapist suspects that his or her client may need medication or any adjunct consultation, the therapist is legally bound to refer the client to the appropriate professional.

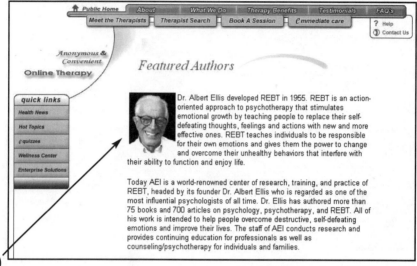

Therapist courtesy of MyTherapyNet

Figure 6.24 Featured Authors Page
1. This page is an example of an author listed on this Web site.

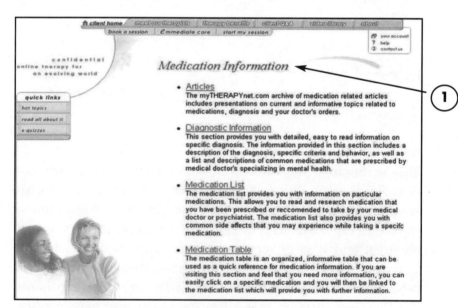

Figure 6.25 Medication Information Page
1. This heading is an example of the type of information that a Web site should be able to provide to the people visiting the site.

Online Quizzes

Online quizzes are popular with both therapists and clients. The therapist uses the online quiz as a diagnostic tool. The online quiz allows clients to receive almost instantaneous feedback. Although therapists refer their online clients to these quizzes, these quizzes may also be used for fun.

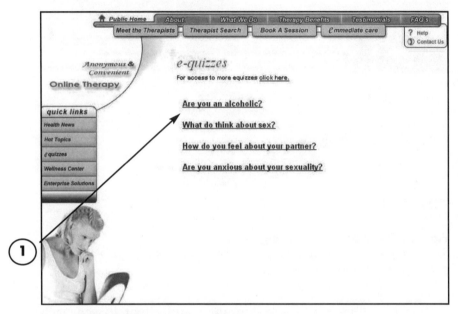

Figure 6.26 Online Quizzes Page
1. This is an example of an e-quiz which the client can fill out online.

Videoconferencing

Videoconferencing enables participants in distant locations to take part in a conference by means of electronic audio- and video communication. It requires both the therapist and the client to have a computer with videoconferencing software, along with a videocamera, speakers, and a microphone for each participant. Some popular Web-based videoconferencing software programs are available from Logitech, a company that manufactures Web-cams, and also CU See Me, a company specializing in web-based videoconferencing software applications.

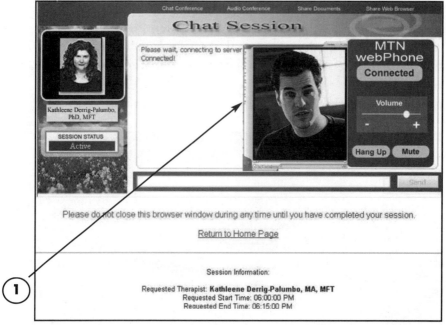

Therapist courtesy of MyTherapyNet

Figure 6.27 Videoconferencing Page
1. This allows therapists to connect with their clients through the video screen and speakers on their computers.

This technology allows a therapist and client to see each other via their monitors. It is a great benefit for both parties, if face-to-face contact is desired. Videoconferencing is a terrific online alternative for those who are not proficient at typing.

Currently, videoconferencing requires a **broadband** connection to the Internet, otherwise the quality may not be optimum.

E-mail
E-mail, or electronic mail, consists of messages, usually text, that are sent from one person to another via computer.

E-mail therapy has been in use since the mid-1990s for online therapy. Some clients find it easier to express lengthy or complex ideas or feelings via e-mail than with instant messaging or face-to-face therapy, knowing that they have time to finish the thought. E-mail therapy allows both the client and the therapist the opportunity to reflect on thoughts, feelings, and other reactions to the other person's words.

Security Problems.
However, it is important to take note that e-mail security can be easily compromised. Computer viruses that can send e-mails to anyone listed in the computer's **address book** may arbitrarily attach themselves to any of the e-mails in a system and send that e-mail to everyone in the address book. This means that a client's confidential e-mail could be broadcast to thousands of people. Although this may not happen with great regularity, it is a distinct possibility, and one that should be carefully considered. However, using e-mail to discuss nonconfidential issues is appropriate and very effective. Some online clinics may offer secure messaging, which provides the function and quality of e-mail without the associated risks.

CONCLUSION

With the numerous choices available for therapists today, it is essential to be well-informed. Therapists are faced with a myriad of possibilities for providing their services online. This chapter has illustrated some of the choices therapists need to make in order to determine the best path for their online practice.

CHAPTER 7

Maintaining an Online Practice

Online practice maintenance requires a shift in the way the therapist thinks about maintaining a traditional, face-to-face practice, but by no means redefines the task. However, what does change is the execution of some of the aspects of the practice and the effect that this change will have in terms of time savings, convenience, and efficiency.

It is important that the practice of online therapy is approached in a way that reduces administrative work for the therapist. For example, integrating the tools the therapist uses for online therapy (i.e., marketing, scheduling, billing, and communication are all linked) is highly recommended. The therapist does not then have to track these elements manually because the software available can be used to very easily and conveniently link the various aspects of the practice, automating practice maintenance as much as possible.

Therapists generally want to focus solely on providing services, and automation makes that possible because a well-run online practice can help one focus more time on serving clients' needs. This is where choosing how to integrate the Internet into a clinical practice is critical. Therapists who conduct their online practices via e-mail and **off-the-shelf** instant message programs are not only risking confidentiality (even "secure" e-mail can be compromised), but will also not have the benefits of the many possible business support services available at some of the higher-end online clinics. For example, therapists often offer e-mail therapy services and use services like PayPal to collect the funds. Since PayPal is a third party, there are obvious questions surrounding confidentiality, but even if one is to disregard that issue, using PayPal does not automatically integrate earnings into personal bookkeeping. E-clinics may also be tempted to allow clients to pay through PayPal. Again, the issue of confidentiality should be considered.

In managing a practice, whether online or traditional, fundamental elements to be aware of are billing, marketing, pricing, administration and service, growth, technical problems, and technological upgrades. Taking each of these elements seriously and devising action plans to continue to support and improve these aspects of the practice are absolutely instrumental in creating a successful online practice, whether individual or via an e-clinic.

MARKETING

Therapists must market themselves. Once a therapist has created a client base, referrals can keep their practice busy, by and large. For most therapists, a constant marketing presence is necessary to maintain the practice at a desired level. Whether one is looking for a part-time or full-time practice, a solid marketing plan is the cornerstone of success.

Therapists should never rely solely on the marketing efforts of others when it comes to their business. Even the most successful online clinics, which see a high level of client flow, need to be supplemented by personal marketing. This will make the difference between simply subsisting or maximizing practice possibilities. One of the most common misconceptions about online businesses is that the business should solely focus its marketing on Internet-based campaigns. Today, the most successful online businesses market in the **real world**. They advertise using all available media: radio, print, and television. They sponsor real-world events and develop joint ventures with real-world organizations and retailers. The most successful Internet businesses most often do not stress that they are Internet businesses alone, because they are not. The Internet is simply a means of ordering or delivering products and services. This is exactly the case for the world of mental health.

Consider that the Internet is used to deliver services and coordinate the online practice. Where is the best place to advertise an online practice? In places where those people will see the ads who do not have the time or the ability to attend traditional face-to-face therapy. Although there may be effective places online to post information about online therapy services, there are many more effective opportunities in the real world. It becomes feasible to market to clients outside of the real-world geographical limitations created by having to travel to see a therapist in person. Therapists' ability to expand the radius of their outreach instantly and exponentially expands their potential client base.

Marketing an online practice can be broken up into print, radio, television, Internet advertising, and guerilla marketing.

REFERRALS

Marketing for therapists also occurs in the form of referrals, both by past and present clients as well as fellow professionals. Therapists with full practices generally spend very little on advertising. Their marketing is over 90% word-of-mouth. Most therapists achieve this form of "network" marketing in the natural course of their careers as they become established. Once established, a therapist may keep a full practice with no more

than a line in the yellow pages as an adjunct to his or her referral business. The key to achieving this level of business success
is taking steps to build a base of clients as well as connecting to
a network of professionals for referrals. One way to do this is
by sending a mailer announcing the business to colleagues.
The cost of brochure creation, duplication, and mailing should
be considered.

Paid advertising response varies greatly across the United
States, especially with respect to therapy services. In some
areas of the country, a Yellow Pages ad can be used successfully
to build a full practice over a few years' time. In other areas of
the country, advertising in a church bulletin or in the local
newspaper may draw the best response. In any scenario, there
is a point of diminishing returns, where an increase in advertising expenditures no longer correlates with an increase in
response-based revenues. All of these factors must be considered when deciding where they place advertising.

Advertising is always a process of testing—it is never
stagnant. Ads are regularly tweaked to continue producing
results. They are run in various media outlets to target specific
demographics, sometimes even at specific times. For instance,
if an issue of the local paper is going to focus on family matters, it may be a good idea to place an ad in that section for
marriage and family therapy. Because there is no standard rule
that works across the board, it is important for the therapist to
carefully analyze the potential advertising opportunity, make
careful notes of the process and results, and compile the results so that more accurate response-rate predictions can be
made in the future, specific to the therapist's particular locale.
The therapist should resist spending a sizeable amount of
money on any one particular form of advertising. It is almost
always advisable to spread a comfortable budget over as many
different mediums as feasible, so that the greatest chance for
success is afforded. Once the medium that is most fruitful has
been identified, a greater percentage of the advertising budget
can be directed to that particular medium.

Again, one practice building method is to build up enough clients over time that a steady stream of referrals result from them. On average, it takes three years to build a full practice. A second method is to find opportunities to be cited as a referral by other pro-fessionals, including other members of the mental health profession and other professions as well. For instance, many lawyers find themselves faced with their clients' emotional issues as well as their legal issues. They are generally more than happy to refer their clients out for anything emotional in nature.

Another source of referrals may come from health management organizations (HMOs). Getting listed with an HMO results in exposure. Currently, there is no code to bill online therapy to an insurance company, and HMOs expect therapists to see their clients in person or by telephone. However, there is a growing acceptance of online therapy as a viable means of access for mental health services, so it is reasonable to expect that in the future insurance carriers will acknowledge this medium and provide for its use.

ADVERTISING

It is important to distinguish between the concepts of advertising and marketing. Marketing is strategy based—it is approaching the offer of services from a general perspective. For instance, a therapist wishing to specialize in addiction might focus upon those individuals who suffer from addiction and their families. Advertising is specific to the medium by which the message is relayed. The therapist specializing in addiction may choose to advertise at rehabilitation clinics, in community papers, or on radio. Advertising is the specific message—marketing is the general strategy.

When considering places to advertise services, the therapist should work from the desired result backwards. For instance, if it is desired to treat adolescents, the therapist should think about where may be a good place to reach parents. The primary advertising mediums are print, radio, television, and online. Within each of these mediums are voluminous choices. The therapist should always think of an advertising campaign as a work in progress, testing different options and carefully recording the results of those efforts. Advertising sources change, and their demographics change over time. It is important for therapists to continually monitor their campaigns and to adjust their strategies as necessary.

Print Ads

As stated previously, therapists should consider where their target market can be found and advertise in those places. Keep in mind, many successful online businesses attribute the majority of their success to conventional advertising Also, online therapy means that therapists may take advantage of the fact that their "storefront" is wherever there are customers.

Print ads include the telephone directory, newspapers, and magazines. The Yellow Pages are a great resource for local contacts. The key factor is determining where to list the online practice. Not all Yellow Pages have an online therapy listing. Therapists will need to check with their particular Yellow Pages to determine the type of listings available. Spending the extra money to get a business-card-sized ad or bigger is usually a valuable investment. It is strongly recommended that the size and content of the therapist's ad work in concert to attract clients. Professional advertising designers have the knowledge and expertise that is necessary to create an ad that will produce results. If therapists absolutely do not wish to hire a professional, they should take the process of designing the ad very seriously, and understand that they may have to conduct live market tests.

Yellow Pages are published once a year, so an ineffectual ad can literally cost the therapist thousands of dollars because the copy can't be changed for a year. Again, if therapists decide against using a professional designer, research is essential.

One way to accomplish this is to collect several volumes of old Yellow Pages from a metropolitan area and look up the psychotherapist listings. See who has been running the bigger ads over multiple years, and see how they have or have not changed the ad copy. If someone is in one year and out the next, the ad probably was not very successful. If someone consistently runs the same ad for three or four years, you can be reasonably assured that it is working for him or her. And therapists should not be afraid to call and ask them how successful their ads have been. Most therapists are thrilled to speak of their successes and share what is working for them.

Newspapers are also a great source for local contacts. For newspaper advertising, there are generally two options available for therapists. The first option is a display ad. In this type of advertising, the therapist buys a certain amount of space in a newspaper (one or two columns wide, say), usually within the general sections of the newspaper. Within that space therapists can use images, text, drawings, logos, or photographs to advertise their online practice. This form of advertising is generally more expensive than **classified advertising**. For example, if adolescents are the therapist's desired clientele, advertising in parenting magazines or at a community center that offers parenting classes is a good idea.

Consider where the target market lies and direct a marketing strategy toward it. Classified advertising, the second option, is usually a few lines of text, sometimes as little as one to two lines, and is found in a specific small ads section of the newspaper. Some classified ads will have individual headings for specific groups. Classified ads can be a good source of new clients. There are thousands of magazines, newspapers, and newsletters across the nation that sell classified ad space. Therapists should once again consider their target market and focus on finding publications that cater to that market. For example, therapists who specialize in women's issues should consider advertising in publications directed to those issues and popular with women who are likely to seek therapy and likely to have issues on which they want to work. In the guerilla marketing section, we discuss how to take this same concept and develop relationships that can provide a steady stream of referrals.

Magazines, newsletters, brochures, and business cards are other options. Magazines vary widely, depending on whether they have a local, national, or international distribution. The higher the distribution, usually the higher the advertising cost. Like newspapers, most magazines have the option of either display or classified ads.

Many organizations publish newsletters that detail their activities. These can be great places to advertise, in particular, because the newsletter is usually focused on a smaller and specific audience. As a result of the smaller audience, newsletter ads are usually reasonably priced. Newsletters also may have display or classified advertising available. The therapist will need to contact the specific newsletter to receive more information. There are tens of thousands of daily, weekly, and monthly newsletters published around the world. Newsletters are published by organizations of all sizes, from nonprofits to corporations. Many nonprofit organizations seek sponsors, which could mean that therapists have room to negotiate the details of how their ad appears and how often. Many other organizations look for guest speakers, which is another great way to become known in a specific community. Remember— because the practice is online, therapists may indeed want to travel to a specific location outside their immediate geographical area if it is determined that there is a market for services in that locale. Many people do not like to see a therapist who is a member of their own community and prefer someone who lives a comfortable distance away from them. Whatever type of marketing is chosen, commitment to an action plan is imperative. People will apply themselves 10% and when they get 10% results, they blame the process instead of the approach. Commit to 110%, do not rely on a single approach but try multiple approaches, all of which can work to counterbalance those that produce less than desirable results.

Brochures can be a great way to reach a larger audience, including a national audience. Prices vary widely, depending on the type of brochure and the targeted audience (local vs. national). Some research will need to be done to determine the best prices.

Most therapists already use business cards for their private practice. Adding the Web site of the therapist's online practice is recommended and can be easily done. Finally, ask successful therapists what they do to maintain their practice size.

Radio and Television

Radio is a great medium for advertising one's online practice, but the ads require repetition to have an effect, and the same time slot should be used for those repetitions. This way, the target listening audience will be reached. Another way to approach radio advertising is to become involved with radio shows that focus on mental health or wellness in general. Many times, the hosts of these shows are enthusiastic to invite guests from their profession to speak on specific topics. Therapists should contact the hosts of radio shows and make them aware of their abilities and willingness to participate. Online therapy allows therapists to reach anyone, anywhere in the world, so the therapist is not constrained to local programming.

Advertising on television is another option. Television may have the largest reach of any medium, but it will be the most expensive. A therapist can choose between local programming, in which the rates can be reasonable, to national spots, in which the rates tend to be very expensive. Just like radio advertising, more research will need to be conducted by the therapist to determine whether television is the right medium for him or her.

Internet Advertising

Internet advertising is either paid or free. Paid ads can include search engines, classified ads, and **affiliate programs** (also known as **associate programs**).

Search engines are tools that enable computer users to locate information on the Internet. **Keywords** are used by the search engines to help the user specify the information he or she is seeking. For example, a user may visit a search engine and type in *online therapy*, and those Web sites that contain the keywords of *online therapy*, will be displayed for the user.

Classified ads on the Internet are similar to classified ads in print media. Some Web sites will not charge for listings to be posted, while others charge a nominal fee. However, it is wise to determine the number of listings posted. There tend to be a large number of postings listed for the classified ads, in particular the free ones, and it can be easy for a listing to get lost. As in newspapers, some Web sites will have specific headings for different groups of classifieds.

Affiliate programs enable companies to advertise on Web sites other than their own. This means therapists are able to advertise their online practice. A quick search on the Internet can reveal more information about this potential marketing medium.

Free ads can include **newsgroups**, message boards, and e-mail campaigns. Newsgroups, which are discussion groups found on the Internet, focus on particular topics. Discussion takes place by posting messages for the viewers to read, having online conversations, and sending e-mail messages to individuals or groups. Thousands of newsgroups, on different subjects, can be found. These newsgroups usually allow free advertising to be posted, particularly if the advertising is related to the subject of the newsgroup. The therapist will need to research a particular newsgroup to determine its advertising policies. Some of these news groups and message boards can be found on large Web sites such as Google.com, MSN.com, and Yahoo.com. Other smaller individual Web sites can be found by using a search engine.

Guerilla Marketing

Guerilla marketing includes using unconventional methods to advertise your online practice; for example, **sponsorships**, support groups, and **community groups.** Sponsorships involve a public endorsement of an activity or product that links its reputation with that of the company or event being sponsored. An example of this can include a therapist endorsing a psychotherapy Web site or perhaps sponsoring a free clinic given by a company.

Support groups can be a way of marketing any online practice. The key here is to ensure that the therapist's online practice is indeed potentially beneficial to the members of the support group. An example might be a support group for men with depression, which might invite a therapist who specializes in that field to come in and talk to the group. The therapist can then make the members aware of his or her online practice and give them the option of contacting him or her online. Taking enough brochures and business cards to such a group is clearly important to maximize the benefit. Contacting the various support groups can help steer the therapist in the right direction.

Marketing with a community group (e.g., Toastmasters, Parents without Partners, PTA) is similar to that of a support group, in that a therapist is able to inform members of a community group of the online practice, thus enabling members to contact the therapist online. Again, the key is to make sure that the online practice will potentially benefit the members of the community group.

If all of your eggs are in a single basket, you are taking a big risk. If you are advertising in the Yellow Pages, for example, it may be advantageous to advertise in two or three different areas. When advertising in the classifieds, run the ad at least three to five times before attempting to determine its effectiveness. If you are running ads in daily newspapers, you should ask the classified ad representative which days are the most popular. These days may be more expensive, but the chance of getting better results is multiplied.

High-profile professionals in the field, such as Dr. Philip Mc-Graw, are expanding the awareness of the importance of good mental health and are helping to remove the stigma of seeking such services. Therapists interested in building this type of exposure can begin this process through media exposure such as cable TV, guest spots on TV shows, radio, and writing articles that are published in educational journals.

PRICING THERAPY SERVICES

Setting an appropriate price point for services requires an understanding of the therapist's target market. Many therapists employ a sliding scale to accommodate lower-income clients. The therapist should be careful not to undersell the market by too wide a margin. When therapists price their services too low, they set a bad precedent for the entire field. Therapy should be reasonable, but not underpriced. Therapists should price their services with the knowledge that they have spent years in school and more years in training to develop the skills to provide these types of services. Too often, therapists get caught up solely in the desire to help their clients and slide their fees when it is not required. It is also very important to remember that people perceive higher-priced products and services as being of better quality. If the quality of the service provided is high, the fee should reflect this.

Much of the downturn in therapist fees since 1990 can be attributed to HMOs, but indirectly, it was the therapists who ultimately agreed to work for reduced fees. There was voluminous research done in the early 21st century, demonstrating a direct correlation between bad mental health and poor economic performance. Mental health issues that relate to poor performance range from insomnia to depression. A study conducted by the University of Michigan revealed that depression costs the American workplace six times the cost of absenteeism. Poor sleep saps over $40 billion annually from the economy. Corporations are beginning to become aware that depression and stress account for billions of dollars in lost revenue annually. These companies are faced with the knowledge that these are costly issues for them, but a history of cutting costs by minimizing access to helpful services still prevails. Meanwhile, HMOs have for years limited the amount of therapy available to their clients. This lack of healthcare coverage for millions of Americans seems to indicate that finding solutions for this problem is not a top priority. However, there is a focus on healthcare, and correspondingly a much higher degree of awareness of the relationship between mental health and physical health, as well as between mental health and productivity. This increased awareness is fueled by research in this area. It is hoped that the compelling nature of these results will help align policies with the need to provide relief in this area. Poor mental health has also been definitely demonstrated to lead to catastrophic physical illnesses, such as cardiac maladies and some forms of cancer.

ADMINISTRATION AND SERVICE

Administering an online practice can be a very streamlined process when compared with the administration necessary to conduct a traditional face-to-face practice. Once again, the automation that can be built into an online practice can free more time for therapists to practice their art and help people. If therapists choose to put together the various components of an online practice themselves, however, it is possible that management can become tedious. Some online clinics aggregate and integrate these administrative chores. The amount of physical labor required to manage the practice will vary depending upon the path the individual therapist chooses.

Providing quality services or products is the cornerstone to the success of a business. If the quality of the service is inferior, the customer will be lost, and any referrals from that individual will be lost. Therefore, many therapists are choosing to take courses in providing online therapy (see Appendix D). Chapters 1 and 3 describe many hints and techniques that provide an enhanced experience for clients, when the therapist knows how to use them. Focusing on knowing how to utilize the available tools may take some initial effort and determination, but ultimately, your online practice benefits greatly from this knowledge.

BILLING

Billing is a key aspect to therapists' online therapy practice. Therapists may have their own online therapy Web site with the latest technology, or be a part of an e-clinic, but if they are not able to bill properly for their services, then having an online practice becomes useless. An e-clinic needs to have its billing practices clearly defined somewhere on the Web site, for both therapist and client to see. Before signing up with an e-clinic, the therapist will also want to know what the billing procedure is and if it will fit his or her needs.

For therapists with an independent online therapy Web site, the billing process needs to be implemented onto the Web site, either by the therapist, if he or she built the Web site, or by the **Webmaster.** The key is to make the billing as efficient as possible for both therapist and clients. It is important that therapists include the different types of payment options that are possible, whether it be cash, check, money order, credit card, or payment through insurance. In most cases, online therapy is accessed after paying for services by using a credit card or an electronic check. The services are paid for at the time they are booked, and generally, the cancellation policies that therapists use for traditional practices are implemented online. For example, if a client cancels with 24 hour notice, the therapy fee is refunded or applied to a future session.

GROWTH

While growth in an online practice is obviously a positive thing, a therapist will need to make adjustments to his or her online practice to ensure that the growth does not affect the practice. For a therapist connected with an e-clinic, growth is usually defined by the number of clients that the therapist is seeing online. Ideally, the e-clinic that the therapist is connected with should easily accommodate this expansion, allowing the therapist a smooth transition as his or her practice continues to grow.

For a therapist with an individual online therapy Web site, one way growth is defined is by the number of visitors to the Web site. In most cases, the therapist's Web site will only be allowed a certain number of visitors or bandwidth. If this number is exceeded, then the Web site might be shut down to additional traffic by the web-hosting company. At this point, therapists will need to determine if they want to pay more money to allow more people to access their Web site. A discussion with the Webmaster will help determine the different options available. For the circumstance in which a therapist's Web site receives such a volume of visitors that he or she would be required to pay for additional band-width to support that number or more, it is important to look at a few factors. First, the therapist should determine what percentage of visitors to the Web site are converting to paying customers. If this number is very low, the Web site needs to be updated to help convert visitors to customers. Also worthy of consideration is marketing other products or services on the site. If a high number of visitors come to a site, it is an indication that it is either well positioned and advertised, or that it has great word-of-mouth advertising because of useful information present on it. Therapists may choose to market a manual or a workshop, which can be made available online via a Web-conference. Therapists should make every effort to offer useful information to their Web site visitors, and to do so in a way that compels the visitors to seek additional services.

TECHNICAL PROBLEMS

No matter how new the computer system is or how many computer classes, if any, a therapist has taken to become more competent on the computer, there will always be technical problems when treating clients online. These can range from simple problems on the online therapy Web site that the therapist is using, to more complex problems with the computer system. For a therapist who is part of a large e-clinic, the e-clinic itself has, or at least should have, an easy way for the therapist to contact the e-clinic in case of any technical difficulties. Sometimes, it might be challenging for a therapist to determine if a particular problem is a technical issue or not. An e-clinic should be able to assist the therapist, regardless of the type of problem that is occurring. Most e-clinics have a tech support team available to help assist the therapists and their clients with any technical issues.

More than likely, therapists will experience technical problems with the computer itself at some point. The computer manufacturer will have a tech support 800 number, to be found either on the manufacturer's Web site or in the brochures that came with the computer. If the problem is with the server, there will likewise be tech support available either via an 800 number or online.

TECHNOLOGICAL UPGRADES

It seems like new computers are coming out every month or so with newer technologies, the latest gadgetry that everyone wants to have, or there are updates that everyone needs to run. For the most part, these new technologies and upgrades, while they can be helpful, are not required. However, some can be extremely useful and are highly recommended. In the case of operating system updates, especially security updates, taking time to regularly check for and run these updates is most often critical.

Most computer systems have automatic updates that ask the computer user to run them. This usually involves making a few clicks, and the updates are completed automatically. In this day and age of new computer viruses coming out almost daily, it is highly recommended to run these updates because they help protect the computer from vulnerabilities.

For therapists who have their own Web site, the Webmaster will be able to help them determine what updates are needed for the Web site. If the therapist is also the Webmaster, then the therapist will need to make his or her own determination of what updates to run. There are many resources available to help determine this and usually a quick search on the Internet will produce these resources.

The most important thing to remember is to persevere. Building a practice and managing it are time and effort intensive prospects. Diligence is the key. Once a therapist is able to effectively build and manage an online practice, the rewards can be tremendous.

CONCLUSION

This chapter has discussed the basic requirements for maintaining an online therapy practice, including marketing; advertising, whether print, radio, television, or the Internet; pricing therapy services, administrative and service issues, billing, growth, and technological problems, including upgrades and updates.

CHAPTER 8

Legal and Ethical Issues

Therapists who are setting up an online practice must learn the legal and ethical issues associated with security and confidentiality of online communications. Many of the misconceptions discussed in Chapter 2 were in relation to some type of legal and ethical concern. Legal and ethical issues tend to be at the forefront of most therapists' minds because our profession is governed by them. Many organizations have developed guidelines, but these are merely *guidelines* and should not be misinterpreted as the *law*; these guidelines are presented in Appendix C. Keep in mind that any medium for providing therapy has its own limitations and therefore should be used appropriately and specifically according to the clients' needs. The 2003 Health Insurance Portability and Accountability Act (HIPAA) guidelines require specific technology protection systems to ensure that client information is secure. The following table summarizes the legal and ethical issues related to online therapy.

Table 8.1 Legal and Ethical Issues Related to Online Therapy

Issue	Solution
Confidentiality Therapists may have their licenses revoked for "Failure to maintain confidentiality, except as otherwise required or permitted by law, of all information that has been received from a client in confidence during the course of online treatment and all information about the client which is obtained from tests and other means."	1. Secure Internet lines for "chat" to take place 2. **Digitally encrypted messages** (128 SSL encryption) 3. **Password protection** 4. No storage of communications on servers
Payment for referral if choosing to be connected with an online therapy company Paying, accepting, or soliciting any consideration, compensation, or remuneration, whether monetary or otherwise, for the referral of professional clients is considered unprofessional conduct. This type of payment is illegal.	1. For online therapy, therapists will set their fee (e.g., $1.60 per minute) with the client ahead of time by posting it on their Web page. 2. In some cases, a percentage of the fee goes to the therapist and the remaining percentage to the company for rent of space, time, and technology. 3. In essence, many online clinics act as a "virtual landlord" receiving rent, per session, from the therapist.
Out-of-state services As of this date, there are no national guidelines regarding out of state services. The out-of-state issue has been controversial since the beginning of online therapy. The controversy is	over the question of where the therapy takes place. 1. Proceed and defend, as necessary, that therapy takes place where the therapist practices and is licensed. (continued on next page)

Adapted from the California Board of Behavioral Sciences (2004), and the American Psychological Association (2004).

2. Only see clients in the state in which you are licensed.

3. Provide other services, such as life coaching, to clients in states other than your licensed state.

Reporting abuse

1. Known or Suspected Cases of Child Abuse

The Child Abuse and Neglect Reporting Act delineates counselors' "duty to report" in the event of information obtained within the context of psychotherapy that constitutes a known or suspected incident of child abuse. Part (b) states that a "health practitioner," "Shall report the known or suspected instance of child abuse to a child protective agency immediately or as soon as practically possible by telephone and shall prepare and send a written report thereof within 36 hours of receiving the information concerning the incident."

2. Known or Suspected Cases of Dependent Adult/Elder Abuse

All fifty states and the District of Columbia have enacted legislation authorizing the provision of Adult Protective Services (APS) in cases of elder abuse. A mandated reporter of dependent adult or elder abuse shall report the known or suspected instance of abuse by telephoning immediately or as soon as possible, and by written report sent within two working days. www.elderabusecenter.org/default.cfm?p=backgrounder.efm

1. Call local (e.g., local to the therapist, that is, in the state in which he or she practices) law enforcement agency, Adult Protective Services (APS), or Department of Children and Family Services (DCFS).

2. Have local law enforcement agency, APS, or DCFS call the law enforcement agency, APS, or DCFS in the client's community.

(continued on next page)

Table 8.1 continued

Handling dangerous client situations	
Handling dangerous client situations *1. Duty to Warn (Tarasoff)* "If there is a duty to warn and protect under the limited circumstances specified above, the duty shall be discharged by the psychotherapist making reasonable efforts to communicate the threat to the victim or victims and to a law enforcement agency." This law does not exist in every state; therefore, this may not be a mandate for you to follow, if one of your online clients states a serious threat of harm to another. *2. Threats of Suicide* *Bellah v. Greenson* (1978) mandates that a therapist take reasonable steps to prevent a threatened suicide. "Reasonable steps" may or may not include a breach of confidence. In the event that a therapist does breach a client's confidence, the law would protect him or her in the event of civil liability. This law does not exist in every state; therefore, this may not be a mandate for you to follow, if one of your online clients states a serious threat of harm to him- or herself.	1. Some large online therapy companies have direct links to 911 in clients' area codes. 2. Obtain physical address and phone number of client and emergency contact before commencing therapy. 3. Therapists should provide clients with community resources, e.g., hospitals, suicide hotlines, shelters, etc. (see Appendix B).

CONFIDENTIALITY

Confidentiality refers to the legal rules and guidelines that obligate a therapist not to reveal information about an in-person or online client. This includes content that is discussed in the therapeutic setting as well as even confirming that a client is in therapy. Confidentiality is derived from the broader right of privacy, granted to all United States citizens by the United States Constitution, which gives each person the right to decide how much of his or her thoughts, feelings, and personal information will be shared with others.

Confidentiality for online therapy has the same rules as traditional therapy. However, therapists must also consider how the online environment affects confidentiality. The rules stay the same, but the medium in which the therapy takes place changes. What must be considered is how this different medium affects confidential information. For example, in a physical office, you may be concerned with other clients listening at your door. The precaution you take could be to have a waiting room. Or you may choose an office that has been soundproofed. Online, you have to consider where the "door" is through which people could listen. Online, you need to be concerned that the chat interface between you and your client cannot be accessed or viewed by a third party. You would therefore make sure that the software you use protects the privacy of users, and that neither other users nor the software or server's employees can "listen in" on your sessions. A therapist may have his or her license revoked for "failure to maintain confidentiality except as otherwise required or permitted by law, of all information that has been received from a client in confidence during the course of treatment and all information about the client which is obtained from tests and other means" (California Board of Behavioral Sciences, 2004).

Security of Communications and Confidentiality

In the real world, traditional therapists choose an office that is in a quiet location and is conducive to practicing therapy. They are concerned about acoustics and whether people in the waiting room or adjacent offices can overhear their conversations with their clients. They also are interested in having a comfortable, peaceful office setting that promotes calm in their clients. Online, the "look" of the office is dictated by the look and brand of software that therapists use to communicate with their clients. The "soundproof" nature of the online office is dictated by the type of security, the software, and the nature of how communications are transmitted by that software.

Therapists should be aware of potential vulnerabilities to computer hacking that may threaten the security of notes stored on the computer. Even when the computer is not connected to the Internet and therefore not vulnerable to having information hacked and stolen from the hard drive, there is still the possibility of theft of the computer. Please refer to Appendix A for more information with regard to confidentiality risks related to the technology of online therapy.

As we have said earlier, online therapy is not a new type of therapy, it is a new medium. All of the fundamental considerations therapists have in their face-to-face practices will remain relevant to their online practice. When storing client notes with an online service such as Yahoo!, therapists should keep track of security codes and passwords. It is always possible for a hacker to gain access to an online file server, so it is important how information is stored on these systems. For example, some online clinics store communications separate from user identities—literally on separate servers.

Some online clinics do not store communications at all. Chat messages are only passed through to the users, not stored by the service's computer servers. Most chat providers and instant message providers do store all communications. Access to these communications is available to countless employees of these organizations, who are not bound by any professional legal or ethical confidentiality agreements. Most chat and instant messaging programs in public use do not even encrypt the messages. This means that anyone with a little knowledge of computer programs can read any messages sent between individuals, even if they are in so-called "private" chat rooms. Therapists should choose a chat software that meets the following criteria: All messages must be encrypted at **128-bit cipher strength**, and the computer servers of the provider of the chat software must not be used to store the messages.

In fact, storing of chat therapy sessions is not advised. There is a carefully thought-out and protected process in place for the procurement by a court of law of any information relating to clients. In face-to-face therapy, a court will typically subpoena client notes, if necessary. In some cases, it is not appropriate to divulge this information, and the process ensures that efforts to subpoena such items are stopped. If a chat session is subpoenaed, it would no longer be the therapist's word versus the word of the client. Actual transcripts of therapy chat sessions would be subpoenaed.

In the real world of traditional therapy, there is no practical way to receive a transcription of actual sessions. In the online therapy world, transcriptions are usually stored using chat software. As a result, an attorney can easily subpoena the records of the software provider—a process not protected by confidentiality. Detailed communications are readily attainable without being subjected to the processes that are in place for mental health related evidence. If your notes are also stored online using storage provided by Yahoo! or a similar service (chat rooms, documents, and journal storage), a court may be able to obtain the word-for-word account as well as your client notes.

We suggest that therapists concerned about confidentiality pay close attention to the software they use to communicate online. Using a proper online clinic will not only aggregate all communications, billing, calendaring, and administration, but will do so with consideration to the very special needs of the mental health field. Once confident that (1) communications cannot be "eavesdropped" on by a third party and (2) instant message conversations are not stored by a server, both therapist and client can feel secure knowing that their session is confidential.

Finally, e-mail is not secure. Even "secure" e-mail has vulnerabilities. There are services that provide security for asynchronous communications; communications of this type are not "live"; for instance, a letter is typed, then sent and read at a later time by the recipient, who then responds in the same manner). It is preferable not to use e-mail for very personal information. There are too many ways for confidentiality to be breached when using e-mail, such as:

1. A third party can "view" the e-mail's contents during delivery (even when security is in place).
2. Someone can view the e-mail after it is downloaded to the computer.
3. A virus can take the contents of the e-mail and send it to everyone in your address book, or anyone to whom you have ever sent an e-mail.

PAYMENT FOR REFERRAL

When discussions and debates on the effectiveness and safety of online therapy began, the issue of fee splitting became a focus and soon a major topic of discussion *Payment for referral* is the legal term for fee splitting. Paying, accepting, or soliciting any consideration, compensation, or remuneration, whether monetary or otherwise, for the referral of professional clients is considered unprofessional conduct. This type of payment is illegal. If a company offers payment for receiving referrals, this is also illegal.

It is reasonable and customary for a therapist to pay rent for space used. Oftentimes this can be on an hourly basis or a flat rate. Some online therapy clinics require therapists to pay for the rent, space, and technology when using the site on a session-by-session basis. Other clinics may require therapists to pay a flat rate every month whether they use the site or not. The way these clinics collect fees for rent may be very similar to that of a traditional face-to-face setting.

OUT-OF-STATE ISSUES

The out-of-state issue has been controversial since the beginning of online therapy. The controversy is over the question of where the therapy takes place. Some state boards, such as the California Board of Behavioral Sciences, have stated that they believe "therapy takes place where the client resides" versus taking place where the therapist resides.

We believe that the therapy takes place in the state in which the therapist is licensed. In our opinion, this makes the most sense for the protection of the client as well as the therapist. We attended a national board meeting where the state board delegates from all 50 states were present. The issue of the locality of therapy in regard to online therapy was the first topic of three to be discussed that day.

The discussion began with this question: "I am a California therapist providing therapy for a client in Illinois. Where does the therapy take place?"* The room was split in half as to opinions of where the therapy took place. Through our discussion we were able to illustrate what occurs if therapy is considered to take place where the client resides. The following is the progression of the discussion and questions presented that day (quotations have been paraphrased for the purpose of this book):

---

* Quotations are paraphrased. We have elected to use the name of the states as an example. The delegate of the state mentioned.

Question: The client has a complaint. Illinois, what would you do?

Illinois: Nothing, since we do not have jurisdiction over the California therapist.

Question: California, what would you do?

California: What could we do if we did not know what was happening and the problem did not arise in the state where we have jurisdiction?

Question: Illinois, since you are not able to do anything and California is not able to do anything, would you have this case transferred to California? (The question was asked this of the entire group and the vast majority responded "No.")

Illinois: No, we would not.

Question: California, would you have the case transferred? (The question was asked of the entire group and once again the vast majority responded "No.")

California: No, we would not.

Question: This does not seem to protect the client. Illinois, if we say that the therapy takes place in the state where the therapist is, and the client has a complaint, then what would happen?

Illinois: The client would contact the California Board.

Question: California, for example's sake, if we say that the therapy takes place in the state where the therapist is and the client has a complaint, then what would happen?

California: If they called, we would take care of it.

Conclusion: At this point, it seems as though protection of the client is best accomplished by adopting the stance that the therapy takes place in the therapist's state of licensure.

One delegate had a very compelling remark regarding this issue. He stated, "I live in an eastern state, and my state borders two other states. I have some clients who walk to my office yet live in another state. I do not want this can of worms to be opened. I would not like to think that because of this stand in online therapy, we would now be jeopardizing traditional therapy. I do not agree. Therapy takes place in the state where the therapist is licensed."

Another issue to take into consideration revolves around international clients. Each country would more than likely have differences in the legal and ethical issues governing psychotherapy. Being aware of international legal and ethical issues may be a huge task to take on and therefore may create problems in this area. Correspondingly, non-U.S. clients may have difficulty seeking a solution for a grievance that they might have.

This controversy is still ongoing. We recommend that therapists practice the way they feel most comfortable. Therapists have the following options and considerations: (1) Proceed and defend as necessary that therapy takes place where the therapist practices. (2) Only see clients in the state in which you are licensed. (3) Provide other services, such as life coaching, to clients in states other than the state in which you are licensed.

REPORTING ABUSE AND HANDLING DANGEROUS CLIENT SITUATIONS

So far, we have discussed the issue of confidentiality and how to maintain it when online. However, confidentiality must be broken in certain situations, regardless of whether therapy is online or face-to-face. In the following situations, confidentiality must be breached while practicing in a face-to-face setting as well as online: (1) a known case of child abuse; (2) a suspected case of child abuse; (3) known or suspected cases of dependent adult/elder abuse; (4) known case of threat to harm other(s) (i.e., duty to warn; Tarasoff).

The Child Abuse Prevention and Treatment Act (CAPTA), last amended June 2003, delineated counselors' "duty to report" in the event that information is obtained within the context of psychotherapy and that obtained information constitutes a known or suspected incident of child abuse. Part (b) states that a "health practitioner" "shall report the known or suspected instance of child abuse to a child protective agency immediately or as soon as practically possible by telephone, and shall prepare and send a written report thereof within 36 hours of receiving the information concerning the incident" (Board of Behavioral Sciences, www.bbs.ca.gov, 2004). It is recommended that therapists practicing online should report incidents to the Child Protective Services agency in the state in which they are licensed. Child abuse reporting laws apply in all states.

A mandated reporter of dependent adult or elder abuse "shall report the known or suspected instance of abuse by telephone immediately or as soon as possible, and by written report sent within two working days . . ." (Board of Behavioral Sciences, www.bbs.ca.gov, 2004; American Psychologists Association, www.apa.gov, 2004). Dependent adult/elder abuse laws do not exist in all states, but there is the federal Older Americans Act, most recently amended in 2000 (see http://wwwelder abusecenter.org). Therapists who need to report abuse from online sessions should report within the state in which they are licensed.

Tarasoff v. Regents of University of California (1976) stated: "If there is a duty to warn and protect under the limited circumstances specified above, the duty shall be discharged by the psychotherapist making reasonable effort to communicate the threat to the victim or victims and to a law enforcement agency." The Tarasoff law does not exist in all states. This law was originated in the state of California. As of 2003, only 23 states had adopted this law.

The Tarasoff law was implemented following a case where a client told his therapist that he was planning to harm his girlfriend. The client had a plan, a specific time to do harm, and a means to carry out the threat. Keep in mind that "serious threat of violence" is not the same as "threat of serious violence."

There was no law, at that time, that covered this within the profession of psychotherapy. The therapist did not have the ability to report because it was considered confidential information. The client carried out the crime and murdered Ms. Tatiana Tarasoff.

Situations in which confidentiality may be breached include:

1.   *Privilege*. Privilege is the therapist's legal right not to have confidential information from online sessions revealed in a legal setting. It is the right of a person to withhold testimony in the courtroom setting. It can be thought of as the legal codification of confidentiality. However, therapists' notes can be subpoenaed, and therapists can be directed to testify by a judge. *Exceptions to privilege*. Privilege is confidentiality in a legal setting. Therefore, an exception to privilege (such as duty to warn and child abuse) means that there are certain circumstances that occur that may be breached if necessary (Child Abuse Prevention and Treatment Act [CAPTA] January 1996 version, last amended September 2000).

2.   *Threats of suicide. Bellah v. Greenson* (1978) mandates a therapist to take reasonable steps to prevent a threatened suicide. "Reasonable steps" may or may not include a breach of confidence. *Bellah v. Greenson* (1978) does not exist in all states. This ruling originated in the state of California.

3.   *Breach of duty arising out of the psychotherapist–patient relationship*. There is no privilege when a client breaches his or her "duty" by not paying his or her fee. This applies in most states. Online therapy solves this problem in some cases by online clinics that have the client pay ahead of time for the session as well as for more additional time, if necessary. Example: A client has not paid the therapist regularly and accumulates a large bill. He doesn't return to

therapy and ignores the invoices from the therapist. With online therapy, the client is not seen unless he or she pays ahead of time. It takes the "money" issue out of the therapy session. If a client wants to continue a session and the therapist has time, the therapist can bill a client on a minute-by-minute basis at some online clinics.

Domestic Violence

Domestic violence is an issue that is regularly presented during online therapy. In most states, domestic violence is not a reportable offense unless a child is witnessing the abuse. At that point, child abuse (willful cruelty) can be reported. Be sure to check with the particular state's guidelines. Oftentimes the computer is the victim's only outlet for help. Resources can be given to clients during their online session with their therapists. Because of fear, domestic violence clients often do not follow through with recommended resources. By visiting the online resource with their client, therapists create both a sense of safety as well as a sense of the urgency for the client to get out of a dangerous situation. See Appendix B for suggestions for managing online domestic violence cases.

Internet Abuse

Internet abuse can take many forms; however, the common trait is that one individual feels threatened or harassed by another, who commits abusive acts online. The following cyberstalking statistics released by Working to Halt Online Abuse (WHOA, 2003) demonstrate how the enforcement of cyberstalking laws has reduced the number of reported cases. The number of cyberstalking cases has decreased from 353 in 2000 to 198 in 2003. Other important facts include:

- The majority of victims who contact WHOA are Caucasian females between the ages of 18 and 30

(39%), followed by Caucasian females ages 31 to 40 (22%).

- By state, California ranks the highest with 13% of cyberstalking cases, followed by Pennsylvania, Florida, New York, Canada, and Texas.
- Over 35% of online harassment cases begin via e-mail, followed by instant messaging programs (17%), message boards (16.5%), chat rooms (8%), and Web sites (7.5%). Almost 66.5% of the cases were resolved with the **Internet Service Provider** that the offender used, with help from WHOA, while 33.5% were referred to law enforcement.
- These statistics are based on questionnaires victims fill out at the WHOA Web site. WHOA. helps over 100 victims each week—and this is just one organization. Others, such as CyberAngels, report helping 55 victims each day and SafetyEd, over 50 each week. This is an estimated 30,000 victims, and these are just the reported cases (WHOA, 2003).

How an Abuser Can Discover Your Internet Activities.
If an abuser gains access to an e-mail account, he or she may be able to read incoming and outgoing mail. If a therapist or client believes his or her account's security has been jeopardized, make sure to change passwords or change e-mail accounts. Use a password that cannot easily be guessed. If an abuser sends threatening or harassing e-mail messages, print and save them as evidence of this abuse. The messages may constitute a federal offense. For more information on this issue, contact your local U.S. Attorney's Office.

If an abuser knows how to read a therapist's or client's computer's history or cache file (automatically saved Web pages and graphics), he or she may be able to see information that has been viewed recently on the Internet. Clear the computer's history or empty the cache files in the Internet browser's settings. Additionally, a victim needs to make sure that the "Use Online Autocomplete" box is not checked. This function will complete a partial Web address while typing a location in the address bar at the top of the browser. It may also complete a username and password. Therapists using the **Internet Explorer** browser can find this box on the Internet Explorer page by clicking on the "Tools" icon at the top, then "Internet Options," and then the "Advanced" tab. About halfway down there is a "Use Inline Autocomplete" box that can be checked and unchecked by clicking on it.

SCOPE OF COMPETENCE

When therapists wish to determine whether they have the competency to deliver therapy online, they must first distinguish between knowledge and mechanical skills. Knowledge is acquired by learning, and therapists can learn about a new area prior to taking on certain cases. For example, information about parenting, custody, and divorce can be acquired by therapists who are considering doing therapy with families going through a divorce. Online therapy falls into the knowledge realm. The mechanical skills necessary to conduct effective online therapy can be learned quickly. When engaging in chat therapy, for example, it is of course important to have adequate typing skills.

Therapists also may use an Internet phone or videoconferencing for online therapy, and in that case, a very basic knowledge of computers and the Internet is all that is required to perform effective online therapy. Therapists must have knowledge of how to connect to the Internet and how to **configure** any sound or video devices that will be utilized. Software that aids in the provision of online therapy must be installed, configured, and coordinated with other aspects of the online practice. Some prominent online clinics consolidate and coordinate such technologies and services. (See Appendix A for a more

detailed look at what a therapist should know from the technological point of view.)

CONTROLLING AND RELEVANT
LEGISLATION TO MANAGE HIPAA

HIPAA standards became enforceable on April 14, 2003. Reactions to the HIPAA regulations among clinicians varies. Some
are frightened, some are frustrated, and many ignore their responsibility. True, at first glance it seems that many clinicians
may not need to be in compliance; however, the impact is
much greater than was generally believed. First, let's consider
who are the *covered entities*. Any mental health clinician, licensed or not, who provides healthcare is considered a covered
entity under the HIPAA rules. That means it applies to psychiatrists, psychologists, marriage and family therapists, social
workers, chemical dependency counselors, coaches, unlicensed
therapists such as interns, trainees, and psychological assis-
tants, and healers who furnish, bill, or are paid for healthcare in the normal course of business. Thus, the HIPAA
accountability umbrella is quite broad in the mental health
arena.

Therapists must comply with HIPAA if they implement any
of the following in their practice:

- Transmit health information via electronic form
  (e-mail, Internet, etc.) to any person, party, or entity,
  including patients.
- Receive faxes from insurance companies regarding
  patients.
- Send faxes via a computer program regarding patients.
- Interact with other businesses that perform the
  above on their behalf (e.g., a company or individual
  performing billing services).

The HIPAA requirements are intended to protect consumers from having health information disclosed or revealed due to carelessness by healthcare providers. For example, several patients diagnosed with cancer received marketing letters promoting specific cancer medication from pharmaceutical companies and hospitals. Their names were being sold to these companies, without their consent, by their diagnosing facilities.

HIPAA places several responsibilities on clinicians, which include the following:

- Create a *notice of privacy practices*. Post it in a conspicuous place in the office, hand it out to all patients, make it available to nonpatients, if requested.
- Complete an *acknowledgment of receipt of notice of privacy practices* document, which establishes that the clinician took reasonable steps to document that the patient received the *notice of privacy practices*.
- Create an *authorization to use and disclose* document, which provides consent to release psychotherapy notes (e.g., to an insurance company, client, attorneys, physicians, other therapists).
- Create and use a *business associate contract* with individuals or entities who interact with the clinician, as defined by HIPAA.
- Create a *complaint* form to address complaints.
- Document *staff review* of HIPAA policies and procedures.

If the HIPAA guidelines are not followed, the penalties are severe. The civil penalties involve $100 for each offense, with an annual cap of $25,000 for repeated violations of the same requirement. The criminal penalties are: (1) for knowingly misusing individually identifiable health information, the clinician can be fined $50,000 and/or spend one year in prison; (2) for misuse under false pretenses, the clinician can be fined up to

$100,000 and/or spend five years in prison; and (3) for offenses to sell or profit from malicious harm, the clinician can be fined $250,000 and/or spend 10 years in prison.

Needless to say, plaintiff attorneys are waiting to initiate legal actions on behalf of clients. They will surely assess if a clinician is HIPAA compliant as part of their malpractice–administrative legal action. Not being compliant will most likely accentuate the legal repercussions felt by the clinician. We strongly suggest that therapists follow the HIPAA guidelines and include HIPAA guideline education on their Web site. Remember, "It never happens until it happens, and when it happens, it's too late."

For a complete copy of HIPAA rules, go to http://www. hhs.gov/ocr/hipaa.

TELEMEDICINE LAW

For the purposes of this section, the term *telemedicine* means the practice of healthcare delivery, diagnosis, consultation, treatment, transfer of medical data, and education using interactive audio, video, or data communications. Neither a telephone conversation nor an electronic mail message between a healthcare practitioner and patient constitutes telemedicine for purposes of this section. The relevant section of law is Section 2290.5 of the Business and Professions Code (Schanz & Cepelewicz, 2001). Please note that the reference to *healthcare practitioner* and *licentiate* in subdivision (b) includes marital and family therapists, psychologists, LCSWs, psychiatrists, and any other licensed professionals in a related field. Note that both verbal and written informed consent is required prior to the delivery of health care via telemedicine. In subdivision (c), there are five mandatory disclosures that must be made. Subdivision (d) contains information about additional contents of the written statement and the requirement of a signature.

This section also states: "(i) This section shall not apply in an emergency situation in which a patient is unable to give informed consent and the representative of that patient is not available in a timely manner." As we have recommended before, it is important for therapists to verbally state the informed consent as well as giving clients a copy via e-mail or a shared document through the virtual office. This allows clients to sign a copy and give approval. Potential clients of an online clinic will need to give their acceptance to the privacy policy, terms, and conditions before becoming a client.

ETHICAL CONSIDERATIONS

There are ethical guidelines and considerations that are important for therapists to follow for the safety of their clients and their practice.

Your Required Documents

Obtaining informed consent: There are four important considerations when obtaining an informed consent from a client online or face-to-face:

1. *The client's competency.* The client needs to have the cognitive ability and functioning necessary to understand the parameters of therapy as explained by the therapist.
2. *The disclosure of material information.* A therapist should explain any information that a "reasonable" person should know before deciding to begin therapy.
3. *The client's understanding of the presented material.* The therapist should use language that a "reasonable" person would understand, whether the parameters of therapy are explained verbally or within a therapeutic contract.

4. *Voluntary consent.* When the client gives consent, he or she must do so free of pressure, influence, or coercion from others.

Suggested Written Format

The following is a suggested outline to follow in constructing a therapeutic contract to be presented to clients online. Once they have read and accepted the informed consent, clients can actually use a feature known as a digital signature. This allows the therapist to take a *virtual computer fingerprint* of the client's computer and personal information. This digital signature covers the mandates in the telemedicine law. The contract form should include the following areas for review: therapy, alternative services, appointments, confidentiality, money, and general issues.

I.   Therapy
  A.   How does online therapy work?
  B.   What are the benefits and limitations of online therapy.
  C.   About how long will it take?
  D.   What should I do if I feel therapy isn't working?
  E.   Will I have to take any tests? If so, what kind?
II.   Alternative Services
  A.   What other types of therapy or help are there (such as face-to-face therapy or support groups)?
  B.   How often do they work?
  C.   What are the risks of these other approaches?
III.   Appointments
  A.   How are appointments scheduled online?
  B.   How long are sessions online? Do I have to pay more for additional time?
  C.   How can I reach you in an emergency?
  D.   If you are not available, who can I talk to that will be there?

E.   What happens if I'm sick and cannot get to my computer?

IV.   Confidentiality

A.   What kind of records do you keep? Who has access to them (servers, Internet company, insurance companies, etc.)?

B.   Under what conditions are you allowed to tell others about the things we discuss (suicidal or homicidal threats, child abuse, court cases, insurance companies)?

C.   Do other members of my family, or of the group, have access to information? How should I protect my password?

V.   Money

A.   What is your fee?

B.   Can I pay for more sessions ahead of time?

C.   Do I need to pay for missed sessions?

D.   Do I need to pay for telephone calls or e-mails?

E.   What are your policies about raising fees? (for example, how many times have you raised them in the past few years)?

F.   If I lose my source of income, can my fee be lowered?

VI.   General Issues

A.   What is your training and experience? Are you licensed? Board certified?

B.   Who do I talk to if I have a complaint about therapy that we can't work out (e.g., the online therapy company, state boards; Handelsman & Galvin, 1988)?

Additional issues can be added or removed from an informed consent based on therapist perference and client base.

UNPROFESSIONAL CONDUCT

As with traditional therapy, online therapists must be aware of what constitutes unprofessional conduct:

False or Misleading Advertising

It is unprofessional conduct to advertise in a way that it incorrect, false, deceptive, or misleading; one cannot advertise services outside of his or her scope of practice and/or competence online.

Payment for Referrals

Paying, accepting, or soliciting any consideration, compensation, or remuneration, whether monetary or otherwise, for the referral of professional clients online is considered unprofessional conduct. This type of payment is illegal. There is new legislation allowing "referral services" to exist, whereby a group of individuals share advertising expenses to solicit business. However, this still does not allow a person to be reimbursed solely for making a referral.

Seeing Another Psychotherapist

There are no specific laws forbidding one therapist from seeing a client at the same time as another psychotherapist. It may happen more with online therapy than traditional face-to-face therapy due to the nature of the medium. Clients have access to many therapists online.

Fradulent Licenses or Degrees

A therapist may not post a license or a degree online that is not valid. This is considered to be unethical and fraudulent. Securing a license or degree in a fraudulent manner is also unethical and considered unprofessional conduct.

The Use of a Controlled Substance

As with traditional face-to-face therapy, a therapist conducting therapy online may not be under the influence of any controlled substance. It is important for the online therapist to keep in mind this requirement. This is particularly true because it is much easier to be using a controlled substance during an online session while it would be almost unthinkable in a face-to-face session. Although therapy is being conducted in a more informal environment in which the client and therapist do not see each other, rules of proper conduct must be followed.

Mandate When a Client Reveals Having Sex With Another Psychotherapist

When a client reveals a previous or ongoing sexual relationship with his or her former therapist, the client's subsequent therapist has a legal obligation to give the client a brochure that explains the client's rights and responsibilities.

CONCLUSION

In all of these circumstances, the same procedures that are followed for face-to-face therapy apply to online therapy, with the following caveat. All states do not have the same laws, so it is important for therapists to report to the state in which they are licensed, not the state in which the client resides. This is the only way that true protection can be afforded to both clients and therapists.

Once again, always keep in mind that the legal and ethical requirements of the mental health profession are consistent regardless of the medium in which the therapy takes place. Do take into account the state in which you are licensed and the particular regulations that apply to you in that state. If questions arise, be sure to consult with an expert. The American

Association of Marriage and Family Therapists, National Association of Social Workers, and American Psychological Association provide access for its membership to highly qualified legal experts. Above all, in order to provide the greatest quality of care to their clients, therapists must protect themselves and their practice and be knowledgeable, especially in areas where the repercussions are serious for either the therapist or the client.

APPENDICES

APPENDICES

APPENDIX **A**

Basic Information and Skills

Your first decision is whether to buy a desktop computer or a laptop. In order to make this decision, you need to have some basic information and you must make an assessment of the skills you have or will acquire. There are pros and cons to each. If portability is desired, a laptop computer is ideal. Laptops are generally more expensive than desktop computers, and processing speed is less than that of equivalent desktop computers. Once you have made this decision you need to be aware of and choose among the various features that will allow your computer system to perform as you require.

CHOOSING AND PURCHASING A COMPUTER SYSTEM

In today's technology marketplace, newer and faster personal computers are being introduced every few months. For this reason, it can be a daunting experience for a therapist to try and find the perfect computer for his or her needs. However, the majority of consumers, which include both therapists and clients, own models that are three to five years old. A desktop computer is generally less expensive than a laptop. The monitor on a desktop computer may be easier on the eyes and the computer components are easier and cheaper to replace. However, a desktop computer can take up a lot of desktop space and be bulky to move and set up.

A laptop can go just about anywhere with the therapist, which makes note taking easier. This can be especially useful when a therapist wishes to provide his or her online services on the road. A laptop can also be used with a docking station in order to access a bigger monitor and keyboard. However, laptops are also more prone to theft and damage, and the flat screen on a laptop may not be as clear as one on a desktop computer and may be harder to read, especially outdoors. The following are some basic points that can help a therapist determine the best computer system for him or her.

Intended Usage

What does the therapist intend to use the computer for? This is one of the key considerations when purchasing the computer system. The main goal is to get a system that will suit the therapist's computing needs. If a therapist is using the computer for professional or business purposes, for example, providing online therapy, the therapist will want to factor stability and service support into his or her purchase decision.

Budget

The therapist will certainly need to consider his or her budget when buying a new computer system. Low-end budget systems will save a therapist a lot of money and are suitable for most home users. High-end systems with the latest Athlon 64 or Intel Pentium 4 processors will cost more, but may be more suitable for those who want to provide therapy online.

System Features

There is a wide range of components to choose from, including memory, video cards, sound cards, optical drives, and so on, when choosing a computer. The most essential components in a computer system are listed below:

Central Processing Unit (CPU).
The CPU is the brain of the computer system, so it is a key consideration when buying a computer. The older chips, such as Intel Celeron and Intel Pentium 3, chips are now becoming obsolete. If a therapist wants his or her system to last for some time, then newer processors such as the Intel Centrino Intel Pentium 4, and the AMD Athlon XP are highly recommended.

Memory.
System memory is very important, as it is relied upon by software programs to maintain satisfactory performance, especially when multitasking. Currently, a therapist will want to look for at least 256 or 512 MB of memory in a computer system. Anything less may pose a problem for business or graphics applications.

Hard Drives.
The general consensus is to get as much hard disk space as one can afford. A typical hard disk by today's standards starts at 40 gigabytes (GB). If a therapist does a lot of downloading off the Internet, edits videos, or has a large collection of MP3s, getting an 80 GB hard disk would be strongly recommended.

Optical Drives.
A CD-ROM drive is now a standard feature in all computers. It is recommended to get at least a 40X CD-ROM read speed. An additional consideration would be whether the therapist wants read–write capability—most computers now come with CD-RW

drives which allow for the writing of information to disc. DVD-ROM drives are also bundled in desktops. Even better, some come with DVD-RW drives, which will save the therapist the cost of buying a separate DVD writer later on. DVD-ROM drives allow for much more data to be stored on each disk and are useful for back-up purposes as well as for transporting very large files.

Monitors.
The key consideration here is whether the therapist wants a CRT or LCD display. It is ideal to go for at least a 17-inch monitor if the therapist wants a CRT display, and at least a 15-inch monitor for LCD displays. Some good brand names include Sony, NEC, Samsung, and ViewSonic.

Graphics.
If advanced graphics capabilities are desired (gaming, artwork), a high-end video card is recommended.

Sound.
If premium sound is a consideration, a high-end sound card may be desired.

Ports.
Check that the system comes with support for the latest USB 2.0 port specification. Firewire ports are also increasingly available on new systems. Firewire allows for extremely rapid data transfer.

Operating System.
The majority of computer systems today ship with Windows XP Home Edition, which is suitable for home users. Business users should also look for Windows XP Professional or Windows 2000 Professional. Although free, open-source operating systems are available such as Linux or Lindows. However, these operating systems may pose compatibility issues with reguard to hardware, software, and communications.

Technical Support.
After-sale support and warranty periods are a prime consideration, especially if a therapist does not have any experience in troubleshooting computers. Most basic warranty periods last for a year or two and are sufficient for the average user. It is not recommended to go for an extended warranty period without reading the fine print. Most of the time, it is not necessary to have overly long warranty periods because the lifetime of a computer will be about four to five years at most.

In summary, buying a good desktop PC is a matter of doing the research and homework by considering each of the factors above. If possible, go to the manufacturer's Web site to look for more in-depth material.

SETTING UP THE COMPUTER

Requirements of setting up the computer will vary widely and depend on the type of computer the therapist has purchased. Each computer will come with instructions on how to set it up, and following these instructions exactly is strongly recommended. Doing so will avoid problems down the road.

Getting Online Service

Choosing the right online service is an important consideration. You may have bought the latest and fastest computer, however, the speed of your Web access will be limited by the speed of your internet connection. The choices are dial-up (the slowest), DSL, cable, or T-1 (which are the fastest). DSL and cable may cost more per month than dial-up, however most users of DSL or cable will see financial savings and time savings over users of dial-up. Consider these other factors when selecting an online or Internet service:

1.   If choosing dial-up, the service should provide a local phone number. Telephone long-distance charges can exceed the cost of the service.

2.   It should provide the services that the therapist needs. If a therapist just needs e-mail, he or she can get a cheaper service than if he or she wants access to financial databases, wire services, and the World Wide Web. However, for a therapist doing online therapy, full access to the Internet is required

3.   The service should be comfortable for the therapist to use. Most services provide tech support via an 800 number or online.

4.   The service should be within the (therapist's) budget. If cost prevents the therapist from signing on, he or she will not get the benefit of the service. Costs range from free to $30 a month, and higher, depending on the location of the therapist and the type of service. Some services also charge by the hour.

SKILLS AND PROGRAMS

Basic computing skills are required to conduct online therapy, and most people have already acquired these skills.

Keyboard and Mouse Skills

Chat therapy requires a degree of typing comfort. In general, the skills needed to comfortably engage in online therapy are the following:

1.   Ability to turn on a computer (don't laugh, therapists and attorneys are notorious in this area).

2.   Ability to access the Internet.

3.   Ability to type (essential for chat therapy).

4.   Ability to configure audio/video connections (a technician can be there to assist; however, it is important to make sure that clear directions on using the camera and troubleshooting tips for common

problems are obtained before use with an actual client).

5.   Ability to use e-mail.

Following onscreen directions is a vital prerequisite to a successful and happy human–computer relationship. Some therapists who may not be as proficient in their typing skills as they would like may attempt to use speech-to-text conversion software. This allows the user to speak into a microphone and have their spoken words converted to text in a document. This software is installed on the user's computer. Each user would require the software to be installed on his or her computer system. At the time of writing, speech-to-text software has not yet been perfected. Once there is an acceptable level of accuracy, it is likely that this feature will be implemented in the major e-clinics and by other chat software developers.

Key Programs

Below are some of the more common programs that a therapist will need to be familiar with in order to successfully navigate through a computer system.

1.   Word processing is a computer program used to create documents that are text-based, such as letters, memos, and reports. It is perhaps the most frequently used computer application. Examples of word processors include Microsoft Word, and WordPerfect.

2.   Electronic mail (e-mail) consists of messages, usually text, sent from one person to another via computer.

3.   Browsers are software programs used for searching and viewing various kinds of Internet resources such as information on a Web site. The most popular Internet browsers are Microsoft Internet Explorer and Netscape Navigator.

4.   Speech-to-text is an application that converts the spoken word to text.

5.   Graphics involve using a computer to create, display, and store pictures.

6.   Video programs.

If the intention is to utilize videoconferencing, using a late model computer with fast processing speeds, a decent amount of RAM, and a broadband Internet connection is recommended. At time of press, Intel Pentium 4, Centrinos, and AMD's Athlon 64 are all appropriate. Processor speeds over 1 GHz are recommended. 256 MB of RAM, or even better, 512 MB, is also recommended. By the time this book is in circulation, **dual-core processors** will be available. This technology will allow computers to increase performance by running simultaneous calculations and operations. Remember, not every therapist or client is going to be equipped with the latest and greatest computer system. The average client will not have such a high-end computer. (If a therapist is trying to have a videoconference with a client who is running Windows 98 on a Celeron 500 mhz processor and a dial-up 56k connection, the client will likely become extremely frustrated with the process.) However, for those engaging strictly in chat therapy, most any computer with an internet connection will suffice, as chat functionality requires very little processing power, and 56k dial-up is sufficient to transmit data in this form.

Ask the client what type of equipment he or she owns. If it is likely that video or even audio will cause the client frustration in setup and troubleshooting, suggest chat therapy. If the client is a good candidate for a solution-focused, cognitive–behavioral approach, then chat therapy might be the perfect solution.

Audio- or videoconferencing requires greater effort in setup and configuration, but once in place is effortless to use. Connecting the microphone, speakers, and camera are the easy part. Most cameras and some microphones use Universal Serial Bus (USB) connections, and most speakers connect both to a power supply and to the computer's sound card, usually via a miniphono jack.

Configuring a sound card, microphone, and camera will require a diligent effort and deliberate reading of paper as well as on-screen directions. Therapists should call a computer technician if difficulties arise. They should also be sure to learn the basic functions of each element so that a rudimentary understanding of the way these components work and are accessed is clear. A good technician will be able to provide the knowledge that is needed. Most mainstream audio/video software comes with superb written and on-screen instructions.

Once all the equipment is connected, the therapist is ready to go! Therapists practicing from a large e-clinic most likely will have their audio and video as an integrated part of the clinic's software. This is the advantage to practicing from an e-clinic. A good e-clinic will provide customized technology solutions specifically suited to the practice of psychotherapy. One should be aware of what components the clinic is using. If the clinic utilizes third-party software solutions, security is compromised, and the therapist may not be providing a safe environment for his or her clients. If therapists decide to use their own software or build their own Web site, they should be aware of their responsibilities to their clients.

Many therapists have used standard e-mail, message boards, and instant message programs to practice online therapy in the past. The fact is that they used those programs because that was the best there was at that time. Now, it is understood that psychotherapy requires specific technologies because the field places specific demands on the manner in which therapy is conducted.

Regardless of how therapists choose to run their online practice, they should be familiar with the technology before using it with a client. Above all, the client comes first, and therapists should be confident and comfortable with the technology they use, because it is likely they may need to coach their clients through it.

Calendars, Billing, and Other Administrative Tools

Most therapists are familiar with some form of electronic calendar, and most have used some type of accounting software. Those who have not will need to spend some time familiarizing themselves with these concepts and utilizing the actual technologies. It is important to become familiar with these types of tools.

Once again, an advantage to being a part of an e-clinic is that the tools are customized for the therapist's practice and therefore simplified because there is only one function that needs to take place—the therapy session. Typically e-clinics will customize accounting, bookkeeping, taxes, health insurance billing, and calendaring for the therapist's particular online practice needs. This software will likely be very intuitive for therapists to use, and learning the full scope of all available functions is usually a quick and easy process.

Sharing Files

Document sharing and resource sharing can be very powerful tools to add to the therapeutic process. Sharing resources is an inherent capacity of online therapy. Therapists can keep an archive of their favorite articles, Web sites, or news reports, and instantly provide that resource to a client during a session. Clients will often share their favorite Web sites/resources with their therapists as an aid to illustrating their thoughts and feelings.

Having an informed consent form electronically signed and filed is a very important function. In fact, a therapist can have any document signed in this fashion with this system. An independent online therapy Web site or an e-clinic should have easy capability for a therapist to upload documents, and for clients to electronically sign these documents. An example of this is adding the electronic signature *button* to a document.

Writing Code

For most therapists, especially those connected to an e-clinic, writing code is something that they will never have to worry about. However, for some therapists, in particular those who own their own independent online therapy Web site, learning to write code can be a very valuable skill. There are many resources available on the Internet that can direct a therapist to learn how to write code. A search on a search engine will result in many options from which a therapist can choose.

Editing and Manipulating Graphics and Photos

The two most commonly used illustration programs are Adobe's Photoshop and Illustrator and Macromedia's Freehand. These programs are full-featured, professional-strength graphics illustration programs suitable for all media. There are passionate adherents of each, just as there are with Netscape and Internet Explorer. If the therapist is focusing on the Web, he or she might also want to consider one of the new hybrid tools, such as Fireworks, which offers good basic illustration features.

COMPUTER PROTECTION

The therapist's computer is like the therapist's home. It contains sensitive and valuable information, so it is a good idea to keep it locked and be careful about who is allowed access. Potential intruders lurk both in cyberspace and amongst those who have physical access to the therapist's computer, and either type may try to steal sensitive information or use it to attack other computer systems. Some individuals simply enjoy sending out viruses that can destroy files and require expensive computer repairs. By taking some basic security steps, the therapist can use his or her computer with confidence and fully protect personal information.

If the therapist accesses the Internet using a high speed or broadband Internet connection (such as a cable modem or DSL), the therapist needs to be especially vigilant about computer security and take additional precautions. Dial-up users should also take precautions and develop the security habits that will protect their computer files now and when they move to broadband.

Always Use Antivirus Software

Keep the software up-to-date. Over 500 new viruses are discovered each month. The therapist is not just protecting him- or herself when using virus software, but also others with whom the therapist communicates. The therapist's computer can become infected and infect other computers with viruses that may be planted in e-mails or attachments to e-mails, in programs or files that the therapist downloads, in floppy disks, and even in Web sites that the therapist visits.

The first line of defense is an antivirus program. This is not the same as a firewall—both are needed because they protect the therapist from different types of attacks. The therapist can buy antivirus software online or in retail stores. Get an antivirus program that updates itself automatically. Look for programs that can also repair damage caused by a virus.

Therapists should not open e-mail or e-mail attachments unless they expect the message and know who it is from. They should only download files and programs and use disks from sources they know and trust. It is best for therapists not to forward e-mail warnings about new viruses to their friends—they could be hoaxes designed to spread a virus instead of warn against them.

Back It Up

Just as the therapist might use a safe-deposit box to guard valuables, he or she should consider safeguarding important items that are in his or her computer so they will not be lost if a virus strikes, if the computer crashes, or there is some other kind of disaster. Financial records, research, writing, original artwork, and work files that would be difficult to reconstruct or replace should be backed up regularly.

Therapists should not rely on paper copies of material that would require inputting the data all over again. They should use floppy disks to back up small files, CDs or removable disk drives for larger files. Some items, such as bank records, should be backed up every time a change is made, while others might require less frequent backups. Set schedules for backing up files and stick to them. Store backups in a locked, fireproof container.

Always Use a Firewall

A firewall is an "internal lock" for information on the therapist's computer. It is like the fence around a fort: It makes it harder for intruders to get into the therapist's computer from cyberspace. This is especially important if the therapist has a high-speed Internet connection through the cable provider or DSL, because the doorway from the therapist's computer to the Internet is open whenever the therapist's computer is on, even if the therapist is not doing anything online at that moment.

Many computer operating systems already have firewalls installed, and users just have to turn them on. There are many other firewalls available to download or buy to help the therapist secure the computer. The therapist needs to check to see if the computer hardware or software already has a built-in firewall. If it does, it may be necessary to turn the firewall feature on. If the therapist does not already have one, he or she can find free firewall software on the Internet or purchase software. Another option is for the therapist to use an external firewall device that connects to the computer. Firewalls differ and some can be customized to suit the therapist's particular needs; the descriptions need to be read carefully.

Learn the Risks and Rules Associated with Sharing Files or the Internet Connection

The therapist can be exposed to danger via e-mail, file sharing, an unprotected broadband connection, or a nonsecure wi-fi connection (also known as wireless fidelity, this mediates a

connection to a network or the Internet without the use of ca-
bles—the signal is sent and received via radio frequencies.)

Disconnect from the Internet When Idle

If the therapist is not using the Internet connection, turn it off.
No one can attack a computer when it is not connected to the
Internet. This is especially important if the therapist has a
high-speed connection.

Use Unique Passwords

Passwords are the keys that unlock access to e-mail, accounts,
and other computer activities. They must be chosen carefully to
prevent intruders from correctly guessing them (based on
knowledge about the therapist) or cracking them (with software programs that try every word in the dictionary until they
get a match). Use a combination of letters and numbers. Avoid
obvious things such as your birth date. Pick passwords that you
can remember. Do not write passwords down where others
may find them. Keep the passwords private and be suspicious
of people who ask for them, claiming to be from companies
that should already have them. Therapists connected with an
e-clinic should have the ability to choose and change their
password whenever they need to do so.

Be in Control of the Computer and the Software

The software and operating system on the therapist's computer
have many security features. Learning how to automatically
update the operating system with security patches, to activate
firewalls and to turn off any extraneous options that leave the
computer vulnerable are highly recommended. If the therapist
shares the computer with roommates, children, or other users,
it is crucial for everyone to follow the same security rules.
Make sure that all users understand the dangers of security
breaches and how to avoid them. Turn the computer off when
no one is using it. Do not share passwords that would enable
others to get into personal accounts that the therapist may

have set up in the computer. Keep the computer in a common area where the therapist can see who is using it and what he or she is doing.

Take Action Immediately

If the therapist thinks he or she has been hacked or infected by a virus, he or she needs to contact their ISP. If the therapist has high-speed Internet access through cable or DSL, unplug the phone or cable line from the computer. The therapist's ISP and software and hardware vendors may offer advice about how to remedy the problem. If the therapist believes that someone has obtained financial or other sensitive information, he or she should contact the financial institution immediately. It is important to determine how the security breach occurred in order to strengthen protection in the future.

Keep Up to Date

Hackers and virus creators are constantly looking for new ways to get around the protections that are put in place to thwart them. To keep the computer secure, the therapist needs to keep one step ahead of them. Take advantage of "patches" that software manufacturers may offer when they discover flaws in their programs that can make them vulnerable to hackers, viruses, and other problems. These patches can often be downloaded at no charge from the manufacturers' Web sites. If the therapist's antivirus software does not automatically update itself to detect and stop new viruses, he or she needs to get updated software at least once a year.

APPENDIX **B**

Online Therapy Resources

ONLINE THERAPY SITES

Therapists searching today for online therapy sites, using a variety of search terms, will find a large selection from which to choose. There are some important distinctions for therapists to remember when trying to locate a particular online therapy site. Below we have listed some definitions that will help therapists distinguish among the various terms. We have also included examples of each.

The listed sites are not ranked in any way, and no endorsement of any particular site, therapist, or company is made by either the authors or the publisher. These sites were found by a simple Internet search, and are listed only as examples of the kinds of sites that therapists might find in their own searches. Included in this list are the Web site names and URLs. New online therapy resources are developing all the time. Therapists are encouraged to use the criteria in this book to do their own searches and find the e-clinic that meets their particular needs.

Table of Services for Online Therapy E-Clinics

	My Therapy Net	Help Horizons	Find-a-Therapist	Online Counsellors	PsychOnline	Therapy In LA	Ask the Internet Therapist
Nationwide	•						•
License Verification	•	•	•				
Chat Room	•	•	•		•		•
Billing	•	•	•		•		
Calender	•	•	•		•		•
Immediate Care for Crisis	•	•	•	•	•		
Virtual Office	•	•	•				
Message Board	•	•	•	•	•		•
Online Therapy Training	•			•			
Confidentiality	•	•	•	•	•	•	•
Security	•	•	•	•	•	•	•
Business Development	•						
Telephone Option	•	•	•			•	•
Face-to-face Option	•	•				•	•
CEU Training	•						
Accounting	•	•	•		•		
Scheduling	•	•	•		•		•
Marketing	•	•	•	•	•	•	•
Investment Opportunity	•						
Newsletters	•			•		•	•
Articles	•	•	•	•	•		•

Effective January 2005
Research conducted online

Ask the Internet Therapist (http://www.asktheinternet
therapist.com)
Find-a-Therapist (http://www.find-a-therapist.com)
Help Horizons (http://www.helphorizons.com)
My Therapy Net (http://www.mytherapynet.com)
Online Counselors (http://www.onlinecounsellors.co.uk)
Psych Online (http://www.psychonline.com)
Therapy in LA (http://www.therapyinla.com)

EDUCATIONAL SITES

International Society for Mental Health Online (http://
www.ismho.org). A nonprofit organization, the International Society for Mental Health Online
(ISMHO) was formed in 1997 to promote the understanding, use, and development of online communication, information, and technology for the
international mental health community. This site
contains many excellent articles on online therapy
via its "White Papers," including "Suggested Principles for the Online Provision of Mental Health Services" and "Myths and Realities of Online Clinical
Work."

Metanoia (http://www.metanoia.org). An independent
consumer guide run by Martha Ainsworth; this site
provides data about therapists who offer services
on the Internet: their credentials, fees, payment
options, services offered, and other relevant facts.

NetPsychology (http://www.netpsych.com). This site explores the uses of the Internet to deliver mental
health services.

Psych Central (http://www.psychcentral.com). Maintained by John Grohol, it is one of the Net's best
annotated guides to the most useful Web sites,
newsgroups, and mailing lists online today in

mental health, psychology, social work, and psychiatry. It receives between 3,000 and 4,000 visitors per day and acts as a reliable and accurate source of mental health information for the over 20 million visitors who have stopped by since it was first introduced.

SELF-HELP SITES

In Chapter 1 Dr. Meichenbaum discusses existing educational sites, such as http://www.kpchr.org/feelbetter, which offers six sessions of cognitive–behavioral interventions, and www.melis sainstitute.org, which offers interventions and education regarding violence protection.

EMERGENCY RESOURCES

AIDS/HIV

AIDS Hotlines: U.S. Public Health Service—24 hours, 800-342-2437. Spanish speaking: 24 hours, 800-344-7432. Hearing impaired: 24 hours, 800-243-7889
KNOW HIV/AIDS—www.knowhivaids.org—866-344-5669

Alcohol and Drug Abuse

National Alcohol and Drug Abuse Hotline—800-252-6465
HHS/SAMHSA Center for Substance Abuse Treatment—800-662-HELP

Child Abuse and Family Violence

Boys Town National Crisis Line—24 hours a day, every day. The only national crisis line that children and parents can call with any problem, any time. You can refer troubled families to the hotline, which is staffed by caring professionals. 800-448-3000, or for TDD call 800-448-1833

Child Find/A Way Out—800-292-9688 (800-A-way-out)

Childhelp USA's National Child Abuse Hotline— 800-422-4453

Children of the Night, short-term crisis—800-551-1300

Children's Rights of America Youth Crisis Hotline— 800-442-4673

Covenant House Nineline—24-hour crisis, 800-999-9999 (TTY, 800-999-9915), is a national crisis hotline for youth under 21 and their families. Since 1987, their crisis workers have provided timely, and some-times lifesaving, intervention for those in need. Their referral database of more than 26,000 agen-cies allows them to connect those in need with the local agencies best equipped to help them. In the past year their workers answered over 61,000 crisis calls and provided more than 11,000 referrals. Their Web site provides educational pieces ad-dressing youth issues for kids and people who want to help kids. http://www.covenanthouse.org/ nineline

Domestic Violence—National Domestic Violence Hot-line, 800-799-SAFE (7233) or 800-787-3224 (TTY) for a referral to a domestic violence shelter or pro-gram in the client's area.

National Child Pornography Tipline and CyberTip-line—Handles calls from individuals reporting the sexual exploitation of children through the pro-duction and distribution of pornography. 800-843-5678 or www.cybertipline.com

National Council on Child Abuse & Family Violence— www.nccafv.org 202-429-6695

Consumer Information

Consumer Product Safety Commission Notify about products, cribs, children's toys that are dangerous or easily broken—800-638-CPSC.

Disability Services

Crisis for the Physically & Mentally Challenged—800-426-4263

Education

National Literacy Hotline—800-228-8813

Gay and Lesbian Issues

Homosexuals Anonymous—800-288-4237

IYG and Out Youth Often Helpline—peer counseling for gay, lesbian and bisexual youth—800-347-8336 and 800-969-6884

The Trevor Project—24-hour suicide prevention hotline for gay youths. Call before you fall: The Trevor Project, a nonprofit organization named for the short film about a 13-year-old boy who attempted suicide because of his sexuality, has established a national toll free, 24-hour suicide prevention hotline for gay youths. 800-850-8078.

Grief

Grief Recovery—www.grief-recovery.com

Family Planning

National Life Center Hotline/Pregnancy Hotline—
800-848-5683

Internet Abuse

Working to Halt Online Abuse (WHOA)—http://www.
haltabuse.org

Legal Services

American Bar Association—pro bono legal services
http://www.abanet.org/legalservices/probono

Mental Health and Crisis Intervention

American Psychological Association Public Education
Line. This is a toll-free call; a live operator answers
24 hours a day, 7 days a week (press "10"). After an
initial discussion, the operator connects the caller
to the American Psychological Association chapter
in the caller's state, who will give the caller a local
referral to psychologists only. Most state APA
chapters keep normal business hours. 800-964-2000
or www.helping.apa.org

American Psychiatric Association Answer Center. Contacting this number is a toll call, and live operators
are only available from 8:30 A.M. to 6:00 P.M. EST.
Otherwise it's somewhat similar to the 1-800 line
for the American Psychological Association. The
operator will refer the caller to the American Psychiatric Association chapter in your state, but the
caller is required to hang up and dial that number;
they cannot automatically connect the caller. The
state chapters, which are open during normal busi-

ness hours, can refer the caller to psychiatrists only, 703-907-7300 or www.psych.org

Counseling On-Line: www.befrienders.org/email.html (a 24-hour confidential e-mail service by the Samaritans)

Knowledge Exchange Network (KEN)—This is a toll-free call, 877-495-0009. Live operators are available from 8:30 A.M. to 5:00 P.M. EST. The operator will first ask if the caller has tried to obtain help through his or her private health insurance plan. However, this number also provides referral to public mental health clinics near the caller's home; the caller will have to hang up and redial to the local number. The KEN line is run by the federal government's Center for Mental Health Services (CMHS) —800-789-2647 or http://www.mentalhealth.org

Metanoia—Contains conversations and writings for suicidal persons to read. http://www.metanoia. org/suicide

National Crisis Helpline—For use in locating the nearest crisis service in the United States-800-999-9999

National Hopeline Network—The Hopeline connects people in immediate distress to a crisis center. Calls are answered by certified counselors 24 hours a day, 7 days a week. When the system is fully operational, the call should be routed to a center nearest the caller's home. A trained counselor should answer within two or three rings, or about 20 to 30 seconds, 800-SUICIDE or www.hope line.org

National Victim Center Infolink—M–F 8:30 A.M.–5:30 P.M.(ESP)—800.FYI.CALL; www.neve.org

On Line Counseling is available at the following addresses and sites: Samaritans http://www.befriend ers.org/email.html (a 24-hour confidential e-mail service) and http://www.kidshelp.sympatico.ca—a

service for young people, which also addresses issues in addition to suicide. Talk to a therapist online—this is a list of over 200 psychotherapists and
other professionally trained counselors who will
interact with young people via the Internet. Some
can respond within 24–36 hours. Most charge a
small fee. Be sure to read the background information.

Samaritans   http://www.befrienders.org/email.html,
http://www.samaritans.co.uk. A 24-hour confidential e-mail service. The Samaritans—trained volunteers—are available 24 hours a day to listen and
provide emotional support. Volunteers can be
phoned or e-mailed. Confidential and nonjudgmental.

1-800-THERAPIST—A free referral service. Callers can
talk to "referral resource counselors" during normal business hours. The advantage to using this
service is that after an initial telephone evaluation,
they can refer the caller to the full range of mental
health clinicians, including a psychiatrist, psychologist, marriage or family therapist, clinical
social worker, licensed professional counselor, or
psychiatric nurse—800-843-7274 or www.1-800-
THERAPIST.com

Missing Children and Runaways

National Center for Missing and Exploited Children—
24-hour hotline at 800-843-5678

National Network of Runaway and Youth Services—
Networks with youth shelters and other community-
based groups. 1319 F Street NW #401, Washington,
DC 20004—202-783-7949

National Runaway Switchboard operates a confidential
hotline for runaway youth, teens in crisis, and con-

cerned friends and family members. All services are free and available 24 hours every day and include crisis intervention; message relay between runaways and their parent/legal guardian; referrals to and conference with community-based resources such as counseling, support groups, alternative housing, and healthcare; Home Free program in partnership with Greyhound Buslines, Inc. to help runaways return home to their families; education and outreach services; free NRS promotional materials for distribution at community events, school assemblies, and health fairs: 24-hour crisis line, 800-621-4000. info@nrscrisisline.org or http://www.nrscrisisline.org

National Youth Crisis Hotline CA—Crisis line for runaways and parents needing immediate assistance, 800-448-4663 (800-HIT-HOME)

Poison Control

American Association of Poison Control Centers— 800-222-1222. Their Web site http://www.aapcc.org enables you to "find your poison center" nationwide, by zip code, state, map, or directory.

Rape and Sexual Assault

The Rape, Abuse and Incest National Network (RAINN)—Operates the National Sexual Assault Hotline, 800-656-HOPE, www.rainn.org

Victims of Crime Resource Center—800-851-3420

Sexual Addiction

National Council on Sexual Addiction and Compulsivity (NCSAC)—www.ncsac.org—770-541-9912 (based in Atlanta, GA), also known as the Society for the Advancement of Sexual Health (SASH)

Suicide Prevention

American Association of Suicidology National Suicide Hotline—24 hours 800:SUICIDE (784-2433)
Suicide Prevention Crisis Lines—Call 911

Youth and Teen Services

Kidshelp: kidshelp.sympatico.ca—A service for young people that also addresses issues in addition to suicide.

APPENDIX C

Online Therapy Guidelines

The following organizations and associations have created these guidelines for the protection of consumers who are the clients of clinicians, counselors, and therapists. These guidelines will be in constant revision and development based on new research in the area of online therapy. It is important to visit the organization's Web site regularly to become informed about the new guidelines.

Although online therapy has been utilized since the mid-1990s, no state laws have been established to govern it. However, many associations and organizations have suggested principles and guidelines for utilizing the Internet for mental health services; for example the American Counseling Association, American Medical Informatics Association, American Psychiatric Association, American Psychological Association, International Society for Mental Health Online, and the National Board of Certified Counselors. Here we present the most recent guidelines from these organizations for your information. We recommend that *all* therapists contemplating setting up an online practice read *all* of these guidelines and also consult their state organization.

AMERICAN COUNSELING ASSOCIATION

The American Counseling Association (ACA) provides guidelines* for confidentiality. This covers the privacy of the client's information and how secure the websites are. It provides informational notices for security of professional sites, professional identification, client's electronic communication's record, and transference of client information. It recommends guidelines for the establishment of the online counseling relationship, appropriateness of the counseling, counseling plan, continuation of counseling, and competence of the counselor and treating minors. It completes the guidelines by exploring some legal considerations. The parenthical cross references refer to other sections of ACA's ethical standards which are not reproduced here.

Additional Ethical Standards for WebCounseling

Confidentiality.

a. Privacy Information.
Professional counselors ensure that clients are provided sufficient information to adequately address and explain the limitations of (i) computer technology in the counseling process in general and (ii) the difficulties of ensuring complete client confidentiality of information transmitted through electronic communications over the Internet through online counseling. (See A.12.a, B.1.a, B.1.g)

---

*Reprinted from Ethical Standards for Internet Online Counseling, 1999. © ACA. Reprinted with permission. No further reproduction without written permission of the American Counseling Association. Available at http://www.counseling.org/Content/NavigationMenu/RESOURCES/ETHICS/ EthicalStandardsforInternetOnlineCounseling/Ethical_Stand_Online.htm

1. SECURED SITES: To mitigate the risk of potential breaches of confidentiality, professional counselors provide one-on-one online counseling only through "secure" Web sites or e-mail communications applications, which use appropriate encryption technology designed to protect the transmission of confidential information from access by unauthorized third parties.

2. NON-SECURED SITES: To mitigate the risk of potential breaches of confidentiality, professional counselors provide only general information from "non-secure" Web sites or e-mail communications applications.

3. GENERAL INFORMATION: Professional counselors may provide general information from either "secure" or "non-secure" Web sites, or through e-mail communications. General information includes non-client-specific, topical information on matters of general interest to the professional counselor's clients as a whole, third-party resource and referral information, addresses and phone numbers, and the like. Additionally, professional counselors using either "secure" or "non-secure" Web sites may provide "hot links" to third-party Web sites such as licensure boards, certification bodies, and other resource information providers. Professional counselors investigate and continually update the content, accuracy and appropriateness for the client of material contained in any "hot links" to third-party Web sites.

4. LIMITS OF CONFIDENTIALITY: Professional counselors inform clients of the limitations of confidentiality and identify foreseeable situations in which confidentiality must be breached in light of the law in both the state in which the client is located and the state in which the professional counselor is licensed.

b. Informational Notices.

1. SECURITY OF PROFESSIONAL COUNSELOR'S SITE: Professional counselors provide a readily visible notice that (i) information transmitted over a Web site or e-mail server may not be secure; (ii) whether or not the professional counselor's site is secure; (iii) whether the information transmitted between the professional counselor and the client during online counseling will be encrypted; and (iv) whether the client will need special software to access and transmit confidential information and, if so, whether the professional counselor provides the software as part of the online counseling services. The notice should be viewable from all Web site and e-mail locations from which the client may send information. (See B.1.g.)

2. PROFESSIONAL COUNSELOR IDENTIFICATION: Professional counselors provide a readily visible notice advising clients of the identities of all professional counselor(s) who will have access to the information transmitted by the client and, in the event that more than one professional counselor has access to the Web site or e-mail system, the manner, if any, in which the client may direct information to a particular professional counselor. Professional counselors inform clients if any or all of the sessions are supervised. Clients are also informed if and how the supervisor preserves session transcripts. Professional counselors provide background information on all professional counselor(s) and supervisor(s) with access to the online communications, including education, licensing and certification, and practice area information. (See B.1.g.)

3. CLIENT IDENTIFICATION: Professional counselors identify clients, verify identities of clients, and obtain

alternative methods of contacting clients in emergency situations.

c. Client Waiver.
Professional counselors require clients to execute client waiver agreements stating that the client (i) acknowledges the limitations inherent in ensuring client confidentiality of information transmitted through online counseling and (ii) agrees to waive the client's privilege of confidentiality with respect to any confidential information transmitted through online counseling that may be accessed by any third party without authorization of the client and despite the reasonable efforts of the professional counselor to arrange a secure online environment. Professional counselors refer clients to more traditional methods of counseling and do not provide online counseling services if the client is unable or unwilling to consent to the client waiver. (See B.1.b.)

d. Records of Electronic Communications.
Professional counselors maintain appropriate procedures for ensuring the safety and confidentiality of client information acquired through electronic communications, including but not limited to encryption software; proprietary on-site file servers with fire walls; saving online or e-mail communications to the hard drive or file server computer systems; creating regular tape or diskette back-up copies; creating hard-copies of all electronic communications; and the like. Clients are informed about the length of time for, and method of, preserving session transcripts. Professional counselors warn clients of the possibility or frequency of technology failures and time delays in transmitting and receiving information. (See B.4.a., B.4.b.)

e. Electronic Transfer of Client Information.
Professional counselors electronically transfer client confidential information to authorized third-party recipients only when (i) both the professional counselor and the authorized recipi-

ent have "secure" transfer and acceptance communication capabilities, (ii) the recipient is able to effectively protect the confidentiality of the client confidential information to be
transferred; and (iii) the informed written consent of the client,
acknowledging the limits of confidentiality, has been obtained.
(see B.4.e., B.6.a., B.6.b.)

Establishing the Online Counseling Relationship

a. The Appropriateness of Online Counseling.
Professional counselors develop an appropriate intake procedure for potential clients to determine whether online counseling is appropriate for the needs of the client. Professional
counselors warn potential clients that online counseling services may not be appropriate in certain situations and, to the
extent possible, informs the client of specific limitations, potential risks, and/or potential benefits relevant to the client's
anticipated use of online counseling services. Professional
counselors ensure that clients are intellectually, emotionally,
and physically capable of using the online counseling services,
and of understanding the potential risks and/or limitations of
such services. (See A.3.a., A.3.b.)

b. Counseling Plans.
Professional counselors develop individual online counseling
plans that are consistent with both the client's individual circumstances and the limitations of online counseling. Professional
counselors shall specifically take into account the limitations, if
any, on the use of any or all of the following in online counseling:
initial client appraisal, diagnosis, and assessment methods employed by the professional counselor. Professional counselors
who determine that online counseling is inappropriate for the
client should avoid entering into or immediately terminate the
online counseling relationship and encourage the client to continue the counseling relationship through an appropriate alternative method of counseling. (See A.11.b., A.11.c.)

c. Continuing Coverage.

Professional counselors provide clients with a schedule of times during which the online counseling services will be available, including reasonable anticipated response times, and provide clients with an alternate means of contacting the professional counselor at other times, including in the event of emergencies. Professional counselors obtain from, and provide clients with, alternative means of communication, such as telephone numbers or pager numbers, for backup purposes in the event the online counseling service is unavailable for any reason. Professional counselors provide clients with the name of at least one other professional counselor who will be able to respond to the client in the event the professional counselor is unable to do so for any extended period of time. (See A.11.a.)

d. Boundaries of Competence.

Professional counselors provide online counseling services only in practice areas within their expertise and do not provide online counseling services to clients located in states in which professional counselors are not licensed. (See C.2.a., C.2.b.)

e. Minor or Incompetent Clients.

Professional counselors must verify that clients are above the age of minority, are competent to enter into the counseling relationship with a professional counselor, and are able to give informed consent. In the event clients are minor children, incompetent, or incapable of giving informed consent, professional counselors must obtain the written consent of the legal guardian or other authorized legal representative of the client prior to commencing online counseling services to the client.

Legal Considerations.

Professional counselors confirm that their liability insurance provides coverage for online counseling services, and that the provision of such services is not prohibited by or otherwise violates any applicable (i) state or local statutes, rules, regulations, or ordinances; (ii) codes of professional membership organizations and certifying boards; and/or (iii) codes of state licensing boards.

Professional counselors seek appropriate legal and technical assistance in the development and implementation of their online counseling services.

AMERICAN MEDICAL INFORMATICS ASSOCIATION

The guidelines* from the American Medical Informatics Association (AMIA) are focused on the medicolegal and administrative issues of using e-mail in a clinical setting. It explores the administrative guidelines for using information via e-mail, patient–provider agreement, and the protocol and procedure for handling messages via e-mail. This paper recommends ideas for workstation screens, forwarding e-mails, mailing lists, categorization and redirection of mail, and archiving backups. These guidelines are geared more toward a medical clinic setting than a psychotherapy situation, but the information is very relevant for the online therapist. The guidelines that appear here are excerpted from the White Paper. *The numbering of footnotes is that of the original source.*

Guidelines for the Clinical Use of Electronic Mail with Patients

White Paper by Beverly Kane, M.D., and Daniel Z. Sands, M.D., M.P.H., for the AMIA Internet Working Group, Task Force on Guidelines for the Use of Clinic–Patient Electronic Mail.

---

*Reprinted from the Journal of the American Medical Informatics Association, *5(1), 1998. Also available at http://www.amia.org/pubs/other/email_guidelines.html. © American Medical Informatics Association.*

Guidelines.

Guidelines for using e-mail in a clinical setting address two interrelated aspects: effective interaction between the clinician and patient . . . and the observance of medicolegal prudence.

In these times of increasingly impersonal, truncated, and regulated care, clinic time with patients is often compromised. If a provider anticipates a need to contact a patient again soon with regard to test results or other follow-up, he or she should inquire about the patient's communication preferences. Informally, the provider can ascertain preference for e-mail, telephone or voice mail, or postal exchange at the time of the visit, and document it in the chart. A more formal arrangement entails the use of informed consent, discussed below. Patients might elect e-mail, telephone or voice mail, personal meeting, or the postal route at different times for different purposes. The provider should confirm on a periodic basis which route to use for communication.

Prescription refills, lab results, appointment reminders, insurance questions, and routine follow-up inquiries are well suited to e-mail. It also provides the patient with a convenient way to report home health measurements, such as blood pressure and glucose determinations.

Issues of a time-sensitive nature, such as medical emergencies, do not lend themselves to discussion via e-mail, since the time when an e-mail message will be read and acted upon cannot be ascertained. Sensitive and highly confidential subjects should not be discussed through most e-mail systems because of the potential for interception of the messages and the potential for transmission of messages to unintended recipients.

Medicolegal and Administrative Guidelines.
- Consider obtaining patient's informed consent for use of e-mail. Written forms should:
  - Itemize terms in Communication Guidelines.
  - Provide instructions for when and how to escalate to phone calls and office visits.

- Describe security mechanisms in place.
- Indemnify the health care institution for information loss due to technical failures.
- Waive encryption requirement, if any, at patient's insistence.

- Use password-protected screen savers for all desktop workstations in the office, hospital, and at home.
- Never forward patient-identifiable information to a third party without the patient's express permission.
- Never use patient's e-mail address in a marketing scheme.
- Do not share professional e-mail accounts with family members.
- Use encryption for all messages when encryption technology becomes widely available, user-friendly, and practical.
- Do not use unencrypted wireless communications with patient-identifiable information.
- Double-check all "To:" fields prior to sending messages.
- Perform at least weekly backups of mail onto long-term storage. Define "long-term" as the term applicable to paper records.
- Commit policy decisions to writing and electronic form.

Patient–Provider Agreement.
In general, the use of e-mail depends upon negotiation between patient and provider. Negotiation should focus on the following issues:

- *Turnaround time.* Ascertain how often both parties retrieve e-mail, and establish a maximal turnaround time for patient-initiated messages. In some messaging cultures, natural selection has evolved a one-business-day turnaround for nonurgent phone calls, and a two- to three-business-day turnaround for e-mail. As e-mail gains ascendancy as a preferred medium, messages may need to be checked and sorted by priority (triaged) several times a day. Often, the context of the patient's message will indicate the expected turnaround time. A patient who inquires about the results of a routine cervical smear will tolerate a longer messaging interval than one who is experiencing even mild side effects from a medication.

- *Privacy*. Indicate whether the office staff or nursing staff will triage messages, or whether mail addressed to the provider's private account will be read exclusively by the addressee. Also, establish with whom the physician may share a patient's e-mail message and under what circumstances, such as when consulting with another physician.
- *Permissible transactions and content*. Especially if other clinic staff will be processing e-mail from patients, establish the extent of action permitted over e-mail-prescription refills, medical advice, test results, release of records, etc.—and the topics. Stanford University Medical Clinic, for instance, forbids discussion of HIV status, mental illness, and worker's compensation claims in electronic mail.
- *Categorial subject headers*. Instruct patients to specify a transaction type in the "Subject:" field of their messages. This convention will facilitate redirection of messages, by software with filtering capabilities, to the pharmacy, lab, nurse, or appointment clerk. Since many e-mail addresses consist of nicknames, patients should also be asked to write their full names and a patient identification number, if any, in the body of the message.
- *Discrete subject headers*. Providers should use discre-

tion in their outgoing message titles. Patients may have fewer safeguards on their desktops than they need for their own privacy. "About Your HIV Test" is not an acceptable subject header.

These points should be discussed with the patient and the discussion documented in the record. A more conservative approach would be to commit the agreement to writing. In that case, have the patient sign the document, give a copy to the patient, and place a copy in the patient's chart. A summary of the policies and standards should be available on the clinic's Web site. For example, the Stanford Medical Group's external Web page on Electronic Mail Services illustrates how these policies can be conveyed to patients.[16]

Handling of Messages

- *Automatic reply to incoming messages.* E-mail software should be configured to send automatic replies in response to all incoming messages from patients. Replies should be of the form, "Your message has been received by Dr. Leslie Smith. I will attempt to process your request within one business day. If you need immediate assistance, please call Pat, my nurse, at 444-555-6666."

In addition, out-of-the-office replies should be activated on any e-mail account that will not be serviced by staff or covering physicians during an absence that exceeds the established e-mail response time. Such messages should include the provider's estimated date of return and instructions on whom to contact for immediate assistance.

Some e-mail programs have sophisticated filtering mechanisms that trigger different automated replies for patients, col-

---

16. Stanford Medical Group. Electronic Mail Services. (http://www-med. stanford.edu/shs/smg/email.html).

leagues, and unknown correspondents. At this writing, about half of the 12 most commonly used e-mail applications provide filtered automatic reply capability.[17] The UNIX "vacation" script affords simple auto-reply but requires UNIX shell privileges, is too cumbersome for the average user, and sends the same message to all parties.

- *Archiving of e-mail transactions.* E-mail exchanges constitute a form of progress note. Unless the provider is using an electronic patient record that allows the inclusion of e-mail messages, each e-mail message should be printed in full and a copy placed in the patient's paper record.

The following steps result in efficient archiving: (1) Include the full text of the patient's query in the email reply. (2) Copy the reply to the sender (provider). When the Internet delivers the provider's copy, which now includes both the original message and the provider's reply, the message should be printed and filed in the chart. Printers must operate in an area that is accessible only to staff and not to other patients.

- *Confirmation of action on patient's request.* A new reply message should be sent out upon completion of patient's request for prescription refills, records transfer, and other transactions.
- *Acknowledgment of messages.* For messages containing important medical advice, patients should be instructed to acknowledge messages by sending a brief reply. When such acknowledgment is expected, the printed (chart) copy should not be filed until this confirmation is received. In the absence of such confirmation, it cannot be assumed that the patient has

---

17. Venditto G. E-mail face-off. Internet World. December 1996; 7:12. (http://pubs.iworld.com/) (search on "e-mail face off").

received, much less read, important instructions. When in doubt, confirm delivery by telephone.

- *Escalation of communication.* E-mail from providers should include a footer (signature file) that invites patients to escalate communication to a phone call or office visit, should they feel that e-mail is insufficient. The footer should give the appropriate contact information. Providers may need to actively discourage the use of e-mail as a substitute for clinical examination.

- *Address book and group mailings.* Each provider should maintain a list of patients who communicate with him or her electronically. The address book feature of nearly all e-mail software permits easy maintenance of such a list. If it becomes necessary to notify the general patient population, or a group of patients, of an impending shutdown for network maintenance, recent mail blackouts, new clinic services, or a change of address, the clinic will have a ready-made mailing list. However, group-addressing, where those in the group see each other's names, should never be used to send mail to patients. Even the fact that a person sees a particular health care provider is confidential information. In addition, patients have become indignant about open inclusion on lists like the age-revealing list of women who are due for mammograms.

When sending out group mailings, use the "blind cc:" (blind carbon copy, or blind courtesy copy) software feature to keep recipients invisible to each other. When using this feature, enter the provider's own name in the "To:" field and place the list of recipients in the "bcc:" field.

- *Emotional content of e-mail.* Irony, sarcasm, and harsh criticism should not be attempted in e-mail messages. The impersonal nature and ambiguity of e-mail often results in real or imagined exaggeration of animosity toward the recipient. Providers must realize that sick, anxious, or angry patients might indeed express stronger sentiments with e-mail than they would face-to-face or over the phone. Clinicians should make an effort to restrain their language despite their own stress and fatigue. Clinicians should be aware that e-mail messages are typically stored for months or years on backup tapes. Pressing the delete button on the keyboard doesn't necessarily erase the message from the system. Such "deleted" messages containing disparaging, flippant, or incriminating remarks have come back to haunt physicians.

Medicolegal Issues

Aspects of electronic messaging of particular interest to risk management and legal departments concern data security and liability for advice. Medicolegal anxiety, however, should not be allowed to disable open communication as the basis for a healthy provider–patient relationship.

The most wary, not necessarily the best, approach dictates that patients be asked to sign printed guidelines by way of informed consent at the time an electronic relationship is established. In addition to the points detailed above, electronic messaging agreements should include, in nontechnical language:

- Description of security mechanisms in place: an explanation of the general nature of the network and its level of security. Is the clinic using an intranet with a firewall? Is the provider or the institution directly on the Internet, or is there an intermediary Internet service provider (ISP) who conceivably monitors transmission? Is encryption software in use?
- Indemnity for technical features: a clause to limit li-

ability for network infractions beyond the control of the health care providers. Examples include system crashes, power outages, and overloads at the ISP level.

- Waiver of encryption requirement: a mechanism for patients to opt out of the use of encryption if they do not wish (or are unable) to comply with the extra processing required. As of this writing there is no widely available, inexpensive, easy-to-use, highly secure, cross-platform encryption program suitable for global use.

Additional Recommendations

- *Workstation screen.* Avoid leaving open e-mail on the computer screen. If the computer is in the same room as other patients, use a password-activated screen saver so that patient files are not visible to other patients, especially if the provider is called out of the room.
- *Forwarding.* Never forward a patient's message or patient-identifiable information to a third party without the express permission of the patient. Text forwarded to a colleague for the purpose of consultation should not contain the patient's name or e-mail address.
- *Mailing lists.* Never use a patient's e-mail address in clinic marketing schemes or supply such addresses to third parties for advertising or any other use.
- *Headers.* Consider the use of a banner at the top of each e-mail message such as:

This is a CONFIDENTIAL medical communication.

Many commercial e-mail programs allow creation of stationery templates. Even simple UNIX-based mail programs such as *pine* can be scripted to create headers and footers.

- *Offsite processing of patient mail.* As with other parts of the medical record, patient-identifiable e-mail must not be taken out of the office. If providers answer e-mail from home, they must take special precautions to prevent other household members from intercepting messages from patients. Providers must not share e-mail accounts or passwords with friends, family, or nonmedical coworkers. Providers who communicate with patients should have their own accounts for professional use. Providers must see to it that e-mail processed off site on home systems or portable computing devices is subsequently printed in the office and included in the medical record.

- *Encryption.* As soon as practicable, clinics should establish a means of secure communication using the data encryption methods described below. Commercial encryption programs, encryption capabilities in commercially available e-mail software, and security features provided by the vendors of major clinical systems are becoming more common. The United States Post Office is testing a postmarking and encoding system specifically aimed at medical, legal, and financial transactions.[18] At least one semiconductor corporation is marketing a decoder ring device that provides security and encryption in a combination of wearable hardware and computer SoftWare.[19]

In March 1997 the Committee on Maintaining Privacy and Security in Health Care Applications of the National Information Infrastructure, under the National Research Council, released a comprehensive preliminary report on the privacy and secu-

18. Marketing News. U.S. Post Office testing electronic postmarks. 1996;30(22):16.
19. Dallas Semicomputer. (http://www.ibutton.com/).

rity of health information.[20] Although the authors did not specifically address e-mail as a separate entity for security purposes, all their findings and recommendations are germane to this topic.

With regard to encryption the authors state: ". . . [S]ecurity tools based on cryptography are still largely undeployed anywhere in the public computing industry, much less in health care. In the sites visited, the committee found almost no use of encryption technologies except in a few localized experimental settings. . . ." Of additional interest is that the Committee acknowledges the tension that will always exist between the need for access and free flow of information and the need for security. Providers should be prepared to encounter patients who are sophisticated Internet users, aware of its privacy limitations, who nevertheless initiate unencrypted e-mail discussions of a surprisingly intimate medical nature. Wireless communications should never be used to transmit unencrypted patient data.

- *Avoidance of computer–human interaction error.* Mistakes due to poor interface design and lack of failsafe mechanisms are particularly troublesome in medical communications. By late 1996, there was litigation pending in the United States courts alleging that a physician inadvertently posted his patient's diagnosis of breast cancer to the public area of a major commercial online service. As the doctor and patient had had prior e-mail exchanges, the mistake

---

20. Committee on Maintaining Privacy and Security in Health Care Applications of the National Information Infrastructure. For the record: protecting electronic health information. Computer Science and Telecommunications Board Commission on physical Sciences, Mathematics, and Applications; National Research Council. Washington, DC: National Academy Press, 1997. (http://www.nap.edu/readingroom/books/ftr/).

was almost certainly due to an interface design characteristic in the client software. Such an error can occur when an e-mail application defaults to a "reply to all" feature rather than the "reply to sender (only)" option. Until foolproof software is available, and until e-mail is routinely encrypted, correspondents must habitually double-check the "To:" box in every message prior to sending.

Site-Specific Policy Formulation.
There is growing evidence to suggest that electronic resources, both e-mail and Web-based self-help documents will result in substantial cost savings to clinics. Savings of time spent on the telephone will result from a reduction in telephone tag and a reduction of repetitious instructions. Many clinics, especially those with capitated plans, anticipate replacing inappropriate office visits with online support, including teleconferencing.

Health care institutions will need to develop written policies to address communication, technical, and medicolegal issues. Questions that must be answered include:

- *Triage.* Who will triage e-mail, and what is to be the response time?
- *Clerical overhead.* Who will print messages and place them in patients' charts?
- *Categorization and redirection of mail.* Will each provider have her own account, or will there be categoric accounts for all billing questions, medical questions, and scheduling questions?
- *Selective access for patients.* Should all patients be given the provider's e-mail address or can the provider give it out on a selective basis?
- *Archiving and backup.* How is e-mail cleared from the server? Does it stay on the provider's local machine or on the clinic or ISP mail server, or both? How are

both repositories archived and cleared? How long should e-mail be stored on backup systems? How will messages be indexed for retrieval?

- *Forbidden topics.* Will the clinic disallow discussion of certain highly sensitive topics such as an AIDS diagnosis or psychiatric conditions?

- *Selective confidentiality.* Will patients be given a choice as to what content from their e-mail messages appears in the chart? If patients can opt to exclude material from the chart, will the clinic establish a secure repository, either electronic or paper-based, to recall the text of the original message? Or will the transaction be more like a phone call where the conversation is relegated to secondhand progress notes? How will providers handle a patient's request to omit material from his or her record when it is the clinic's policy to print all mail? Be aware that altering or expurgating a message, or sequestering an archive of private material, may be against state law and leave the clinic on shaky legal ground.

- *Encryption.* Will encryption systems be required? If so, how soon and what kind? Will patients be given the encryption software by the clinic?

- *Clinic-provided e-mail accounts.* Should clinics provide patients with e-mail accounts on the institutional server? Will such accounts be inside or outside the clinic's firewall?

- *Outcomes evaluation.* How will the efficacy and usefulness of e-mail with patients be evaluated? Will it be possible to determine utilities based on a monetary cost-benefit analysis, patient satisfaction, provider perception, or clinical outcomes?

A survey or focus group conducted among both staff and patients before instituting an e-mail policy will reveal important additional considerations innate to each venue. Seeking buy-in from all users and stakeholders will foster maximal cooperation with the new directives.

All policy decisions regarding electronic mail should be placed in the institution's policies and procedures manual, given to all staff in paper form, and be available in electronic form on individual workstations or on the clinic's internal Web site.

E-mail storage and retrieval must eventually be integrated with a comprehensive electronic medical record (EMR) and with patient education resources, some of them Web-based. EMRs over secure internal Internet sites, called intranets, seen destined to be the future of clinical computing services, and they will subsume e-mail functions. E-mail and other computer-based resources are not an entirely satisfactory substitute for face-to-face clinical evaluation, however. Ultimately, quality-of-care outcome assessments of adjunctive forms of communication must be benchmarked against physical contact.

These guidelines were endorsed by the Board of Directors of AMIA in June 1997. Members of the task force are: Beverley Kane, MD, *Chair*, Ted Cooper, MD, Tom Ferguson, MD, Joseph Kannry, MD, Tim Kieschnick, Gretchen Murphy, Edward Anthony Oppenheimer, MD, Thomas Payne, MD, Larry Pfisterer, and Daniel Z. Sands, MD, MPH.

AMERICAN PSYCHIATRIC ASSOCIATION

The American Psychiatric Association (APA) is a medical specialty society recognized worldwide that supports the ethical use of telemedicine as reflected in this position statement.* Its member physicians work together to ensure humane care and effective treat-

---

*ment for all persons with mental disorders, including mental retarda-
tion and substance-related disorders.*

Position Statement on the Ethical Use of Telemedicine

The American Psychiatric Association supports the use of
telemedicine as an appropriate component of a mental health
delivery system to the extent that its use is in the best interest
of the patient and is in compliance with the APA policies on
medical ethics and confidentiality.

In December 1995 the Board of Trustees voted to approve the
Position Statement on the Ethical Use of Telemedicine as an of-
ficial position statement of the APA.

AMERICAN PSYCHOLOGICAL ASSOCIATION

In the following statement, the American Psychological Association
(APA) does not give specific guidelines for online therapy; however,
readers are referred to the APA* Ethical Principles of Psychologists
and Code of Conduct *(2004). It recommends that the clinician up-
hold the same guidelines as in a traditional setting to protect the client.
The APA states that guidelines for online therapy are in the works by
the committee and that they would be added to the general ethics code
in the future. The APA issued new general guidelines in 2003, but these
did not involve a statement on telemedicine or online therapy.*

Statement on Services by Telephone, Teleconferencing, and
Internet

Statement of the Ethics Committee of the American Psychological Association

The American Psychological Association's Ethics Committee
issued the following statement on November 5, 1997, based on
its 1995 statement on the same topic.

---

*Reprinted from http://www.apa.org/ethics/stmnt01.html. Copyright 1997 by
The American Psychological Association. Reprinted with permission.

The Ethics Committee can only address the relevance of and enforce the "Ethical Principles of Psychologists and Code of Conduct" and cannot say whether there may be other APA Guidelines that might provide guidance. The Ethics Code is not specific with regard to telephone therapy or teleconferencing or any electronically provided services as such and has no rules prohibiting such services. Complaints regarding such matters would be addressed on a case by case basis.

Delivery of services by such media as telephone, teleconferencing and the Internet is a rapidly evolving area. This will be the subject of APA task forces and will be considered in future revision of the Ethics Code. Until such time as a more definitive judgment is available, the Ethics Committee recommends that psychologists follow Standard 1.04c, Boundaries of Competence, which indicates that "In those emerging areas in which generally recognized standards for preparatory training do not yet exist, psychologists nevertheless take reasonable steps to ensure the competence of their work and to protect patients, clients, students, research participants, and others from harm." Other relevant standards include Assessment (Standards 2.01–2.10), Therapy (4.01–4.09, especially 4.01 Structuring the Relationship and 4.02 Informed Consent to Therapy), and Confidentiality (5.01–5.11). Within the General Standards section, standards with particular relevance are 1.03, Professional and Scientific Relationship; 1.04 (a, b, and c), Boundaries of Competence; 1.06, Basis for Scientific and Professional Judgments; 1.07a, Describing the Nature and Results of Psychological Services; 1.14, Avoiding Harm; and 1.25, Fees and Financial Arrangements. Standards under Advertising, particularly 3.01–3.03 are also relevant.

Psychologists considering such services must review the characteristics of the services, the service delivery method, and the provisions for confidentiality. Psychologists must then consider the relevant ethical standards and other requirements, such as licensure board rules.

INTERNATIONAL SOCIETY FOR MENTAL HEALTH ONLINE

In these guidelines the International Society for Mental Health Online (ISMHO)* concentrates on informed consent and information that would be beneficial for both the client and the therapist; for example, the possible misunderstandings that can occur due to the lack of visual cues, turnaround time of e-mail therapy, and privacy. ISMHO also explores the potential benefits and risks, safeguards, and alternatives to online therapy. Boundaries of competence, requirement for the online therapist to develop a safe practice, the structure of online services, and most important, emergency procedures and protocols are discussed.

Suggested Principles for the Online Provision of Mental Health Services

Online mental health services often accompany traditional mental health services provided in person, but sometimes they are the only means of treatment. These suggestions are meant to address only those practice issues relating directly to the online provision of mental health services. Questions of therapeutic technique are beyond the scope of this work.

The terms *services*, *client*, and *counselor* are used for the sake of inclusiveness and simplicity. No disrespect for the traditions or the unique aspects of any therapeutic discipline is intended.

1.   Informed consent

        The client should be informed before he or she consents to receive online mental health services. In particular, the

---

*The Suggested Principles for the Online Provision of Mental Health Services are Copyright © 2000 International Society for Mental Health Online & Psychiatric Society for Informatics. All rights reserved. The document may be freely reproduced without permission provided that the source is cited and no fee is assessed to access the information. The document is available at http://www.ismho.org/suggestions.html

client should be informed about the process, the counselor, the potential risks and benefits of those services, safeguards against those risks, and alternatives to those services.

a.   Process

   1.   Possible misunderstandings

The client should be aware that misunderstandings are possible with text-based modalities such as e-mail (since nonverbal cues are relatively lacking) and even with videoconferencing (since bandwidth is always limited).

   2.   Turnaround time

One issue specific to the provision of mental health services using asynchronous (not in "real time") communication is that of turnaround time. The client should be informed of how soon after sending an e-mail, for example, he or she may expect a response.

   3.   Privacy of the counselor

Privacy is more of an issue online than in person. The counselor has a right to his or her privacy and may wish to restrict the use of any copies or recordings the client makes of their communications. See also below on the confidentiality of the client.

b.   Counselor

When the client and the counselor do not meet in person, the client may be less able to assess the counselor and to decide whether or not to enter into a treatment relationship with him or her.

   1.   Name

The client should be informed of the name of the counselor. The use of pseudonyms is common online, but the client should know the name of his or her counselor.

   2.   Qualifications

The client should be informed of the qualifications of the counselor. Examples of basic qualifications are degree, license, and certification. The counselor may also wish to provide supplemental information such as areas of special training or experience.

3. How to confirm the above

    So that the client can confirm the counselor's qualifications, the counselor should provide the telephone numbers or Web page URLs of the relevant institutions.

c. Potential benefits

    The client should be informed of the potential benefits of receiving mental health services online. This includes both the circumstances in which the counselor considers online mental health services appropriate and the possible advantages of providing those services online. For example, the potential benefits of e-mail may include: (1) being able to send and receive messages at any time of day or night; (2) never having to leave messages with intermediaries; (3) avoiding not only intermediaries, but also voice mail and "telephone tag"; (4) being able to take as long as one wants to compose, and having the opportunity to reflect upon one's messages; (5) automatically having a record of communications to refer to later; and (6) feeling less inhibited than in person.

d. Potential risks

    The client should be informed of the potential risks of receiving mental health services online. For example, the potential risks of e-mail may include (1) messages not being received and (2) confidentiality being breached. E-mails could fail to be received if they are sent to the wrong address (which might also breach confidentiality) or if they just are not noticed by the counselor. Confidentiality could be breached in transit by hackers or Internet service providers or at either end by others with access to the e-mail account or the computer. Extra safeguards should be considered when the computer is shared by family members, students, library patrons, etc.

e. Safeguards

The client should be informed of safeguards that are taken by the counselor and could be taken by himself or herself against the potential risks. For example, (1) a "return receipt" can be requested whenever an e-mail is sent and (2) a password can be required for access to the computer or, more secure, but also more difficult to set up, encryption can be used.

1. Alternatives

The client should be informed of the alternatives to receiving mental health services online. For example, other options might include (1) receiving mental health services in person, (2) talking to a friend or family member, (3) exercising or meditating, or (4) not doing anything at all.

g. Proxies

Some clients are not in a position to consent themselves to receive mental health services. In those cases, consent should be obtained from a parent, legal guardian, or other authorized party—and the identity of that party should be verified.

2. Standard operating procedure

In general, the counselor should follow the same procedures when providing mental health services online as he or she would when providing them in person. In particular:

a. Boundaries of competence

The counselor should remain within his or her boundaries of competence and not attempt to address a problem online if he or she would not attempt to address the same problem in person.

b. Requirements to practice

The counselor should meet any necessary requirements (for example, be licensed) to provide mental health services where he or she is located. In fact, requirements where the client is located may also need to be met to make it legal to provide mental health services to that client. See also the above on qualifications.

c. Structure of the online services

The counselor and the client should agree on the frequency and mode of communication, the method for determining the fee, the estimated cost to the client, the method of payment, etc.

d. Evaluation

The counselor should adequately evaluate the client before providing any mental health services online. The client should understand that that evaluation could potentially be helped or hindered by communicating online.

e. Confidentiality of the client

The confidentiality of the client should be protected. Information about the client should be released only with his or her permission. The client should be informed of any exceptions to this general rule.

f. Records

The counselor should maintain records of the online mental health services. If those records include copies or recordings of communications with the client, the client should be informed.

g. Established guidelines

The counselor should of course follow the laws and other established guidelines (such as those of professional organizations) that apply to him or her.

3. Emergencies

a. Procedures

The procedures to follow in an emergency should be discussed. These procedures should address the possibility that the counselor might not immediately receive an online communication and might involve a local backup.

b. Local backup
    Another issue specific to online mental health services is that the counselor can be a great distance from the client. This may limit the counselor's ability to respond to an emergency. The counselor should therefore in these cases obtain the name and telephone number of a qualified local (mental) health care provider (who preferably already knows the client, such as his or her primary care physician).

NATIONAL BOARD OF CERTIFIED COUNSELORS

The Guidelines* from the National Board of Certified Counselors (NBCC) were published on November 3, 2001. It defines Internet Counseling and what is appropriate for the use of this medium. It offers standards for the ethical practice of Internet counseling including the counseling relationship, confidentiality, and the therapist's licensure and certification credibility.

Standards for the Ethical Practice of Web Counseling

This document contains a statement of principles for guiding the evolving practice of Internet counseling. In order to provide a context for these principles, the following definition of Internet counseling, which is one element of technology-assisted distance counseling, is provided. The Internet counseling standards follow the definitions presented below.

A Taxonomy for Defining Face-To-Face and Technology-Assisted Distance Counseling.
The delivery of technology-assisted distance counseling continues to grow and evolve. Technology assistance in the form of

---

*Reprinted with the permission of the National Board for Certified Counselors, Inc™ and Affiliates, 3 Terrace Way, Suite D, Greensboro, NC 27403-3660. Available at http://www.nbcc.org/ethics/webethics.htm.

computer-assisted assessment, computer-assisted information systems, and telephone counseling has been available and widely used for some time. The rapid development and use of the Internet to deliver information and foster communication has resulted in the creation of new forms of counseling. Developments have occurred so rapidly that it is difficult to communicate a common understanding of these new forms of counseling practice.

The purpose of this document is to create standard definitions of technology-assisted distance counseling that can be easily updated in response to evolutions in technology and practice. A definition of traditional face-to-face counseling is also presented to show similarities and differences with respect to various applications of technology in counseling. A taxonomy of forms of counseling is also presented to further clarify how technology relates to counseling practice.

Nature of Counseling.
Counseling is the application of mental health, psychological, or human development principles, through cognitive, affective, behavioral or systemic intervention strategies, that address wellness, personal growth, or career development, as well as pathology.

Depending on the needs of the client and the availability of services, counseling may range from a few brief interactions in a short period of time, to numerous interactions over an extended period of time. Brief interventions, such as classroom discussions, workshop presentations, or assistance in using assessment, information, or instructional resources, may be sufficient to meet individual needs. Or, these brief interventions may lead to longer-term counseling interventions for individuals with more substantial needs. Counseling may be delivered by a single counselor, two counselors working collaboratively, or a single counselor with brief assistance from another counselor who has specialized expertise that is needed by the client.

Forms of Counseling.

Counseling can be delivered in a variety of forms that share the definition presented above. Forms of counseling differ with respect to participants, delivery location, communication medium, and interaction process. Counseling *participants* can be individuals, couples, or groups. The *location* for counseling delivery can be face-to-face or at a distance with the assistance of technology. The *communication medium* for counseling can be what is read from text, what is heard from audio, or what is seen and heard in person or from video. The *interaction process* for counseling can be synchronous or asynchronous. Synchronous interaction occurs with little or no gap in time between the responses of the counselor and the client. Asynchronous interaction occurs with a gap in time between the responses of the counselor and the client.

The selection of a specific form of counseling is based on the needs and preferences of the client within the range of services available. Distance counseling supplements face-to-face counseling by providing increased access to counseling on the basis of necessity or convenience. Barriers, such as being a long distance from counseling services, geographic separation of a couple, or limited physical mobility as a result of having a disability, can make it necessary to provide counseling at a distance. Options, such as scheduling counseling sessions outside of traditional service delivery hours or delivering counseling services at a place of residence or employment, can make it more convenient to provide counseling at a distance.

A Taxonomy of Forms of Counseling Practice. Table 1 presents a taxonomy of currently available forms of counseling practice. This schema is intended to show the relationships among counseling forms.

Table 8.1: A Taxonomy of Face-To-Face and Technology-Assisted Distance Counseling

Counseling

- Face-To-Face Counseling
  - ▸ Individual Counseling
  - ▸ Couple Counseling
  - ▸ Group Counseling

- Technology-Assisted Distance Counseling

  - ◆ Telecounseling

    - Telephone-Based Individual Counseling
    - Telephone-Based Couple Counseling
    - Telephone-Based Group Counseling

  - ◆ Internet Counseling

    - E-Mail-Based Individual Counseling
    - Chat-Based Individual Counseling
    - Chat-Based Couple Counseling
    - Chat-Based Group Counseling
    - Video-Based Individual Counseling
    - Video-Based Couple Counseling
    - Video-Based Group Counseling

Definitions

Counseling is the application of mental health, psychological, or human development principles, through cognitive, affective, behavioral or systemic intervention strategies, that address wellness, personal growth, or career development, as well as pathology.

Face-to-face counseling for individuals, couples, and groups involves synchronous interaction between and among counselors and clients using what is seen and heard in person to communicate.

Technology-assisted distance counseling for individuals, couples, and groups involves the use of the telephone or the computer to enable counselors and clients to communicate at a distance when circumstances make this approach necessary or convenient.

Telecounseling involves synchronous distance interaction among counselors and clients using one-to-one or conferencing features of the telephone to communicate.

Telephone-based individual counseling involves synchronous distance interaction between a counselor and a client using what is heard via audio to communicate.

Telephone-based couple counseling involves synchronous distance interaction among a counselor or counselors and a couple using what is heard via audio to communicate.

Telephone-based group counseling involves synchronous distance interaction among counselors and clients using what is heard via audio to communicate.

Internet counseling involves asynchronous and synchronous distance interaction among counselors and clients using e-mail, chat, and videoconferencing features of the Internet to communicate.

E-mail-based individual Internet counseling involves asynchronous distance interaction between counselor and client using what is read via text to communicate.

Chat-based individual Internet counseling involves synchronous distance interaction between counselor and client using what is read via text to communicate.

Chat-based couple Internet counseling involves synchronous distance interaction among a counselor or counselors and a couple using what is read via text to communicate.

Chat-based group Internet counseling involves synchronous distance interaction among counselors and clients using what is read via text to communicate.

Video-based individual Internet counseling involves synchronous distance interaction between counselor and client using what is seen and heard via video to communicate.

Video-based couple Internet counseling involves synchronous distance interaction among a counselor or counselors and a couple using what is seen and heard via video to communicate.

Video-based group Internet counseling involves synchronous distance interaction among counselors and clients using what is seen and heard via video to communicate.

Standards for the Ethical Practice of Internet Counseling.
These standards govern the practice of Internet counseling and are intended for use by counselors, clients, the public, counselor educators, and organizations that examine and deliver Internet counseling. These standards are intended to address *practices* that are unique to Internet counseling and Internet counselors and do not duplicate principles found in traditional codes of ethics.

These Internet counseling standards of practice are based upon the principles of ethical practice embodied in the NBCC Code of Ethics. Therefore, these standards should be used in conjunction with the most recent version of the NBCC ethical code. Related content in the NBCC Code are indicated in parentheses after each standard.

Recognizing that significant new technology emerges continuously, these standards should be reviewed frequently. It is also recognized that Internet counseling ethics cases should be reviewed in light of delivery systems existing at the moment rather than at the time the standards were adopted.

In addition to following the NBCC® Code of Ethics pertaining to the practice of professional counseling, Internet counselors shall observe the following standards of practice:

Internet Counseling Relationship.
1.   In situations where it is difficult to verify the identity of the Internet client, steps are taken to address

impostor concerns, such as by using code words or numbers.

2.   Internet counselors determine if a client is a minor and therefore in need of parental/guardian consent. When parent/guardian consent is required to provide Internet counseling to minors, the identity of the consenting person is verified.

3.   As part of the counseling orientation process, the Internet counselor explains to clients the procedures for contacting the Internet counselor when he or she is offline and, in the case of asynchronous counseling, how often e-mail messages will be checked by the Internet counselor.

4.   As part of the counseling orientation process, the Internet counselor explains to clients the possibility of technology failure and discusses alternative modes of communication, if that failure occurs.

5.   As part of the counseling orientation process, the Internet counselor explains to clients how to cope with potential misunderstandings when visual cues do not exist.

6.   As a part of the counseling orientation process, the Internet counselor collaborates with the Internet client to identify an appropriately trained professional who can provide local assistance, including crisis intervention, if needed. The Internet counselor and Internet client should also collaborate to determine the local crisis hotline telephone number and the local emergency telephone number.

7.   The Internet counselor has an obligation, when appropriate, to make clients aware of free public access points to the Internet within the community for accessing Internet counseling or Web-based assessment, information, and instructional resources.

8.   Within the limits of readily available technology, Internet counselors have an obligation to make their

Web site a barrier-free environment to clients with disabilities.

9.   Internet counselors are aware that some clients may communicate in different languages, live in different time zones, and have unique cultural perspectives. Internet counselors are also aware that local conditions and events may impact the client.

Confidentiality in Internet Counseling.

10.   The Internet counselor informs Internet clients of encryption methods being used to help insure the security of client/counselor/supervisor communications.

Encryption methods should be used whenever possible. If encryption is not made available to clients, clients must be informed of the potential hazards of unsecured communication on the Internet. Hazards may include unauthorized monitoring of transmissions and/or records of Internet counseling sessions.

11.   The Internet counselor informs Internet clients if, how, and how long session data are being preserved. Session data may include Internet counselor/Internet client e-mail, test results, audio/video session recordings, session notes, and counselor/supervisor communications. The likelihood of electronic sessions being preserved is greater because of the ease and decreased costs involved in recording. Thus, its potential use in supervision, research, and legal proceedings increases.

12.   Internet counselors follow appropriate procedures regarding the release of information for sharing Internet client information with other electronic sources.

Because of the relative ease with which e-mail messages can be forwarded to formal and casual referral sources, Internet counselors must work to insure the confidentiality of the Internet counseling relationship.

Legal Considerations, Licensure, and Certification.

13.　　　Internet counselors review pertinent legal and ethical codes for guidance on the practice of Internet counseling and supervision.

Local, state, provincial, and national statutes as well as codes of professional membership organizations, professional certifying bodies, and state or provincial licensing boards need to be reviewed. Also, as varying state rules and opinions exist on questions pertaining to whether Internet counseling takes place in the Internet counselor's location or the Internet client's location, it is important to review codes in the counselor's home jurisdiction as well as the client's. Internet counselors also consider carefully local customs regarding age of consent and child abuse reporting, and liability insurance policies need to be reviewed to determine if the practice of Internet counseling is a covered activity.

14.　　　The Internet counselor's Web site provides links to websites of all appropriate certification bodies and licensure boards to facilitate consumer protection.

APPENDIX D

Online Therapy Education

For someone interested in participating in an online therapy workshop, the options are currently limited. As online therapy continues to grow and expand, the number of options will expand along with it. Below are some examples of online therapy workshops currently available. The listed sites are not ranked in any way, and no endorsement of any particular site, therapist, or company is made by either the authors or the publisher. The information below was retrieved in November of 2004 and may be changed by press time.

ONLINE THERAPY WORKSHOPS

MyTherapyNet "Online Therapy Workshop"

This course, presented both online and in person, is a 5-hour course focusing on online therapy. This course includes a sample presentation of an e-clinic, clinical issues, legal and ethical perspectives, sample online sessions, and role play. This course will enrich and enhance your private practice by providing you with detailed knowledge on how to be effective in this medium, and how to best advertise your services. As an online professional, you will be able to advertise your virtual office in both the conventional media as well as online. Your potential market is exponentially increased through having an online presence. As an online therapist, you will possess the necessary tools to take maximum advantage of your practice and provide the quality of services that your clientele expect. As a certified online therapist, you will be able to advertise your certification and enhance your marketability. If you provide services through MyTherapyNet.com, your certification can be displayed on your professional profile page. It will also provide you with the tools that will facilitate your online experience and improve your abilities as an online therapist. This course also enables you to conduct a sample online therapy session. See www.mytherapynet.com; www.etherapyinstitute.com

AAMFT "Online Therapy and Life Coaching: Enhance Your Practice"

This course, presented nationwide and in person, is combined with life coaching. The online therapy course includes a sample presentation of an e-clinic, clinical issues, legal and ethical perspectives, sample online sessions, and role play. The life coaching course includes distinctions between coaching and psychotherapy, cornerstones of effective coaching, a basic model of coaching, styles of coaching, and legal and ethical issues of coaching (see http://www.aamft.org/institutes/online_therapy.asp).

OnlineCounsellors.co.uk: "Online Training Program"

Designed for qualified practitioners who wish to explore and develop their online presence, this 6-week certificated course of study introduces online therapy from both a theoretical and practical stance, based on actual research and international expert opinion. All study takes place online; you choose the times suitable for you to take part. Onlinecounsellors.co.uk does not expect you to launch into live online sessions with no grounding in the method. Although this is interactive training, there are no role-playing sessions with other trainees. Instead, a new training system has been developed to enable you to experience online e-mail and Internet relay chat therapy sessions that include you as the observer, guiding you to learning points and allowing you to add your own thoughts and feelings about the sessions taking place.

A discussion board allows you to interact with other trainees and the trainers to explore your learning in a supportive environment, and you have full access to the most up-to-date resources in online therapy research papers and Web sites, including a guide to standardized Online Therapy Netiquette for Practitioners. Also available is a subscription to The Online Therapy Netiquette for Practitioners and to The Online Therapy Network, a members benefit package. See www.Online Counsellors.co.uk

Internet Guided Learning: "Navigating the Mental Health Internet"
This course, presented online, contains seven lessons on navigating the mental health Internet, of which one lesson is devoted entirely to online therapy (see http://www.internet guides.com/nmhi/navhome.html).

Ofer Zur "Telehealth: Clinical, Ethical and Legal Issues"
This online course is offered for continuing education credits for psychotherapists. It covers the legal, ethical, clinical, and risk management considerations of 1) using e-mail for in between in-person session contacts with clients or offering online counseling services with no in-person contact, 2) providing assessment or treatment services to an individual in a different location utilizing interactive televideo communications and other Web technology, and 3) using the telephone for crisis intervention or other contacts between in-person sessions, con-

ducting telephone sessions with patients who are not able to attend in-person sessions for a period of time, or providing clinical services entirely by telephone to an individual in a different geographical area. See http://www.drzur.com/homeon line.html.

Glossary

Glossary terms have been set in boldface type on their first appearance in the book.

ASCII: an ASCII file contains text only. When you save a file as ASCII text, you save only the characters, not the size, the font, the style, the color, or the format.

address book: a section of e-mail for storing e-mail addresses; allows you to quickly send e-mail without having to remember long addresses; usually has a place to store additional information such as phone numbers, street addresses.

affiliate programs: a means by which companies may advertise on Web sites other than their own.

alerts: a notification that is automatically generated by a computer that allows a user to be notified of a certain situation.

antivirus protection: a program that protects a computer from viruses.

associate programs (see *affiliate programs*)

asynchronous communication: a method of transmission in which one character is sent one bit at a time; also referred to as *serial transmission*; opposite of synchronous communication; communications that do not occur in real time.

audioconferencing: conferencing conducted using audio components, whereby the participants verbally converse with each other.

audiotherapy: therapy conducted using audio components, resulting in the therapist and client verbally conversing with each other throughout the session.

automatic billing: billing that is completed by a computer system, rather than manually.

avatar: the "body" you "wear" in a virtual community; an animated, articulated representation of a human that represents you, the user, in any virtual environment.

back-up: a copy of a computer file, especially for storage on a floppy or CD.

backdoors: holes in the security of a system deliberately left in place by designers or maintainers.

blog: (see *Weblog*)

broadband: high-speed Internet connections that usually take the form of cable modem, DSL, or T1 lines.

browser: a software program used for searching and viewing various kinds of Internet resources such as information on a Web site.

bulletin boards (see *message boards*)

button: a region of the screen you can click on to perform a function or answer a question.

cable modem: a type of modem that connects to a local cable TV line to provide a continuous connection to the Internet.

calendaring: computing infrastructure that supports the electronic scheduling of people and resources.

CD-ROM: short for Compact Disc-Read-Only memory, a type of portable disk capable of storing large amounts of data

chat: any system that allows any number of logged-in users to have a typed, real-time, online conversation, either by all users logging into the same computer, or more commonly nowadays, via a network.

chat rooms: (see also *therapist-assisted chat rooms*) Web sites that contain individual pages ("rooms") in which you can "chat" with random surfers or arrange rendezvous; the chat takes the form of inputting lines of text, often with the option of complementary "emotion" signifiers (see *emoticons*), and waiting for a typed response

classified advertising: a form of advertising common in newspapers and other periodicals; usually text based.

clicks: selecting particular actions located within a Web page.

community group: a group of people organized for a specific purpose to benefit the community at large.

compact disk (CD): an optical disc on which data are encoded.

computer-assisted education: the science and art of providing health education with the assistance of a computer.

computer-guided therapy: self-help by interaction with a computer system that itself asks the questions and uses clients' answers to direct the interview and give individually tailored advice.

computer-mediated counseling: counseling that is made possible by the use of a computer.

configure: to change software or hardware actions by changing settings.

database: an organized body of related information.

decryption: the process of converting coded data to plain text.

digital signature: an electronic signature that can be used to authenticate the identity of the sender of a message or the signer of a document.

digital subscriber line (see *DSL)*

digitally encrypted message: a message whose language has been digitally converted into code, as to restrict access to that message from an outside source.

disk (see *floppy disk*)

distance therapy: methods of therapy received by the client when he or she is not located in the physical proximity of the therapist's office.

document sharing: the ability of two or more persons to share and view the same document from different locations.

download: transferring files or information from a remote computer to your computer.

DSL (digital subscriber line): a method for moving data over regular phone lines. A DSL circuit is much faster than a regular phone connection, and the lines used are the same as those used for regular phone service.

dual-core processor: an integrated circuit to which two or more processors have been attached for enhanced performance, reduced power consumption, and more efficient simultaneous processing of multiple tasks.

e-clinic: nationwide (or global) operations that administer online therapy sites.

e-mail (electronic mail): messages, usually text, sent from one person to another via computer.

electronic signature database: a collection of signatures acquired through electronic means and held in a database.

embedded image: an image that is enclosed inside a document or program.

E-mmediate Care: a program on MyTherapyNet that allows clients to receive therapeutic services immediately, or close to immediately.

emoticon: a combination of keyboard characters meant to represent a facial expression; frequently used in electronic communications to convey a particular meaning, much like tone of voice is used in spoken communications.

encrypted e-mail: a message that is sent via computer with extra security attached to it

face-to-face therapy (f2f): type of therapy in which therapist and client are in close proximity to each other, usually in the same room.

file: a body of encoded information (either data or program, or both) that can be read only by a computer.

file, graphics: a file format designed specifically for representing graphic images.

file, picture: a file format designed specifically for representing pictures.

file, sound: a file format designed specifically for representing sounds.

file, video: a file format designed specifically for representing video.

file transfer protocol (FTP): a way of transferring files over the Internet from one computer to another.

firewall: an "internal lock" to protect information on a computer.

floppy disk: a removable storage medium; a convenient way to transfer files between computers (see also CD-ROM)

hacker: a computer expert who taps into a computer system to gain access to data.

hard drive: data storage device found in a computer.

hardware: the mechanical, magnetic, electronic, and electrical components making up a computer system (see *software*).

home page: Originally, the Web page that your browser is set to use when it starts up. The more common meaning refers to the main Web page for a business, organization, person, or simply the main page out of a collection of Web pages.

hosting company: infrastructure that supports the storage and "serving" of web sites. Websites are stored on webservers, which are specially configured computers that allow Internet users to access the websites stored therein.

hypertext: any text that contains links to other documents.

hypertext link: an easy method for retrieving information by choosing highlighted words or icons on the screen; clicking on the link will take you to related documents or sites. (*see also* uniform resource locator)

hypertext mark-up language (HTML): the coded format language used for creating hypertext documents on the World Wide Web and controlling how Web pages appear.

instant messaging: a service that alerts users when friends or colleagues are online and allows them to communicate with each other in real time through private online chat areas, such as AOL Messenger, Yahoo! Messenger, or MSN Messenger.

interactive: computer programs that accept input from the user while the program is running.

interface: a connection between two dissimilar devices.

Internet: the publicly available, internationally interconnected, system of computers.

Internet 2: a nationwide project to develop the next generation of computer network applications to facilitate the research and education missions of universities.

Internet Explorer: a popular Web browser, created by Microsoft, used to view pages on the World Wide Web.

Internet phone: technology that enables users of the Internet to place voice telephone calls through the Internet, thus bypassing the long-distance network.

Internet protocol (IP): a standardized method for transporting information across the Internet in packets of data.

Internet protocol address: an identifier for a computer.

Internet service provider (ISP): a company that provides access to the Internet.

keyboard: a bank of keys arranged on a board for the purpose of operating a computer or other machine.

keywords: words that are entered into the search form or search window of an Internet search engine to locate the Web pages or sites that include the keyword and information related to it.

link (see *hypertext link*)

live (going live): making a Web site viewable on the Web.

log off: to terminate communication with a computer operating system.

log on: the act of connecting with a computer system and entering your user identification and password.

measurement tool: a tool, such as a questionnaire, survey or interview, to be used to measure functionality and progress.

media rich: an Internet advertising term for a Web page that uses graphic technologies such as streaming video, audio files, or other similar technology to create an interactive atmosphere with viewers.

message board: a Web-based message center where users can post text communications for one another.

modem: a device or program that enables a computer to transmit data over analogue telephone lines.

monitor: a CRT (cathode ray tube) used to display television or computer generated text or images.

mouse: handheld mobile device used to control cursor movement and to select functions on a computer display.

multimedia: information presented in more than one format, such as text, audio, video, graphics, and images.

navigate: to move around on the World Wide Web by following hypertext paths from document to document.

newsgroups: discussion groups on the Internet, each of which is focused on a particular topic.

off-the-shelf: describes a ready-to-use hardware or software product that is packaged and ready for sale, as opposed to one that is proprietary or has been customized.

128 bit cypher strength: the length of the "session key" generated by every encrypted transaction; the longer the key, the more difficult it is to break the encription code; 128 bit is currently the longest key available.

online brochure: a relatively static or fixed Web site of one to four "pages."

online clinic: a Web site that features online therapy.

online journaling: the act of keeping a journal through the use of a computer.

online slang: jargon occurring chiefly in casual and playful speech, made up typically of short-lived coinages and figures of speech that are deliberately used in place of standard terms for added raciness, humor, irreverence, or other effects.

online therapy: the technology of providing psychotherapy through the computer: also referred to as *e-therapy.*

optimization: changes made to a Web page to improve the positioning of that page with one or more search engines; a means of helping potential customers or visitors to find a Web site.

password: a unique string of characters that a user types as an identification code to restrict access to computers and sensitive files. The system compares the code against a stored list of authorized passwords and users. If the code is legitimate, the system allows access at the security level approved for the owner of the password.

password protection: technology that allows a user to employ advanced protection for a password.

payment services: a computer-mediated service that allows for payments to be made for services rendered.

personal Web site: a Web site owned and operated by a single individual.

privilege: the therapist's legal right to refuse to reveal confidential information from online sessions in a legal setting.

program (see also *software*): a sequence of instructions that a computer can interpret and execute.

programming: the process of creating a sequence of operations that direct a computer to perform a desired task.

proprietary software: software with which users do not have, in general, more rights than the right to use.

public chats: chat rooms that are open to the general public.

public message boards: software used to communicate between a group of individuals; for example, members of a support group.

publish: to send forth information from one source to a particular Web page.

ranking: the listing of a particular Web site in comparison to another Web site.

real time: Relating to computer systems that update information at the same rate they receive information.

real-time chat: live dialogue via the Internet, conducted by typing on the computer keyboard; the participating users are getting the messages and responding to each other immediately, as opposed to messages sent back and forth by e-mail.

real world: the outside (physical) world as opposed to virtual world of digital communication.

run: the continuous period of time during which a computer operates.

search engine: a tool that enables users to locate information on the Internet; search engines use keywords entered by users to find Web sites that contain the information sought.

server: a computer on a network that is dedicated to a particular purpose and which stores all information and performs the critical functions for that purpose. For example, a Web server would store all files related to a Web site and perform all work necessary for hosting the Web site.

software: a computer program that provides the instructions which enable the computer hardware to work. System software, such as Windows or MacOS, operate the machine itself, and applications software, such as spreadsheet or word processing programs, provide specific functionality.

sound card: a type of expansion board on PC–compatible computers that allows the playback and recording of sound.

speech-to-text software: computer programs that convert speech into the written word as one speaks aloud into a microphone.

speed: the length of time it takes a computer to complete a particular application.

sponsorship: a partnership between companies in which the sponsor publicly endorses an activity and ties its reputation to that of the company or event being sponsored.

streaming: a technique for transferring data such that it can be processed as a steady and continuous stream.

surfers: a computer user who randomly peruses the different Web sites on the Internet.

synchronous communication: Real-time communications in which users who are in conversation see the messages being typed immediately as they are typed or upon a user "sending" a message.

T1 line: a type of high-speed Internet connection that provides a great deal of bandwidth.

telecommunication: communication over long distances, especially by telephone, radio, satellite, television, and the Internet.

telehealth: the use of electronic communication networks for the transmission of information and data focused on health promotion, disease prevention, and the public's overall health.

telemedicine: the exchange of medical information from one site to another via electronic communications to improve patient care and education.

terminal: an input/output device consisting of a keyboard and a monitor (CRT).

text editor: any program that performs even the most basic word processing and saves files to standard ASCII text.

text messaging: a wireless service that involves the transmission of a short text message and its receipt by a wireless handset pager.

therapist gallery: a listing of therapists located in a particular e-clinic.

third-party software: also known as bundled software; an additional software component that is included in another software.

Trojan horse: a program containing additional hidden code that allows the unauthorized collection, exploitation, falsification, or destruction of data.

uniform resource locator (URL): the name/address of a resource on the Internet. (*see also* hypertext link)

universal serial bus (USB): a standard port that enables the connection of an external device (such as a digital camera, scanner, mouse) to a computer.

upload: to transmit a file of data from your computer to another computer.

user name: the name that identifies a user to a computer network; generally used in conjunction with a password to establish the user's right to access a host; also called *account name* or *user ID*.

videoconferencing: teleconferencing in which video images are transmitted among the various geographically separated participants in a meeting.

videotherapy: therapy conducted using video components, resulting in the therapist and client hearing and seeing each other throughout the session.

virtual community: a community of people sharing common interests, ideas, and feelings over the Internet or other collaborative networks.

virtual reality (VR): an environment that is simulated by a computer.

virus: a computer program that can reproduce by changing other programs to include a copy of itself; it is a parasite program, needing another program to survive.

Web-based treatment interventions (WBTIs): self-help treatment intervention modules on Web sites.

Webcam: a digital camera that uploads images to a Web site for broadcast.

Web conferencing: a conference conducted via the World Wide

Web between two or more participants in different locations; text, audio, or video may be used to communicate in real time or in an asynchronous environment.

Webmaster: the person responsible for administering a Web site.

Web logs (blogs): a frequent, chronological publication of personal thoughts and Web links.

Web site: a collection of pages or files linked together and available on the World Wide Web; Web sites are established by companies, organizations, and individuals.

Web site sharing: the ability to share Web sites with two or more people who are in different locations.

wi-fi: short for wireless fidelity; allows for connection to networks without the use of wires.

Word: a word processing program that can be used to create, edit, format, and save documents.

word processing: a computer program, such as Word, used to create documents that are text-based (e.g., letters, memos, term papers). It is the most common computer application.

World Wide Web (Web, WWW): a hypertext system that operates over the Internet.

worm: computer programs that replicate themselves and that often, but not always, contain some function that will interfere with the normal use of a computer or a program.

References

American Bar Association. *Pro bono and public services*. Retrieved November 17, 2004, from www.abanet.org//legalservices/probono.

American Counseling Association (ACA) (1999). *Additional ethical standards Webcounseling*. Retrieved November 1, 2004, from http://www.counseling.org/Content/NavigationMenu/RESOURCES/ETHICS/EthicalStandardsforInternetOnlineCounseling/Ethical_Stand_Online.htm.

American Medical Informatics Association (AMIA) (1998). Guidelines for the clinical use of electronic mail with patients. *Journal of the American Medical Informatics Association, 5*(1). Retrieved November, 1, 2004, from http://www.amia.org/pubs/other/email_guidelines.html.

American Psychiatric Association Ethics Committee. (1995). *Position statement on the ethical use of telemedicine.* Washington, DC: Author. Retrieved November 16, 2004, from http:/www.psych.org/edu/other_res/lib_archives/archives/199515.pdf.

American Psychological Association Ethics Committee (1997). *Services by telephone, teleconferencing, and Internet.* Retrieved November 1, 2004, from http://www.apa.org/ethics/stmnt01.html.

American Psychological Association (2004). *Ethical principles of psy-*

chologists and code of conduct. Retrieved November, 16, 2004, from http://www.apa.org/ethics/code.html.

American Telemedicine Association. (2004). *ATA adopts telehomecare clinical guidelines.* Retrieved November 16, 2004, from http://www.atmeda.org/news/list.html.

Association for Counselor Education and Supervision. (1993). Ethical guidelines for counseling supervisors. *ACES Spectrum, 53*(4), 5–8.

Barak, A. (1999). Psychological applications on the Internet: A discipline on the threshold of a new millennium. *Applied and Preventive Psychology, 8,* 231–246.

Barnett, D. (1982). A suicide prevention incident involving the use of a computer. *Professional Psychology, 13,* 565–570.

Behavior Online. (1999). *Clinical application of email* [online panel discussion]. Retrieved November 16, 2004, from www.behavior.net/chatevents/transcript99-2.html.

Beck A. T. (1979). *Cognitive therapy and the emotional disorders.* New York: Meridian Books.

Bellah v. Greenson (1978). 146 *Cal. Rptr.* 535. Cal. App.

Benjamin, A. D. (1987). *The helping interview* (3rd ed.). Boston: Houghton Mifflin.

Berg, I. K. (2004). *Student's corner.* Retrieved November 16, 2004, from www.brief-therapy.org/insoo_essays.htm.

Bernard, J. M., & Goodyear, R. K. (1992). *Fundamentals of clinical supervision.* Needham Heights, MA: Allyn & Bacon.

Boscolo, L., Cecchin, G., Hoffman, L., & Penn, P. (1987). *Milan systemic family therapy: Conversation in theory and practice.* New York: Basic Books.

Botella, C., Banos, R. M., Villa, H., Perpina, C., & Garcia-Palacios, A. (2000). Telepsychology: Public speaking fear treatment on the Internet. *CyberPsychology and Behavior, 3,* 959–968.

Brandt, D. (1998). *Is that ALL there is? Balancing expectation and disappointment in your life.* Atascadero, CA: Impact.

Brenner, C. (1973). *An elementary textbook of psychoanalysis.* Garden City, NY: Anchor Books.

Buchanan, T. (2002). Online assessment: Desirable or dangerous? *Professional Psychology: Research and Practice, 33,* 148–154.

Budman, S. H. (2000). Behavioral health care dot-com and beyond: Computer-mediated communications in mental health and substance abuse treatment. *American Psychologist, 55*(11), 1290–1300.

Burgower, B. H. (2001). *Is online help safe?* Retrieved November 11, 2004, from http://my.webmd.com/content/Article/12/1674_50618. htm.

Burns, D. (1985). *Intimate connections: The new and clinically tested program for overcoming loneliness developed at the Presbyterian-University of Pennsylvania Medica.* New York: William Morrow.

Burton, D. C. (1997). Kentucky advances mental health services through Kentucky telecare and the state mental health network [online]. *Telehealth News, 1*(2). Retrieved November 5, 2004, from http://www.telehealth.net/telehealth/newsletter_2.html.

California Board of Behavioral Science. (2004). *Laws and regulations.* Retrieved November 16, 2004, from http://www.bbs.ca.gov/law-reg.htm

Celio, A. A., Winzelberg, A. J., Wilfley, D. E., Eppstein-Herald, D., Springer, E. A., & Dev, P. (2000). Reducing risk factors for eating disorders: Comparison of an internet- and a classroom-delivered psychoeducational program. *Journal of Consulting and Clinical Psychology, 68*, 650–657.

Chafe W., & Tannen, D. (1987). The relationship between written and spoken language. *Annual Review of Anthropology, 16*, 383–407.

Child Abuse Prevention and Treatment Act (CAPTA) (1996, ammended 2003). 42 U.S.C. 5101, et seq. Retrieved November 5, 2004, from www.acf.hhs.gov/PROGRAMS/cb/initiatives/capta/legalissues.htm.

Childress, C. (1998). *Potential risks and benefits of online psychotherapeutic interventions.* Retrieved November 5, 2004, from http://ismho.org/issues/9801.htm.

Chomsky, N. (1957). *Syntactic structures.* The Hague: Mouton.

Clawson, V. K., Bostrom, R. P., & Anson, R. (1993). The role of the facilitator in computer-supported meetings. *Small Group Research, 24*, 547–565.

Colon, Y. (1999). Digital digging: Group therapy online. In J. Fink (Ed.), *How to use computers and cyberspace in the clinical practice of psychotherapy* (pp. 66–81). Northvale, NJ: Aronson.

Department of Health and Human Services (1999). *Executive summary.* Retrieved November 4, 2004, from http://www.surgeon general.gov/library/mentalhealth/home.html.

deShazer, S. (1985). *Miracle question.* Retrieved July 13, 2004, from http://www.brief-therapy.org/steve_miracle.htm.

DiPietro, R. (Ed.). (1982). *Linguistics and the professions: Proceedings of the second annual Delaware Symposium on Language Studies.* Norwood, NJ: Ablex.

Duncan, B., Miller, S., & Sparks, J. (2000). *The heroic client: A revolutionary way to improve effectiveness through client-directed, outcome-informed therapy.* Jossey-Bass: San Francisco.

Ellis, A. (1970). *The art and science of love.* Secaucus, NJ: Lyle Stuart. (Originally published 1960).

Ellis, A. (1986). *How to live with a neurotic.* North Hollywood, CA: Wilshire. (Originally published 1957)

Ellis, A. (1994). *The essence of rational emotive behavior therapy* (REBT): *A comprehensive approach to treatment.* Retrieved Feb. 25, 2005, from http://www.rebt.org/dr/pamphletofthemonth.asp.

Employment Policy Foundation. (2001). Computer ownership and Internet access: Opportunities for workforce development and job flexibility. *Technology Forecast,* January 11, 1–5. Retrieved November 16, 2004, from http://www.epf.org/research/newsletters/2001/tf20010111.pdf

Epston, D. (2002). *Narrative therapy.* Retrieved from www.narrative approaches.com

Federal Register. (1998). *Payment for telecommunications in rural health professional shortage area.* Washington, DC: Government Printing Office.

Fenichel, M. (1987). *Language and the way we think.* Retrieved November 4, 2004, from http://www.fenichel.com/language.shtml.

Fenichel, M. (1997). *Internet addiction: Addictive behavior transference or more.* Retrieved November 4, 2004, from http://www.fenichel.com/addiction.shtml

Fenichel, M. (2000). *Town hall meeting: APA 2000.* Retrieved November 16, 2004, from http://www.fenichel.com/TownHall.shtml

Fenichel, M. (2002). *The here and now of cyberspace.* http://www.fenichel.com/herenow.shtml.

Fenichel, M., & Dan, P. (1980). Heads from *Post* and *Times* on Three-Mile Island. *Journalism Quarterly, 77*(2), 338–339, 368.

Fenichel, M., Suler, J., Barak, A., Zelvin, E., Jones, G., Munro, K., Meunier, V., Walker-Schmucker, W. (2004). *Myths and realities of online clinical work.* Retrieved November 11, 2004, from http://ismho.org/casestudy/myths.htm.

Ferguson, T. (1998). Digital doctoring: Opportunities and challenges in electronic patient–physician communication. *Journal of the American Medical Association, 280*(15), 1361–1362.

Finn, J., & Lavitt, M. (1994). Computer-based self-help for survivors of sexual abuse. *Social Work With Groups, 17*(1/2), 21–47.

Finn, J. (1995). Computer-based self-help groups: A new resource to supplement support groups. *Social Work with Groups, 18*(1), 109–117.

Finn, J. (1996). Computer-based self-help groups: Online recovery for addictions. *Computers in Human Services, 13*(1), 21–41.

Gabriel, M., & Holden, G. (1999, February). *New uses of technology in support of clinical social work.* Paper presented at New York University, New York.

Galinsky, M. J., Schopler, J. H., & Abell, M. D. (1997). Connecting group members through telephone and computer groups. *Social Work, 22*(3), 181–188.

Glueckauf, R. L. (2002). Telehealth and chronic disabilities: New frontier for research and development. *Rehabilitation Psychology, 47*(1), 3–7.

Glueckauf, R. L., Pickett, T. C., Ketterson, T. U., Loomis, J. S., & Rozensky, R. H. (2003). Preparation for the delivery of telehealth services: A self-study framework for expansion of practice. *Professional Psychology: Research and Practice, 34,* 159–163.

Glueckauf, R. L., Whitton, J. D., & Nickelson, D. W. (2002). Telehealth: The new frontier in rehabilitation and health care. In M. J. Scherer (Ed.), *Assistive technology and rehabilitation psychology: Shaping an alliance* (pp. 197–213). Washington, DC: American Psychological Association.

Grohol, J. (1997). *Why online psychotherapy?* Retrieved November 24, 2004, from www.psychcentral.com/archives/n102297.htm.

Grohol, J. (1999). *Best practices in e-therapy: Definition and scope of e-therapy.* Retrieved November 16, 2004, from http://www.ismho.org/issues/9902.htm.

Gustafson, D. H., Hawkins, R., Boberg, E., Pingree, S., Serlin, R., Graziano, F., & Chan, C. L. (1999). Impact of a patient-centered, computer-based health information/support system. *American Journal of Preventive Medicine, 16,* 1–9.

Gustafson, D. H., Hawkins, R., Pingree, S., McTavish, F., Arora, N. K., & Mendenhall, J. (2001). Effect of computer support on younger women with breast cancer. *Journal of General Internal Medicine, 16,* 435–445.

Handelsman, M., & Galvin, M. (1988). Facilitating informed consent for out-patient psychotherapy. A suggested written format. *Professional Psychology Research and Practices, 19,* 223–225.

Harrar, W. R., VandeCreek, L., & Knapp, S. (1990). Ethical and legal aspects of clinical supervision. *Professional Psychology: Research and Practice, 21,* 37–41.

Harris Poll. (2001). *Cyberchondriacs update.* Retrieved November 16, 2006, from http://www.harrisinteractive.com/harris_poll/index.asp?p:d-229.

Holland, N. N. (1996). The internet regression. In J. Inler (Ed.), *The psychology of cyberspace.* Retrieved November 16, 2004, from http://www.rider.edu_~/suler/psycyber/holland.html.

Hopps, S. L., Pépin, M., & Boisvert, J. M. (2003). The effectiveness of cognitive–behavioral group therapy for loneliness via inter-relay-chat among people with physical disabilities. *Psychotherapy: Theory, Research, Practice, Training, 40*(1–2), 136–147.

International Society for Mental Health Online (ISMHO) (2000a). *The online clinical case study group of the International Society for Mental Health Online: A report from the Millennium Group.* Retrieved November 16, 2004, from http://ismho. org/casestudy/cesgmg.htm.

International Society for Mental Health Online. (2000b). *Suggested principles for the online provision of mental health services.* Retrieved October 30, 2004, from http://www.ismho.org/suggestions.html.

Jacobs, M. K., Christensen, A., Huber, A., Snibble, J. R., Dolezal-Wood, S., & Alexandra Polterok, A. (2000). A Comparison of Computer-Based Versus Traditional Individual Psychotherapy. *Rehabilitation Psychology, 47,* 8–30.

Johnson, L.D., Miller, S.D., & Duncan, B.L. (2000). *The session rating scale 3.0.* Chicago: Authors.

Joinson, A. M. (2001). Self-disclosure in computer mediated communication: The role of self-awareness and visual anonymity. *European Journal of Social Psychology, 31,* 177–192.

Kanz, J. E. (2001). Clinical-supervision.com: Issues in the provision of online supervision. *Professional Psychology: Research and Practice, 32,* 415–420.

Keefe, F. J., & Blumenthal, J. A. (2004). Health psychology: What will the future bring? *Health Psychology, 23*(2), 156–157.

Kiesler, S., Siegel, J., & McGuire, T. W. (1984). Social psychological aspects of computer-mediated communication. *American Psychologist, 39,* 1123–1134.

King, S. A. (1994). Analysis of electronic support groups for recovering addicts. *Interpersonal Computing and Technology, 2*(3), 47–56.

King, S., Engi, S., & Poulos, S. T. (1998). Using the Internet to assist family therapy. *British Journal of Guidance and Counseling, 26*(1): 43–52.

King, S. A., & Poulos, S. T. (1998). Using the Internet to treat generalized social phobia and avoidant personality disorder. *Cyberpsychology and Behavior, 1*(1) 29–36.

Kitchener, K. K. (1988). Dual role relationships: What makes them so problematic? *Journal of Counseling and Development, 67,* 222–226.

Kruger, L. J., Maital, S. L., Macklem, G., Shriberg, D., Burgess, D. M., Kalinsky, R., & Corcoran, K. (2001). Sense of community among school psychologists on an Internet site. *Professional Psychology: Research and Practice, 32*(6), 642–649.

Kraus, R., Zack, J., & Stricker, G. (2003). *Online counseling: A handbook for mental health professionals.* Amsterdam: Elsevier.

Kurpius, D., Gibson, G., Lewis, J., & Corbet, M. (1991). Ethical issues in supervising counseling practitioners. *Counselor Education and Supervision, 31,* 57–58.

Lange, A., Van de Ven, J-P., Schrieken, B., & Emmelkamp, P. M. G. (2001). Interapy: Treatment of posttraumatic stress through the Internet: A controlled trial. *Journal of Behavior Therapy and Experimental Psychiatry, 32,* 73–90.

Lange, A., Rietdijk, D., Hudcovicova, M., van de Ven, J. P., Schrieken, B., Paul, M. G., & Emmelkamp, P. M. G. (2003). Interapy: A controlled randomized trial of the standardized treatment of posttraumatic stress through the Internet. *Journal of Consulting and Clinical Psychology, 71*(5), 901–909.

Laszlo, J. V., Esterman G., & Zabko, S. (1999). Therapy over the Internet? Theory, research and finances. *Cyber Psychology & Behavior, 2*(4), 293–307.

Lebow, J. (1998). Not just talk, maybe some risk: The therapeutic potentials and pitfalls of computer mediated conversation. *Journal of Marital and Family Therapy, 24*(2), 203–206.

Lenhardt, A., Horrigan, J., Rainie, L., Allen, K., Boyce, A., Madden, M., & O'Grady, E. (2003). *The ever-shifting Internet population: A new look at Internet access and the digital divide.* Retrieved November 16, 2004, from http://www.pewinternet.org/ppf/r/88/report_display. asp

Liss, H. J., Glueckauf, R. L., & Ecklund-Johnson, E. P. (2002). Research on telehealth and chronic medical conditions: Critical review, key issues, and future directions. *Rehabilitation Psychology, 47,* 8–30.

Luce, K. H., Winzelberg, A. J., Osborne, M. I., & Zabinski, M. F. (2003). Internet-delivered psychological interventions for body image dissatisfaction and disordered eating. *Psychotherapy: Theory, Research, Practice, Training, 40*(1–2), 148–154.

Magaletta, P. R., Fagan, T. J., & Peyrot, M. F. (2000). Telehealth in the Federal Bureau of Prisons: Inmates' perceptions. *Professional Psychology: Research and Practice, 31*(5), 0735–7028.

Maheu, M. M., & Gordon, B. L. (2000). Counseling and therapy on the Internet. *Professional Psychology: Research and Practice, 31,* 484–489.

Maheu, M. M., Whitten, P., & Allen, A. (2001). *E-health, telehealth, and telemedicine: A guide to start-up and success.* San Francisco: Jossey-Bass.

Mathy, R. M., Kerr, D. L., & Haydin, B. M. (2003). Methodological rigor and ethical considerations in Internet-mediated research. *Psychotherapy: Theory, Research, Practice, Training, 40*(1–2), 77–85.

McKay, G. H., Glasgow, R. E., Feil, E. G., Boles, S. M., & Barrera, M. (2002). Internet-based diabetes self-management and support: Initial outcomes from the Diabetes Network Project. *Rehabilitation Psychology, 47,* 31–48.

Meichenbaum, D. (1995). *A clinical handbook/practical therapist manual for assessing and treating adults with posttraumatic stress disorder (PTSD).* Miami, FL: Melissa Institute Press.

Meichenbaum, D. (2000). *A clinical handbook for Donald Meichenbaum's presentation at The Evolution of Psychotherapy.* Miami, FL: Melissa Institute Press.

Meichenbaum, D. (2003). *The treatment of individuals with anger control and aggressive behavior.* Norwalk, CT: Crown House Publishing.

Michaelson, K. (1996). Information, community and access. *Social Science Computer Review, 14*(1), 57–59.

Miller, S. D., & Duncan, B. L. (2000a). Paradigm lost: From model-driven to client-directed, outcome-informed clinical work. *Journal of Systemic Therapies, 19,* 20–34.

Miller, S. D., & Duncan, B. L. (2000b). *The outcome rating scale*. Chicago: Authors.

Miller, S. D., Duncan, B. L., & Hubble, M. (2004). Beyond integration: The triumph of outcome over process in clinical practice. *Psychotherapy in Australia, 10*(2), 2–3.

Miller, S. D., Duncan, B. L., Brown, J., Sorrell, R., & Chalk, M. B. (in press). Using outcome to inform and improve treatment outcomes. *Journal of Brief Therapy.*

Miller, S. D., Duncan, B. L., Brown, J., Sparks, J., & Claud, D. (in press). The outcome rating scale: A preliminary study of the reliability, validity, and feasibility of a brief visual analog measure. *Journal of Brief Therapy.*

Murphy, L., & Mitchell, D. L. (1998). When writing helps to heal: E-mail as therapy. *British Journal of Guidance and Counselling, 26*(1), 21–32.

MyTherapynet. (2004). *Public resources.* Retrieved Jan. 15, 2005, from MyTherapynet.com/PublicResources)

National Board for Certified Counselors (NBCC). (2004). *Standards for the ethical practice of web counseling.* Retrieved November 1, 2004, from www.nbcc.org/ethics/wcstandards.htm

National Center for Educational Statistics. (2005). *Internet access in U.S. schools and classrooms.* Retrieved February 25, 2005, from http://nces.ed.gov/pubsearch/pubsinfo.asp?pubid_2005015.

National Institute of Justice. (1999). *Telemedicine can reduce correctional health care costs: An evaluation of a prison telemedicine network* (Report No. NCJ 175040). Washington, DC: U. S. Department of Justice.

Nickelson, D. W. (1998). Telehealth and the evolving health care system: Strategic opportunities for professional psychology. *Professional Psychology: Research and Practice, 29*(6), 527–535.

Norcross, J. C., Hedges, M., & Prochaska, J. O. (2002). The face of 2010: A Delphi poll on the future of psychotherapy. *Professional Psychology: Research and Practice, 33,* 316–322.

North, M. M., North, S. M., & Coble, J. R. (1998). Virtual reality therapy: An effective treatment for phobias. *Studies in Health Technology and Informatics, 58,* 112–119.

North, M. M., North, S. M., & Coble, J. R. (1997). Virtual reality therapy for fear of flying. *American Journal of Psychiatry, 154*(1), 130.

Office of Justice Programs. (1999). *Mental health and treatment of in-*

mates and probationers (Report No. NCJ 174463). Washington, DC: U. S. Department of Justice.

O'Hanlon, W. H., & Weiner-Davis, M. (1989). *In search of solutions: A new direction in psychotherapy.* New York: Norton.

O'Hanlon, B., & Wilk, J. (1987). *Shifting contexts: The generation of effective psychotherapy.* New York: Guilford Press.

Pastore, M. (2000a). *Broadband consumers set to hit 35 million by 2005.* Retrieved November 24, 2004, from http://www.clickz.com/stats/sectors/hardware/article.php/5921_364921

Pastore, M. (2000b). *Half of U.S. households use PCs.* Retrieved November 24, 2004, http://www.clickz.com/stats/sectors/demographics/article.php/301081

Pastore, M. (2000c). *The mess known as online healthcare.* Retrieved November 12, 2004, from http://www.clickz.com/stats/sectors/healthcare/article.php/379231

Pew Internet and American Life Project. (2000). *The online healthcare revolution: How the Web helps Americans take better care for themselves.* Retrieved November 16, 2004, from http://www.pewinternet.org/reports/toc.asp?Report=26.

Pew Internet and American Life Project. (2002). *Vital decisions: How Internet consumers decide what information to trust when they or their loved ones are sick.* Washington, DC: Author. Retrieved November 16, 2004 from http://www.pewinternet.org/reports/toc.asp?Report=59

Proudfoot, J., Goldberg, D., Mann, A., Everitt, B., Marks, I., & Gray, J. A. (2003). Computerized, interactive, multimedia cognitive–behavioural program for anxiety and depression in general practice. *Psychological Medicine, 33,* 217–227.

Rabasca, L. (2000). Taking telehealth to the next step. *APA Monitor, 31,* 36–37.

Raine, L. & Horrigan, J. (2005). *A decade of adoption: How the internet has woven itself into American life.* Retrieved January 31, 2005, from http://www.pewinternet.org/PPF/r/148/report_display.asp http://www.pewinternet,org/pdfs/Internet_Status_2005.pdf.

Reid, W. J. (1992). *Task strategies: An empirical approach to social work practice.* New York: Columbia University Press.

Richman, W. L., Kiesler, S., Wiesband, S. & Drasgow, F. (1999). A meta-analytic study of social desirability distortion in computer-administered questionnaires, traditional questionnaires, and interviews. *Journal of Applied Psychology, 84*(5), 754–775.

Ritterband, L. M., Gonder-Frederick, L. A., Cox, D. J., Clifton, A. D., West, R. W., & Borowitz, S. M. (2003). Internet interventions: In review, in use, and into the future. *Professional Psychology: Research and Practice, 134*(5), 527–534. ơv 34

Riva, G. (2001). Shared hypermedia: Communication and interaction in Web-based learning environments. *Journal of Educational Computing Research, 25,* 205–226.

Riva, G. (2003). Virtual environments in clinical psychology. *Psychotherapy: Theory, Research, Practice, Training, 40*(1–2), 68–76.

Riva, G., Bacchetta, M., Baruffi, M., Rinaldi, S., & Molinari, E. (1998). Experiential cognitive therapy: A VR based approach for the assessment and treatment of eating disorders. In G. Riva, B. Wiederhold, & E. Molinari (Eds.), *Virtual environments in clinical psychology and neuroscience: Methods and techniques in advanced patient–therapist interaction* (pp. 120–135). Amsterdam: IOS Press.

Riva, G., Bacchetta, M., Baruffi, M., Rinaldi, S., & Molinari, E. (1999). Virtual reality based experiential cognitive treatment of anorexia nervosa. *Journal of Behavioral Therapy and Experimental Psychiatry, 30*(3), 221–230.

Riva, G., Bacchetta, M., Baruffi, M., Cirillo, G., & Molinari, E. (2000). Virtual reality environment for body image modification: A multidimensional therapy for the treatment of body image in obesity and related pathologies. *CyberPsychyology and Behavior, 3*(3), 421–431.

Riva, G., Bacchetta, M., Baruffi, M., Rinaldi, S., Vincelli, F., & Molinari, E. (2000). Virtual reality-based experiential cognitive treatment of obesity and binge-eating disorders. *Clinical Psychology and Psychotherapy, 7*(3), 209–219.

Riva, G., Bacchetta, M., Cesa, G., Conti, S., & Molinari, E. (2001). Virtual reality and telemedicine based experiential cognitive therapy: Rationale and clinical protocol. In G. Riva & C. Galimberti (Eds.), *Towards cyberpsychology: Mind, cognition and society in the Internet age* (pp. 273–308). Amsterdam: IOS Press.

Riva, G., Wiederhold, B., & Molinari, E. (1998). *Virtual environments in clinical psychology and neuroscience: Methods and techniques in advanced patient–therapist interaction.* Amsterdam: IOS Press.

Rothbaum, B. O., Hodges, L. F., Anderson, P., Price, L., & Smith, S. (2002). 12-month fellow-up of virtual reality and standard exposure therapies for fear of flying. *Journal of Consulting and Clinical Psychology, 70,* 428–432.

Rothbaum, B. O., Hodges, L., Watson, B. A., Kessler, G. D., & Opdyke, D. (1996). Virtual reality exposure therapy in the treatment of fear of flying: A case report. *Behaviour Research and Therapy, 34*(5–6), 477–481.

Saab, P. G., Coons, H. L., Christensen, A. J., Kaplan, R., Johnson, S. B., Ackerman, M. D., Stepanski, E., Krantz, D. S., & Melamed, B. (2004). Technological and medical advances: Implications for health psychology. *Health Psychology, 23*(2), 142–146.

Safran, J. D., & Muran, J. C. (2000). *Negotiating the therapeutic alliance.* New York: Guilford Press.

Sander, F. M. (1996). Couples group therapy conducted via computer-mediated communication: A preliminary case study. *Computers in Human Behavior, 12*(2), 301–312.

Schopp, L., Johnstone, B., & Merrell, D. (2000). Telehealth and neuropsychological assessment: New opportunities for psychologists. *Professional Psychology: Research and Practice, 31*(2), 179–183.

Seligman, M. E. P. (1995). The effectiveness of psychotherapy. The *Consumer Reports* study. *American Psychologist, 50*(12), 965–974.

Schanz, S., & Cepelewicz, B., (2001). *Telemedicine law and practice: Practical guide.* Kingston, NJ: CRI Publishers.

Steward, D. (2003). *In defense of exceptions to confidentiality. Virtual Mentor, 5*(10). Retrieved November 16, 2004, from http://www.amc/assn.org/ama/pub/category/11112.html

Stofle, G. (2001). *Choosing an online therapist: A step-by-step guide to finding professional help on the Web.* Harrisburg, PA: White Hat.

Stofle, G. (2002). Chatroom therapy. In R. C. Hsiung (Ed.), *E-therapy: Case studies, guiding principles, and the clinical potential of the Internet* (pp. 92–135). New York: Norton.

Ström, L., Petterson, R., & Andersson, G. (2000). A controlled trial of self-help treatment of recurrent headache conducted via the Internet. *Journal of Consulting and Clinical Psychology, 68,* 722–727.

Ström, L., Pettersson, R., & Andersson, G. (2004). Internet-based treatment for insomnia. A controlled evaluation. *Journal of Consulting and Clinical Psychology, 72*(1), 113–120.

Suler, J. (2000). Psychotherapy in cyberspace: A 5-dimensional model of online and computer-mediated psychotherapy. *Cyber psychology and Behavior, 3,* 151–159.

Suler, J., Kraus, R., Zack J., & Stricker, G. (2003). *Online counseling: Handbook for mental health professionals.* San Diego, CA: Elsevier Academic Press.

Surgeon General. (1999). *Mental health: A report of the Surgeon General.* Washington, DC: General Printing Office.

Tarasoff v. Regents of Univ. of Cal., (1976), 17 Cal.3d 425, 435, 131 Cal. Rptr. 1423.

VandenBos, G. R., & Williams, S. (2000). The Internet versus the telephone: What is telehealth, anyway? *Professional Psychology: Research and Practice, 31,* 490–492.

Viljoen, J. (2003). dissertation, *Living with Fire.* Department of Religious Studies, University of South Africa. Chapter 4 retrieved July 15, 2004, from http://www.narrativeapproaches.com/narrative%20papers%20folder/vijoen4.htm

Walsh, F. (1997). Family therapy: Systems approaches to clinical practice. In J. R. Brandell (Ed.), *Theory and practice in clinical social work* (pp. 132–163). New York: Free Press.

Walther, J. B. (1996). Computer mediated communication: Impersonal, interpersonal, and hyperpersonal interaction. *Communication Research, 23,* 3–43.

Weinberg, N., Schmale, J., Uken, J. S., & Wessel, K. (1995). Computer-mediated support groups. *Social Work with Groups, 17*(4), 43–54.

Weinberg, N., Schmale, J., Uken, J. S., & Adamek, M. (1995). Therapeutic factors: Their presence in a computer-medicated support group. *Social Work with Groups, 18*(4), 57–69.

White, M., & Epston, D. (1990). *Narrative Means to Therapeutic Ends.* New York: Norton.

Winzelberg, A. J. (1997). The analysis of an electronic support group for individuals with eating disorders. *Computers in Human Behavior, 13,* 393–407.

Winzelberg, A. J., Epstein, D., Eldredge, K., Wilfley, D., Dasmahapatra, R., Dev, P., & Taylor, C. B. (2000). Effectiveness of an Internet-based program for reducing risk factors for eating disorders. *Journal of Consulting and Clinical Psychology, 68,* 346–350.

Winzelberg, A. J., Taylor, C. B., Sharpe, T. M., Eldredge, K. L., Dev, P., & Constantino, P. S. (1998). Evaluation of a computer-mediated eating disorder intervention program. *International Journal of Eating Disorders, 24,* 339–349.

Woody, R. H. (1984). *The law and the practice of human services.* San Francisco: Jossey-Bass.

Working to Halt Abuse (2005). *Online harassment/stalking statistics.* Retrieved March 3, 2005, from http://www.haltabuse.org/resources/stats/index.shtml.

Yager, J. (2001). E-mail as a therapeutic adjunct in the outpatient treatment of anorexia nervosa: Illustrative case material and discussion of the issues. *International Journal of Eating Disorders, 29,* 125–138.

Zarr, M. L. (1984). Computer-mediated psychotherapy: Toward patient-selection guidelines. *American Journal of Psychotherapy, 38*(1), 47–62.

Index